The Great Depression
of Debt

The Great Depression of Debt

Survival Techniques for Every Investor

332.024

Brussee

Warren Brussee

WILEY

John Wiley & Sons, Inc.

Published by John Wiley & Sons, Inc., Hoboken, New Jersey.
Published simultaneously in Canada.

Although care was taken in gathering and analyzing this book's data, there is always the possibility of error. Anyone using this book's information to influence investment direction, or for any other decision, should personally verify the data, calculations, and conclusions to their own satisfaction. For these reasons, the author cannot take responsibility for any losses or unfavorable outcomes related to the use of data or information in this book.

For general information on our other products and services or for technical support, please contact our Customer Care Department within the United States at (800) 762-2974, outside the United States at (317) 572-3993 or fax (317) 572-4002.

Wiley also publishes its books in a variety of electronic formats. Some content that appears in print may not be available in electronic books. For more information about Wiley products, visit our web site at www.wiley.com.

Library of Congress Cataloging-in-Publication Data:

Brussee, Warren.
    The great depression of debt : survival techniques for every investor / Warren Brussee.
        p. cm.
    Includes bibliographical references and index.
    ISBN 978-0-470-42371-4 (cloth)
1. Portfolio management.   2. Investments.   3. Depressions.   I. Title.
    HG4529.5.B785 2009
    332.024–dc22   2008040320

Printed in the United States of America

10   9   8   7   6   5   4   3   2   1

To my wife Lois and my daughters Michelle and Cheri.
They believed in me as a writer and researcher
even as I expanded into areas
beyond Six Sigma and statistics.

Contents

Preface

In the late nineties, two other people and I developed a real-time computerized stock investment program to identify insider trading that had caused a stock's price to go up. The program used statistical tests to identify signs that employees had seen a new product, or other positive development, that they felt would positively affect their company, triggering the purchase of an unusual amount of stock.

This computer program was successful in the positive nineties' stock market. Over a period of two years, several millions of dollars were successfully invested. However, the market changed in 2000, and the algorithms were no longer finding investment opportunities. The good thing was that the computer program took us out of the market. However, I wanted to invest in *all* markets, so I began to look for algorithms that worked in the "new market" after 2002. When reviewing the economy, I became aware of some dire problems. Those insights triggered the eventual writing of my 2004 book *The Second Great Depression*.

I had written two earlier books, *Statistics for Six Sigma Made Easy* and *All About Six Sigma*, so I felt comfortable in my ability to select and analyze data. The essence of Six Sigma is getting good data and analyzing that data to reach conclusions. The economy and the stock market have reams of data from which the premise of a debt-caused depression emerged.

In my depression book I also told a story. There were many supporting graphs and charts that showed how we were on the precipice of a depression. But the events leading up to the present, starting with the nineties, were just as important as the graphs. Just as someone can't understand the Great Depression without understanding the years preceding it, current graphs on the economy make little sense without understanding the mind-set of the people who brought the economy and the stock market to be where they now are. This understanding also assists in making some determination on what is likely to happen in the near future

Following is an excerpt from my 2004 book *The Second Great Depression*.

Come 2008, the number of people giving up on making house payments will skyrocket. Since many of the recent mortgage loans are adjustable rate, have teaser rates, or require little or no collateral, banks will be forced to foreclose on homes and sell them, causing a glut of homes on the market and a deflation of home values. In the 2000 market drop, almost no banks went belly up because people had not bought stocks on leverage. This is not true in housing, where people and banks are leveraged. As the current inflated home values go down, many people will have mortgages greater than the value of their homes, and they will happily give their homes back to the bank rather than fight their mortgage payments. Unless the federal government comes to their rescue, many banks will fail in this downturn. This is because banks got too confident and optimized bottom line results with little consideration for the risks they were taking with marginal mortgage loans.

You will be able to get a great deal on a used SUV, especially a Hummer! The automotive market will be for cars getting great gas mileage, and Detroit will again be caught off guard and all geared up for the gas guzzlers. Sound familiar? This will cause massive layoffs at Detroit carmakers, and all the under-funded automakers' pension funds will become zero-funded. Millions of Japanese high mileage cars with new technologies, like hybrid engines, will have been on the road for many years. But the American automakers, with little on-road experience with these new technologies, will be a car-generation or two behind.

(Brussee, Warren T., *The Second Great Depression*, Booklocker.com, 2005)

Most of my predictions are proving themselves true. But it is time to relook at the predictions that I made for the years *beyond* 2008, to see if they are still true. And, with the benefit of four more years of data, we want to see if we can discover even *more* insights into the future.

This required writing this new book, *The Great Depression of Debt!* Although many of the predictions made in my earlier book remain largely unchanged, the addition of current data and updated charts with current information, enable us to take a closer look at today's bleak economy and subsequently give my earlier predications more substance and scope. With this knowledge, this book will provide you with the steps that you need to take advantage of the dramatic shifts in consumer spending, the mortgage industry, and the stock market.

The Next Great Depression

A recession occurs when there is a significant decline in economic activity spread across more than a few months. This decline is shown in real GDP, real income, employment, industrial production, and wholesale-retail sales. When the recession becomes severe or long enough, it transitions into an economic depression. As I write this book in late 2008, all the measures of economic activity are declining, so we certainly qualify for a recession. And given the depth of the housing, mortgage, debt, and credit issues, we appear well on the way to a full-blown depression.

The U.S. economy began to slow in 2007, and the GDP went negative in the fourth quarter of 2007. Some people only look at the GDP (Gross Domestic Product) when determining whether we are in a recession/depression. However, the government's definition of a recession includes many additional factors, such as unemployment. And, as mentioned earlier, a depression is just a severe and extended recession.

In the Great Depression the GDP went down four years in a row starting in 1930; it then went up the next four years, down the next year, then up again as we entered World War II. But we generally consider the whole period of 1929 through 1940 a depression because of its severity, because unemployment stayed very high, and because other economic measures remained weak even during the years when the GDP was rising.

The start of the current recession/depression was delayed almost a year longer than I expected because people continued to do cash-out refinances on their homes well into 2007, even though homes had already begun to drop in price. However, this delay is only going to make the recession/depression worse because of the increased number of people with mortgages greater than the values of their homes. As I write, 10 percent of homeowners are upside down on their mortgages, and this is increasing at a relentless pace as homes continue to drop in value and more homes come into the market due to record foreclosures. This, in turn, hurts all the credit markets as "mortgage walkers" abandon their homes, causing mortgage-backed securities to continue to lose value. In addition, an extra 1.5 million homes were built in response to the demand caused by the increased number of people able to buy houses based on foolish mortgages. These extra homes are now an albatross around the neck of the housing recovery. Home prices will continue to drop for years; and home building will be largely stagnant, driving related unemployment up. And, of course, all of this is in addition to the underlying problem that consumers have been spending more than their incomes, which is now reversing out of necessity. This reduced spending is causing a severe slowing of the economy, exacerbating the economic problems related to housing.

These problems are so severe that it will take until 2012 or 2013 before the economy bottoms out and our economy again begins to grow. In the meantime, the stock market will drop dramatically, unemployment will be over 15 percent, and the dollar will lose its position as lead currency. Our country will be humbled as it is forced to adapt to a far lower and simpler standard of living.

Although the turnaround of the economy is likely to happen in approximately 2013, it will be somewhere around 2020 before our country's economy fully recovers.

Acknowledgments

I would like to thank Chris Welker, Roy McDonald, and Jeff Kolt for their valuable feedback on the initial manuscript. Like most writers, at some point in writing I become blind to my own words, and I read what I *mean* to say rather than what I actually write. My reviewers shake me out of that fog with both their helpful suggestions and polite corrections. This book would not be possible without them.

Part I

THE ESSENCE OF WHY WE WILL
HAVE A DEPRESSION

P art I discusses the historical elements, starting in the 1990s, that
set us up for this depression. This history shows how people got
so enamored with stock market gains and using debt to finance
their standard of living that they no longer felt the need to save. This
started a series of bubbles that are now breaking because the consumers'
debt level is now at its maximum.

There are many parallels between now and the years preceding the
Great Depression, except that this current depression is likely to be inflationary rather than deflationary. There are other economic conditions
that may exacerbate this depression, but the depression's trigger was consumer debt, forcing spending to decline. As the consumer continues to
reduce spending, industry is slowing and unemployment increasing. As
resets on mortgages raise house payments, people are being forced into
foreclosures, and the banks holding those mortgages have to be rescued
by the government. This is causing a domino effect as the depression
spreads.

The Fed will try to stop the depression through interest rate adjustments and various financial incentives to individuals and banks. But it is fruitless to try to get people who have already spent too much to spend even more. Eventually, the government will have to turn to job creation in an effort to get the economy going, but this will trigger high inflation rates as the government is forced to print money to pay for all this.

Chapter 1, The Crazy Nineties: Craziness in the 1990s' stock market prices was one of the precursors for this depression. People stopped saving and began to rely on their stock market investments for their financial future.

Chapter 2, The Debt Bubble: The American economy has been fueled by consumers who reduced their savings and began spending more than what they could afford. This created debt and housing bubbles.

Chapter 3, Why Are the Good Times Ending and the Bubbles Breaking? The growth of stock buyers aged 30 through 54 has leveled off, and the number of households owning mutual funds has peaked. There is no longer a growing demand for stocks. And the bubbles are, by necessity, breaking.

Chapter 4, Current Times Compared to 1929–1930: There are similarities of the years just prior to the Great Depression and the current times.

Chapter 5, What This Depression Will Be Like: Starting in 2008, this depression will affect many. Unemployment and inflation will grow, and houses will deflate in value. The market will eventually drop 65 percent, and the economy will go to its knees.

Chapter 6, What Else May Deepen the Depression: The wars in Iraq and Afghanistan, terrorists, energy prices, a drop in the dollar's value, the deficit, the balance of payments, inflation, and interest rates may all deepen this depression; but debt is the depression trigger.

Chapter 7, Could the Fed Have Stopped This Depression? No! In fact, the Fed's past decisions have just delayed the inevitable, trading several short recessions in the past for this depression.

Chapter 8, Now That It Has Started, How Are We Going to Work Our Way Out of This Depression? Effective job creation in alternative energy, electric cars, and the required infrastructure will be key; along with training for related skills. Reducing debt and a return to saving will be required.

Chapter 1

The Crazy Nineties

This chapter shows how, in the 1990s, an increasing number of people started investing in the stock market. This increase caused an increase in demand for stocks, driving up stock prices. As stock prices rose, investors became so enamored with their gains that they no longer felt it necessary to save. And they increased their debts in the faith that their gains in the stock market would enable them to pay down their debts at a later date. This caused the stock bubble of the nineties and set up many people for the inevitable break of the stock market bubble.

The Lure of the Markets

I had two neighbors in the late 1990s, one a retired doctor and the other a retired small-business owner, who were never seen in the daytime when the stock market was trading. But, in the evenings, they would have smiles on their faces from ear to ear! These neighbors felt that they had discovered the secret to wealth: day trading! Neither of them ever shared with me their methods of playing the market, but their wives worried that they were buying stocks based on hunches, rumors, recent headlines, and so on. Apparently they were not making any in-depth analysis of stocks, nor did they make any effort to see if they were doing any better than the market in general. All they cared about was that, on an almost daily basis, their on-paper worth was increasing. They believed that they had discovered the secret to making great amounts of money!

They weren't alone in their craziness. Something strange was happening to much of the country during the nineties. Computer nerds, who were never thought to be giants in the practical world of business, were given almost unlimited funds to pursue their latest business ideas related to the Net or other software ventures. These newly ordained entrepreneurs told everyone that their dot-com businesses did not have to make a profit; that the idea was to develop a customer base using information technology, and the profits would come later. They used esoteric measures, like "eyeballs," to determine how many people were visiting their web sites, which they felt was a measure of their business success. Or they counted how many other worthless web sites were sending visitors to *their* worthless site. They didn't even bother estimating when they would make a profit, nor was there any analysis of what those future profits would be. They said that the important criterion in these new-era businesses was generating customers; profits would just naturally come later. Some of their projections of customer base growth took them quickly to exceed the population of the world, but no matter. Venture capitalists and investors believed them. So did my neighbors. We *all* believed!

Not only were investors like my neighbors sucked in; grizzled CEOs of large companies, who should have known better, gazed at these dot-com companies in awe. These were the same executives who, just a few years before, were trying to look, act, and dress like the Japanese, who were the previous rock stars of industry. These techie-wannabe executives tried to do high-fives and make their companies look and perform like the dot-coms. These executives took crash courses on using the Net, but only after one of their in-house techies bought them computers and taught them how to boot up. GE's CEO Jack Welch even bragged that investors looked at GE as being equivalent to a dot-com company. He made all GE executives take courses on surfing the Net, and each individual business within GE had to set up their own web site where customers could peruse that business's management and product lines. Any project having interaction with the Net got priority corporate funding. Jack Welch and many other corporate heads also did what was necessary to make their stock prices act like dot-com stocks. It didn't seem to matter that most of the perceived financial gains during this era came from accounting creativity that made bland corporate performance look stellar by pushing costs into future years and doing other financial wizardry.

Baby boomers, who were wondering if they were going to be able to keep up with the gains realized by their parents' generation, suddenly saw their salvation. Like my day-trader neighbors, the baby boomers would buy stocks in this new-era stock market and watch their riches grow. As more and more of them bought stocks, the demand drove prices up to ridiculous levels. The feeding frenzy had begun. As a result of all this buying pressure, in the later years of the last century the stock market performed brilliantly.

It wasn't just naïve investors who became overconfident in their abilities related to the market. In 1994, Bill Krasker and John Meriwether, two winners of the Nobel Prize in Economics, started a company called Long-Term Capital Management (LTCM). These two individuals had done massive data analysis on the "spreads" between various financial instruments, such as corporate bonds and Treasury bonds. When these spreads became wider than what was statistically expected (based on their computer program), LTCM would buy the financial instrument likely to gain from the correction that was expected to occur shortly.

Using this methodology, LTCM was unbelievably successful for four years. By leveraging their money, they had gained as much as 40 percent per year for their investors, and Bill Krasker and John Meriwether became very wealthy.

They were so successful that, by 1998, LTCM had $1 trillion in leveraged exposure in various financial market positions. Then, LTCM became victim of the "fat tail" phenomena, which is where a normally balanced distribution of data now has a lot of data far out to one end of the distribution tail. The reason this happened is that everyone who played in similar financial markets all decided to get out at once, and

LTCM was seeing results that their computer models had predicted would *not statistically happen in more than a billion years!* Unbeknownst to them, because of the sudden exit of the others playing this financial game, the relationships of the spreads between various financial instruments had changed, which made the earlier computer-generated probability predictions invalid.

The risks that LTCM had taken were so dangerous that LTCM was close to upsetting the whole world's financial institutions. Fed Chairman Alan Greenspan and several of the world's major banks got together to offer additional credit to LTCM to successfully avert this potential global financial disaster.

Long-Term Capital Management lost over $4 billion, and the relaxed credit that was established by the banks to save LTCM later enabled companies like Enron to do their thing. This story is indicative of the overconfidence shown throughout the nineties. If LTCM had not been leveraged to such an extreme level, they probably would have survived this event. But they had gotten overconfident and greedy. Many people in the nineties thought they could get something for nothing by playing financial games, which in this case included being leveraged to the hilt.

The Potential Stock Gains

Anyone who was able to capitalize on the market gains of the nineties was fortunate indeed. In fact, if you bought the S&P 500 stocks in 1994 and sold them in 1999, your investment tripled in value. Figure 1.1 is a graph of the real gains (discounting the effect of inflation) of the S&P 500 stocks since 1900 showing how unusual and dramatic those 1994–1999 gains were, as evidenced by the huge upward spike near the right-hand side of the graph.

However, buying stocks in 1994 and selling in 1999 is not the normal way people invest, nor were many people fortunate enough to time the market that well. The general way of saving is to invest on a consistent basis and then hold the stocks. This is also the savings method advised by most market "experts." If someone saved a fixed amount every year, starting in 1994, the same beginning year as above, and was still investing this fixed amount through the first quarter 2008, he or

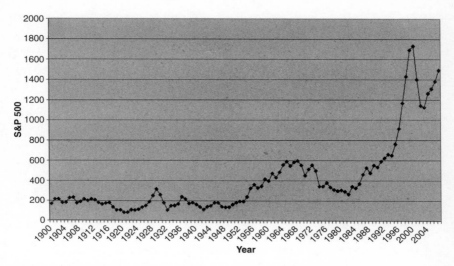

Figure 1.1 Real (Without Inflation) S&P 500 Value History (2007 Dollars)
SOURCE: Stock Data, www.econ.yale.edu/~shiller/data/ie_data.htm.

she would only be ahead 51 percent (including inflation). This assumes a 1.5 percent annual mutual fund management cost, which is typical of what most 401(k) pension savings programs charge. If TIPS were available at this time, this 51 percent gain is almost identical to what someone would have gotten with basically zero risk Treasury Inflation Protected Securities (TIPS) paying 3 percent for much of the time period. TIPS will be discussed in Chapter 9. So, even for those who started to invest in the dramatic market of the nineties, without some fortunate market timing, the gains realized by most investors were not all that phenomenal.

Others have come to similar conclusions on the stock market. John Bogle, founder of the very successful Vanguard Group, estimates that the average return for equity funds from 1984 through 2001, a time period that includes the great stock market bubble of the nineties, was just slightly more than inflation! Contributing to this disappointing performance were the fees charged by mutual funds and the "churning" of stocks—constant stock turnover—which not only adds trade costs, but also causes any gain to be taxed as regular income rather than at the reduced tax rate of capital gains.

However, in most people's memories, the nineties were a time of great gains made in the stock market. They can't get out of their minds the 200 percent gain that could have been realized by buying in 1994 and selling in 1999.

The Cause of the Nineties' Stock Market Jump

Let's try to identify what made the stock market grow the way it did at the end of the last century. When we look for the most likely cause, let's keep in mind Occam's Razor, a logical principle attributed to the mediaeval philosopher William of Occam, which emphasizes that the simplest and most logical explanation is usually the best.

Between the years 1990 and 2000, due to the baby boomer surge, the number of people in the age group 30 through 54 increased almost 25 percent. These are the primary stock buying ages. Below the age of 30, people are involved with getting an education or starting their careers. Once people become 55, some of them begin to move investments into more conservative areas, getting ready for retirement. Figure 1.2 shows the nineties' 25 percent increase in potential stock purchasers, ages 30 through 54.

Figure 1.2 also shows that, after 2005, the number of people in the stock buying years is declining as the baby boomers age. Just as the nineties' increased number of people of stock-buying age increased the demand for stocks, driving prices upward, now that the number of people in this age group is declining, there is a reduced demand for stocks and a downward pressure on stock prices. This is in addition to the downward price pressure caused by the general slowing of the economy as the depression deepens. At the time of writing, the S&P 500 has dropped 22 percent from its 2007 high.

At the same time as this surge of potential stock buyers, there was an increase in awareness of and participation in the stock market. Stock ownership by families went from 23 percent to 52 percent between 1990 and 2001, largely due to the growing number of 401(k) pension plans whose regular savings from income were designated for mutual funds. This is shown in Figure 1.3.

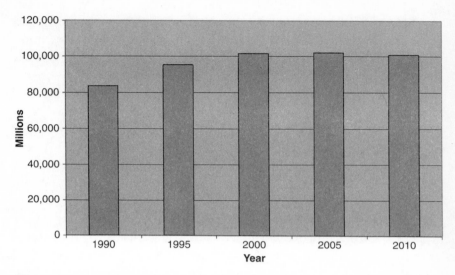

Figure 1.2 Population 30 through 54 Years of Age
SOURCE: U.S. Census Bureau, www.census.gov/population/estimates/nation/intfile2-1.txt.

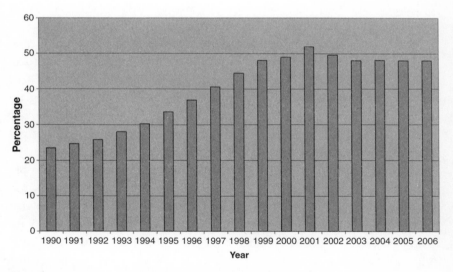

Figure 1.3 Percentage of Households Owning Mutual Funds
SOURCE: U.S. Census Bureau, www.ici.org/pdf/fm-v15n6.pdf.

This increased stock market interest, coupled with the previously noted increase of people aged 30 to 54, meant that there were almost three times as many potential stock buyers at the end of last century than at the beginning of 1990. This put an unusual pressure on the demand side of the traditional relationship between supply and demand. This is not a difficult concept, and its importance has been known for hundreds of years. There are other more esoteric explanations given for the nineties stock price rise, but this is the simplest and most likely cause.

We must emphasize the importance of this increased demand. A relatively small percentage of stocks are in play on any given day. When one of these stocks becomes available for sale, if there are a large number of people interested in buying that stock, the stock will trade at a higher price than normal due to the demand. Simply put, that is what happened in the nineties. People weren't analyzing whether a stock was priced correctly or doing any in-depth analysis of a company's potential. There were just a lot of people who wanted to buy stocks at any price because they believed that the price would go even higher in the future.

This motivation to buy stocks did not just affect individual investors; it also affected the professionals picking stocks for mutual funds. Every week, the increasing number of automatic investment dollars generated by 401(k) savings plans was dumped on mutual fund managers' desks. These fund managers could delay the investment of this money for a few days or weeks if they thought the market would go lower. But they would eventually have to jump into the stock market, driving up demand. No mutual fund manager could keep large portions of her investment money out of the stock market for extended periods of time. After all, the customers wanted to invest in the stock market.

Media coverage of the market became intense, and many people began to actively trade stocks on the Internet. The almost instant investment information on the Web enabled many people to become day traders or self-proclaimed investment experts. The trade costs of playing the market dropped dramatically with the advent of discount brokers and online trading. The almost continuous rise of the stock market just fed the self-aggrandizing of these investors.

Many people began to extrapolate their paper gains for the next 20 years and could see themselves as millionaires with little more effort than the few minutes it took at a computer keyboard to enter their current stock picks. This was how they were going to get their proverbial pot of gold. There was no point in trying to save outside of the stock market. Even if the market took a temporary drop, the stock market gurus assured them that it would always come back and go even higher.

At no point did these people stop to wonder if the stocks they were buying were overpriced or whether the companies really had growth potential. Nor did they ever stop to think that there was not enough money in the world for every investor to become truly wealthy. They couldn't conceive that, when they finally decided to sell their stocks, there could be no one to buy them—that everybody would already be fully invested, with no additional money to put into the market. Sure, if their timing was right, they could be one of the lucky early sellers and do very well. But the following sellers would do worse; and the next sellers even worse, until perceived stock gains miraculously turned into losses. The demand-versus-supply relationship would be turned on its head, with more stocks available than there would be buyers for them.

In the nineties, there was no reason for investors to question the wisdom of what they were doing. The Motley Fool crew was on the radio on weekly broadcasts explaining how *they* were doing it. Investment groups were rampant, including a group of grandmothers who got national attention based on their claim of beating the market experts. People regularly monitored the ongoing media competition between the dartboard stock picks and the market experts. Chat lines gave "inside information" on stocks. Anyone *not* playing the market was obviously naïve or stupid.

TV business news guests were explaining how the information age was enabling companies to realize efficiencies-through-knowledge with little capital investment, thereby justifying the unusually high stock prices. Instant information enabled companies to have minimum inventory and to adjust product mix quickly if consumer tastes changed. This was predicted to eliminate the normal up-and-down cycles in the economy. The market would just consistently go up!

Industrial processes could be fine-tuned, using information system feedback, and methodologies like Six Sigma promised only three defects-per-million-parts-produced if data were used to drive decision making. There was no need to invest in new production equipment because the old-era equipment would run so much better with this new-era information knowledge.

There were books that touted the Dow at 36,000 or even 100,000. No matter that the rationale for the high Dow values was based on fantasy future earnings that would never come to be. Also, these books stated that there was no more risk in investing in the stock market than in other, more traditionally conservative investments, such as bonds. All the stock investor had to do was wait out any downturn of the market—the market always came back and would go on to even higher levels. Of course, the books didn't mention that when the effect of inflation was included, it may take well over 20 years before the investment would recover, and most people's investment window couldn't tolerate that. All the misleading information on the market's potential would have been humorous if it weren't for the fact that many people were risking their lifetime savings on the unrealistic dream of getting rich with little effort!

The Bubble Begins to Break

Then, in 2000, the Motley Fool began to lose money. It was starting to become obvious that information technology in most cases only produced more junk mail and junk information. People already had more information than they could handle *before* the information era started. Often, the additional information just caused people to spend more time sorting.

Someone discovered the accounting error in the Grandmas' claimed gains in the market. The Grandmas forgot that they were regularly infusing additional funds into their investment club, which was not factored in when they calculated their supposed gains. Efficiency gains touted in government statistics on productivity were found to be largely due to changes in the government's accounting system baseline, such as counting productivity gains based on the increased speeds of computer processing rather than any real gains truly affecting productivity. The hyped image of the new-era economy was beginning to get blurry.

I started to see our neighbors out walking during the day, no longer day trading in the stock market. They grumbled that the market was *no longer acting rationally*! Again, they did not choose to share their results with me, but their wives indicated that all their paper gains had been lost, along with a bundle more. The market fooled many people in the nineties because it seemed so logical, and it just kept going up; investors began to feel invincible in their stock-purchase decision making.

This nineties' stock market price bubble is obvious in retrospect when we look back at the Gross Domestic Product (GDP) for this period and see that it was literally unaffected by all the fuss. The GDP is the total market value of all final goods and services produced in the United States in a given year, equal to total consumer, investment, and government spending, plus the value of exports, minus the value of imports. If companies had really gotten superb performance during the late nineties, it would have been evidenced in some measurable effect in the GDP. After all, at some point the value of these new-era companies should have increased the output of the country in a very measurable manner. Instead, the GDP just marched on pretty much as it had in the past. Figure 1.4 is a graph of the GDP through 2006 in logarithmic scale showing this lack of a GDP spike. The graph is shown in logarithmic format because a constant improvement will show itself as a straight line when plotted logarithmically. (For anyone wanting an explanation on how a logarithmic chart makes a constant proportional improvement appear as a straight line, see Appendix C. But it is not necessary to understand this to be able to read this chart or understand the information.)

Figure 1.4 shows that in the nineties there was no sudden change in the ongoing quantitative gain in the GDP. The line showing the GDP just continued upward at the same rate it had for the 45 years before the nineties. The new-era, information-driven society had absolutely no effect on the GDP.

Besides being invisible to the GDP, the stock dividends did not justify the high prices of stocks. Figure 1.5 is a chart showing that, in the nineties, the stock price versus dividend *ratio* just took off and still remains high at the end of 2007, compared to price/dividend ratios before the nineties. The price/dividend ratio at the time of writing in August 2008 is 48.1. The high price/dividend ratio means that people are paying far more for the same amount of stock dividend that they were previously getting at a much lower stock price.

So dividends didn't seem to justify the high stock prices. Some investors felt that the high prices were justified because *future* dividends would jump dramatically as the expected gains realized by the new-era

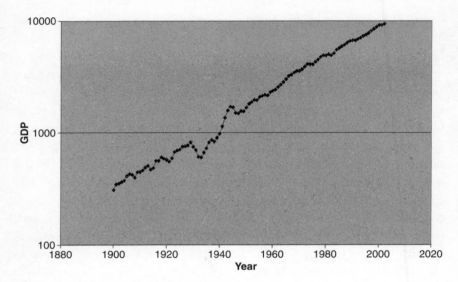

Figure 1.4   Real GDP (1996 Dollars)
SOURCE: U.S. Department of Commerce, Bureau of Economic Analysis, www.measuringworth.com/
uscompare/sourcegdp.php and www.bea.gov/national/nipaweb/TableView.asp?SelectedTable=6&First
Year=2006&LastYear=2008&Freq=Qtr.

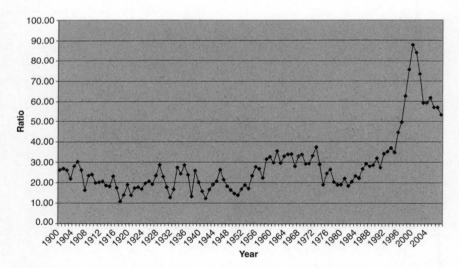

Figure 1.5   Year-End Price/Dividend Ratio
SOURCE: Stock Data, www.econ.yale.edu/~shiller/data/ie_data.htm.

technology took hold. Figure 1.6, plotted logarithmically, shows that dividends have grown consistently since the early sixties, and there was no spike related to the nineties' stock price increases.

Note that Figure 1.6 includes many years after the stock price spurt started in 1994, and the dividends showed no corresponding jump related to the nineties economy. The straight line superimposed over the 40 years between 1965 and 2005 is there to emphasize that the average dividend had been growing at a reasonably uniform rate during that period. The rise in dividends starting in 2005 was the result of a change in tax treatment of dividends that encouraged companies to increase their dividends.

Dividends are the criteria we should use to measure long-term company performance because they are the profits that the owners actually get out of their investments. If you bought a pizza restaurant, you may choose to use initial earnings to expand or improve the restaurant, but at some point you will want to take some money out of the company for personal use. That is the whole purpose of investing. Dividend payout can be delayed while growing a business; but if the earnings *never* generate dividends, then real earnings were either never there, were wasted

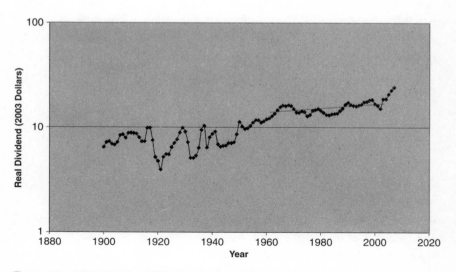

Figure 1.6 S&P 500 Real Dividends Since 1900
SOURCE: Stock Data, www.econ.yale.edu/~shiller/data/ie_data.htm.

on bad investments, or were used to enrich others' pocketbooks rather than the owners of the business. Someone may choose to buy stock in a company that is temporarily investing in growing the business rather than paying dividends. But if this were to go on for too many years, prospective stock purchasers will begin to turn away because they will begin to doubt whether the company will *ever* pay dividends. Then the stock price will level off and eventually start to drop. The fact that Microsoft is now paying dividends is evidence that even the ultimate high-tech company had to eventually turn to paying out cash.

Published earnings are so easily manipulated, as evidenced by the failures of Enron and the like, that it is now difficult to evaluate the real worth of a company using their earnings reports, especially if a company is very large and diverse. In the nineties, companies became expert at making earnings appear to be whatever they wanted. Real spending on research and development (R&D) was reduced and replaced by "accounting R&D" that labeled any project with even minimal risk as being R&D. This gave the misleading appearance of continuing investment for future growth while getting the resultant tax benefits. Individual pieces of equipment, which were previously depreciated separately, were now "bundled" together and then amortized over a larger number of years. This reduced current expenses and made profits appear larger. No matter that this action would make it far more difficult to replace individual pieces of equipment in the future as new technology made them outmoded, because to replace one piece the whole bundled assembly had to justify recapitalization. Items that previously had been expensed were now classified as investments, making current earnings appear more robust by delaying current costs into the future while showing high investment numbers. Outsourcing generated instant gains but sacrificed the manpower skills needed to grow future businesses. The list goes on. Note that all these changes were legal and separate from the more obvious shenanigans of the likes of Enron.

Since the price/earnings ratio is by far the most popular measure to determine if stocks are overpriced, I am including Figure 1.7 for the edification of those who want to see it for a reference. This chart shows that the price/earnings ratio was reasonably uniform (with the exception of the one year in the Great Depression when earnings basically vanished) until 1993, when the ratio just took off. This chart shows that the

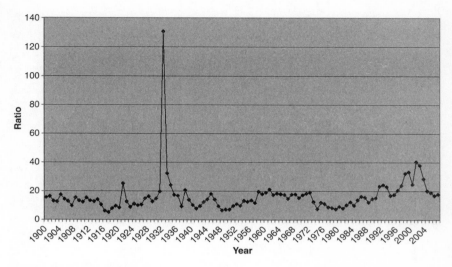

Figure 1.7 S&P 500 Price/Earnings Ratio
SOURCE: Stock Data, www.econ.yale.edu/~shiller/data/ie_data.htm.

price/earnings ratio has recently come down close to the historical high level reached in the sixties. But note, from Figure 1.1, the large market drop that followed the sixties.

However, this book will *not* be using this graph or earnings in any analysis because of the aforementioned reasons, that the earnings are too easily manipulated, making this ratio almost meaningless in this author's opinion.

Summary

We have seen by looking at the GDP and dividends that there was no real performance improvement that justified the dramatic rise in stock prices in the nineties. *The most logical reason for the rise in stock values in the nineties is that the price increase was due to the unusually high demand for stocks, driven by the increase of the buyer base overwhelming the supply of available stocks.* Sure, there were some new dot-com companies that were added to the milieu of stocks (of which many eventually rewarded their investors by

(Continued)

going belly-up), but the pressure was intense on almost all the stocks to be bid up due to the high demand. This is what caused the stock market price jump in the nineties.

This craziness in stock market prices started a series of events that are the precursors for the depression that has now started. Along with the "irrational exuberance" of stock prices, people stopped saving because they thought that their stock market gains would guarantee their future. In fact, they began to believe that speculating in the stock market was actually a form of saving. They also became irrationally exuberant about going into debt, with no concern on how they were going to pay it all back. After all, they were going to become rich through their stock market investments and the ever-increasing values of their homes!

Chapter 2

The Debt Bubble

In this chapter, we will see that, while stocks were being bid-up in the nineties for no real reason other than demand, the continuing growth of the American economy was fueled by consumers who reduced their savings and began spending more than what they could afford. This created a debt bubble. People often used the extra money they got from the reduction of their savings rate and their increase of debt to buy SUVs that got terrible gas mileage or to purchase large homes with little or no down payment. These purchases not only increased their debt, but also put in place higher energy and maintenance costs for future years. In just one generation, we had converted from an economy based on savings and hard work to a debt-driven economy, where people spent whatever was needed to support the lifestyle they believed they deserved, whether they could afford it or not. *This chapter will show that, at some point, living beyond one's income had to come to an unhappy end, and this is what is triggering the current depression. In my first book on the depression, this was a prediction. It has now become a reality.*

Reduced Savings

During the nineties, perhaps in celebration of their seeming success in making loads of money in stocks, consumers went on a spending spree. In order to support this spending spree, consumers reduced their savings rate as a means of getting additional ready cash. Why bother saving additional money when their current investments were obviously going to make them wealthy. By 2005, the savings rate, as a percent of disposable income, was down to 0.5 percent, having dropped from almost 8 percent in 1990. And the savings rate has stayed that low into 2008. Figure 2.1 illustrates this reduction in personal savings.

The Personal Savings Rate, as defined by the Bureau of Economic Analysis of the U.S. Department of Commerce, is what is *left over* from personal income after subtracting personal taxes, Social Security, Medicare, and personal outlays for food, housing, clothing, and so on. Personal income, in this definition, includes wages, dividends, interest, and rental income. Note that Figure 2.1 does *not* include any capital gains or losses due to stock market evaluation.

Figure 2.1 requires further discussion because many people wonder how you can have savings rates approaching zero when they know so

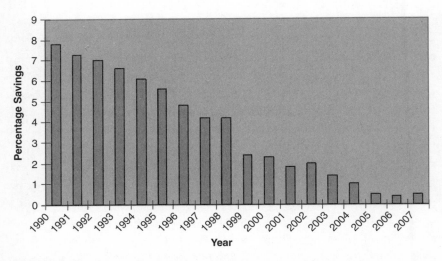

Figure 2.1   Personal Savings Rate (Percentage of Disposable Income)
SOURCE: Bureau of Economic Analysis of the U.S. Department of Commerce, www.ebri.org/pdf/publications/books/databook/DB.Chapter%2009.pdf.

many people who are still saving through their 401(k) plans where they work. The explanation is that Figure 2.1 is the *average* savings rate. So if five people are saving $5,000 per year through their 401(k) plans, but one person takes $25,000 out of *his* savings for any reason, the average savings rate for those six people is zero. On the average, people are not getting ahead on their savings, which does not bode well for baby boomers. Given the large number of people approaching retirement age, the savings rate should be increasing, not decreasing. The reason that the reduction in savings rate did not substantially reduce the demand for stocks in the nineties is that the huge increase in the number of people buying stocks, because of the increase of potential stock buyers mentioned in Chapter 1, easily overwhelmed any effect of the reduced savings rates.

Increasing Debt

In addition to the extra funds that were now available to consumers because they had reduced their savings rate, a debt bubble was growing because consumers were spending more than they earned. Figure 2.2

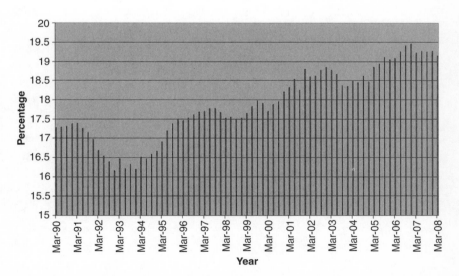

Figure 2.2   Quarterly Financial Obligations Ratio March 1990 to March 2008
SOURCE: The Federal Reserve Board, www.federalreserve.gov/releases/housedebt/about.htm.

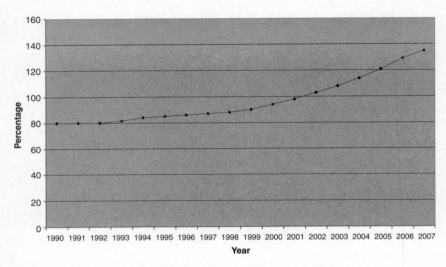

Figure 2.3   Total Household Debt as Percentage of Disposable Income
SOURCE: Federal Reserve Board's Flow of Funds. Bureau of Economic Analysis.

shows the consistent growth of the quarterly financial obligation ratio, which is the ratio of total debt obligation versus after-tax income. This debt obligation includes credit card debt, auto payments, and rent or house payments

This Financial Obligations ratio has been at record highs in recent years. But debt obligations are not the only things eating at disposable income. Increased energy prices, higher food costs, and rising medical costs are reducing the amount of *available* disposable income left over for debt payments.

In Figure 2.3, you can see that consumer debt continues to rise unabated; it is 135 percent of disposable income in 2007. People have not stopped spending more than they earn.

Although we know that consumer debt cannot just keep rising, we would like to make some estimate of how much longer the upward trend can continue. This will give us some idea of when a stock market drop would be expected, since a severe drop in consumer spending will follow when the consumer debt and the quarterly financial obligations ratio hit maximum.

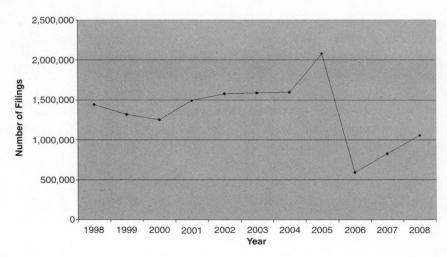

Figure 2.4 Number of Bankruptcy Filings (2008 is an estimate)
SOURCE: www.creditslips.org/creditslips/2008/06/may-2008-bankru.html.

Per Figure 2.3, the 135 percent reading for 2007 is a milestone of note because Japanese consumers, who had a similar jump in consumer debt in the 1980s, had 130 percent of disposable income debt just before entering their long and continuing recession. Since at that point the Japanese were still saving at an 11 percent rate, their personal debt did not have the degree of severity it does in the United States, where current savings rates are close to zero. So, as I write, we should be expecting the market to be dropping. And, indeed, from its high in 2007 to mid-2008, the stock market has dropped nearly 20 percent, which is traditionally the criterion for a bear market.

As debt continues to grow, so does the number of bankruptcies. In Figure 2.4, you can see how bankruptcy filings were growing steadily starting in 2001; but then, in 2005, they skyrocketed because of a coming change in the bankruptcy law that was going to make it far more difficult to declare bankruptcy in future years. However, even with that tighter law in effect, you can see how bankruptcy filings have again begun to grow and have almost doubled since 2006.

The 2005 changes that make it more difficult to declare bankruptcy may have helped credit card companies, but they did little to help the economy. People over their debt limits have just been kept in an extended state of poverty, with dramatically reduced spending ability and with a resultant slowing of the economy. In fact, by reducing the accountability of the credit card companies for their cavalier attitude in mailing out millions of credit cards to anybody and everybody, the credit card companies have just been encouraged to continue their practice of extending credit to everyone, with a growing number of people getting into financial problems.

The Fed's Actions

As we have mentioned, the stock market was going crazy in the nineties, and the great jump in stock prices was one of the causes of consumers having the confidence to spend wildly. Fed Chairman Alan Greenspan was certainly aware of the influence of stock market prices on the rest of the economy. In December 1996, at a speech to the American Enterprise Institute, he made his now famous "irrational exuberance" comment about the high stock market prices. He stated that "we should not underestimate or become complacent about the complexity of the interactions of the asset markets and the economy." That was Greenspanese for *an overpriced market could eventually cause problems in the rest of the economy.* Yet, while he was making this statement, the Fed was allowing the M3 money supply (Figure 2.5), which had been reasonably stable for five years, to start rising dramatically. The M3 money supply includes cash, checking and savings accounts, money market accounts, CDs, euro deposits, and repurchase agreements. This represents the quantity of money (in the generic sense) that can be used to purchase goods, services, and securities. So this increase in the money supply just exacerbated the already irrational exuberance in both the stock market and in consumer spending because it put an unexpected and unneeded shot of extra money into the economy.

Note that in 2006 the government stopped publishing M3 reports, triggering all sorts of conspiracy theories claiming that the government was trying to hide their money creation. However, there is an M2

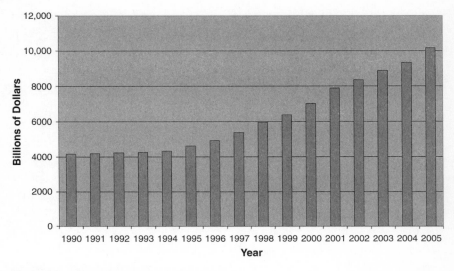

Figure 2.5   M3 Money Supply Since 1990
SOURCE: Federal Reserve Statistical Release: Money Stock Measures.

money supply calculation that continues. Although M2 is not quite as inclusive as M3, it shows that money creation has continued into 2008.

In 2001, when the stock market took its sudden drop, to make sure consumers *kept* spending at a rate they could not afford, the Fed began lowering its federal funds rate—the interest rate banks charge each other for overnight loans—from 5.5 percent all the way down to 1 percent in 2003. Since that initial lowering of interest rates, the value of the dollar against other currencies has been dropping dramatically, especially against the euro. In mid-year 2008, the euro costs approximately 50 percent more in dollars than it did in 2000. This makes imports more expensive, so theoretically consumers should have switched to lower cost domestic goods, helping the United States economy grow. However, this didn't happen! Consumers kept buying their European cars, even though they cost more with the lower value of the dollar. According to the U.S. Census Bureau, the trade deficit has gone from $380 billion in 2000 to $700 billion in 2007. Consumers in the United States continued to buy what they wanted, from wherever they wanted, with no regard for prices or for what additional debts were required. Only in 2008 did consumers finally start to reduce the money they spent on imports (with the exception of oil).

This buying overseas caused another problem other than increasing our deficit. Foreign countries, which have been the beneficiary of the trade deficit, now "own" over half of the U. S. national debt, because these foreign countries used the extra funds they accumulated because of our trade deficit to buy U.S. stocks and bonds. Now, if these countries get tired of the current decline in the dollar, which makes their investments net losers, they will instead use the deficit funds to buy investment instruments elsewhere, for example in Europe. However, the United States *needs* these countries to buy our bonds because that is how we fund our deficit spending. So, if the foreign investors start to hesitate to buy our treasury bonds, the interest on the bonds will have to be raised high enough that the foreign investors won't want to go elsewhere. This scenario is exactly what Fed chief Greenspan was warning everyone in a speech he made at a banking conference in Germany in November 2004. He warned that such an event would increase the interest charges on our deficit and render it "increasingly less tenable." That was Greenspanese for *we won't be able to afford it*.

When there is an expansion of the money supply, as was seen in Figure 2.5, there is always a fear that inflation will grow. Because of that concern, the Fed started raising their overnight funds rate from 1 percent starting in 2004. This continued until the funds rate was 5.25 percent in 2006. Then, as the economy started to show signs of slowing in 2007, the Fed dramatically lowered rates all the way down to 2 percent by May of 2008. In Figure 2.6, you can see the wild gyrations of overnight fund rates that the Fed has put the country through.

Now, in the middle of 2008, the Fed is in a quandary. The economy is slowing, which would normally trigger a further *lowering* of the overnight funds rate. But, at the same time, inflation is rearing its head, especially related to energy and food costs. To slow inflation, the knee-jerk reaction is normally for the Fed to *raise* the overnight funds rate. So the Fed is between the proverbial rock and hard place.

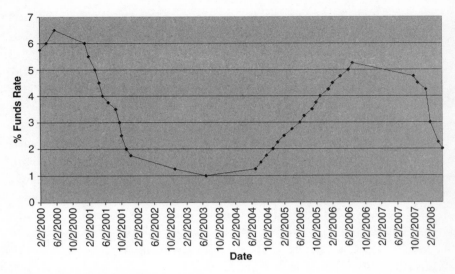

Figure 2.6 Fed Overnight Funds Rate
SOURCE: The Federal Reserve Board, www.federalreserve.gov/fomc/fundsrate.htm.

The Housing Bubble

The data on the housing bubble is almost unique in its continuity and consistency. Watching it unfold has been like watching a Shakespearian tragedy. It was obvious from the very beginning that by the end there were going to be a lot of bodies lying around. People who chose to ignore the signs, as many still are doing as I write this book in 2008, were just in denial. The housing bubble is just part of the total consumer debt issue; and even without the housing issues, we would still be heading for a depression. But the housing problems are just making everything come to a tipping point much sooner. If other consumer debts were not at their maximum, then perhaps consumers would have some wiggle room to adapt to higher payments that are coming on many mortgages. But there is no extra money available since future discretionary funds have already been spent! In fact, consumers have already spent one and one-third years' worth of future discretionary funds. That is why we are heading into a depression!

Let's journey back to when the housing bubble really took off. As interest rates began to drop in 2001, as we saw in Figure 2.6, and creative mortgages were introduced, people started to gravitate toward Adjustable Rate Mortgages (ARMs) and other creative (and risky) loans. These loans enabled people to buy their first homes, or more expensive homes to replace their existing homes, which they previously could not "afford." By 2003, 28 percent of people opted for ARMs. The interest rates on about half of ARMs are tied to the one-year Constant Maturity Treasury (CMT) index. ARMs have a set amount of interest in addition to the CMT rate. Interest rates on adjustable rate mortgages are adjusted periodically. One-year ARMs are adjusted annually based on the one-year CMT. We can see how the one-year CMT index closely tracks the Fed overnight funds rate by looking at Figure 2.7 and comparing it to Figure 2.6. Many of the remaining adjustable rate mortgages are tied to the three-year or five-year CMT indexes, and those rates are adjusted every three or five years accordingly.

You can see in Figure 2.7 that the CMT got as low as 1.0 percent in 2003. This low rate, along with the crazy mortgages being offered, enabled people to enter the housing market who were never there

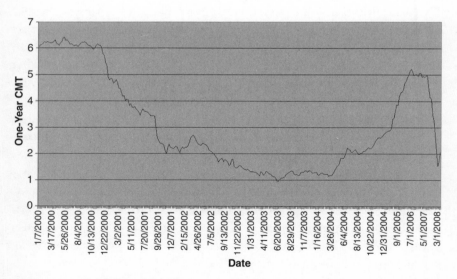

Figure 2.7   One-Year CMT from January 2000 to May 2008
SOURCE: Federal Reserve Board, www.mortgage-x.com/general/indexes/default.asp.

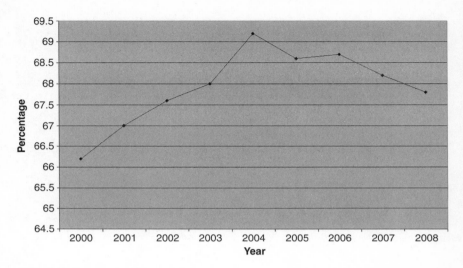

Figure 2.8 Home Ownership Rates
SOURCE: U.S. Census Bureau, www.census.gov/hhes/www/housing/hvs/historic/histt14.html.

before. This caused a huge increase in home ownership, as you can see in Figure 2.8.

Figure 2.8 shows that the percentage of families owning their own homes peaked in 2004. This peak was at the highest since data on home ownership has been collected. At the time, President Bush, Greenspan, and others were pointing with pride to their accomplishment of making the dream of home ownership within the reach of so many. That dream was to quickly turn into a nightmare, not only for many of those who bought homes they truly couldn't afford; but also for those involved in the mortgage business, those who bought securities based on related mortgages, and home owners who happened to live in areas that were about to be inundated by foreclosed homes.

The resultant increased demand for housing caused prices of new and existing homes to skyrocket, as seen in Figure 2.9. Figure 2.9 is plotted without the inclusion of the effect of inflation. The chart was plotted this way to show that home prices have historically gone up in price with inflation. With inflation removed, any increase shown in Figure 2.9 is therefore the result of the housing bubble. And all bubbles eventually break. All of them!

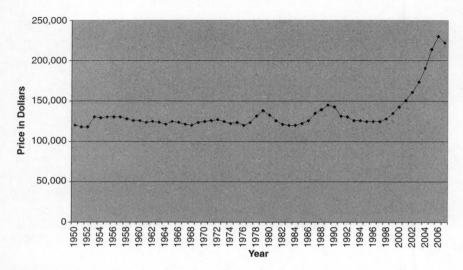

Figure 2.9   Real (Without Inflation) Median Home Prices in 2007 Dollars
SOURCE: S&P/Case-Shiller Home Price Index, www.mysite.verizon.net/vodkajim/housingbubble.

Looking at Figure 2.9, you can see how home prices were pretty much flat with inflation removed; but beginning in 2001 or 2002, the prices jumped at least 50 percent more than would have been expected if there had not been the demand caused by very low interest rates and aggressive mortgages. And, as of the beginning of 2008, even though home prices have begun to drop, they will have to drop another 33 percent to get down to pre-bubble levels. People who are predicting an economic turnaround starting in the second half of 2008 are ignoring this data. The drop in housing prices is just beginning and will continue well into 2012.

Housing increasing in price in excess of inflation was non-sustainable for several reasons. First, unless building and labor costs had also risen in the same proportion as the home prices, which they didn't in this time period, then new homes could be built at a lower cost than existing homes, making it impossible to sell existing homes unless their prices drop. Second, as the prices of homes rise in excess of wages, they become increasingly unaffordable, lowering demand and therefore prices. Homes, unlike stocks, have very effective self-correcting price mechanisms.

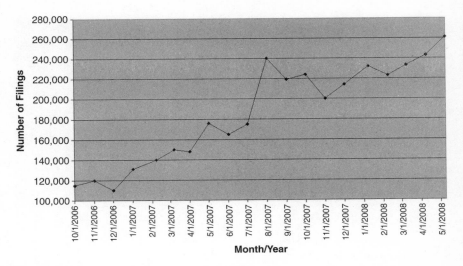

Figure 2.10 U.S. Foreclosure Filings by Month
SOURCE: Realtytrac. www.realtytrac.com/ContentManagement/pressrelease.aspx?ChannelID=9&Item ID=1442&accnt=64847.

One of the contributors to the current drop in home prices is the large number of homes being foreclosed starting in 2007, which added to the inventory of available homes. This is evident in Figure 2.10.

As is shown in Figure 2.10, foreclosures have more than doubled since late 2006. Given the excess number of houses now on the market due to overbuilding to support the increased demand, and the addition of the large number of foreclosed homes, the inventory of homes that are for sale is now extremely high. This can be seen in Figure 2.11. With this large inventory of unsold homes causing an excess of supply versus demand, it is likely that home prices will drop even lower than their pre-bubble equivalent level before prices start to recover.

Note in Figure 2.11 that the housing inventory in months of sales was still growing as of the middle of 2007. This is because builders were making exceptional profits in 2002 through 2005, both due to higher prices and higher demand. And they don't want the good times to end. So, even though they have been reducing their housing starts, they have not reduced them enough to make up for the additional homes coming on the market. Until they reduce their build rate substantially, and the housing

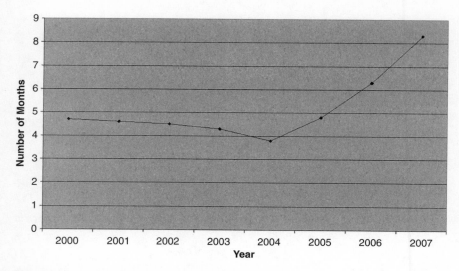

Figure 2.11   Housing Inventory in Months of Sales
SOURCE: www.calculatedrisk.blogspot.com/2008/05/historical-housing-graphs-months-of.html.

prices and inventories drop substantially, there will be no housing recovery! Of course, the unemployment in the building industry resulting from this slowdown will greatly worsen the economic slowdown.

Is Housing Starting to Turn Around?

As I write this in mid-2008, the media has been quoting economists as saying that, because of the reduced rate in the drop in housing sales, the "housing bottom may be near." Even if this rate of decline is really starting to level off, let's look at what this means. Since home ownership peaked in 2004, and sales of new homes peaked in 2005, the housing market volume has been in a downspin for 2.5 to 3.5 years. On any uniform curve, like a sine wave, the inflection point (the point of maximum rate of change) is halfway through the curve. This rationale says that, if we have just passed the inflection point, we have 2.5 to 3.5 more years before housing bottoms out.

Let's look at the timing from a housing price perspective. Median housing prices peaked in 2007, and, according to the Standard & Poors/Case-Shiller U.S. National Home Price Index, home prices have dropped 16 percent in the last year. However, to get down to the level where housing prices would be if they had increased at a historical rate of slightly more than inflation, home prices have to drop another 33 percent. If the price drop continues at its current pace, this will take about two years.

We will now look at this in another way: excess build/sales. If we look at the build/sales rate of homes from 1998 through 2001, and compare that to the build/sales rate between 2002 and 2006, we see that the United States built/sold about 1.5 million extra homes between 2002 and 2006 in order to satisfy a temporary increase in demand (speculators and people who could not realistically afford homes). At the current lower build/sales rate, we are slowly reducing that excess. But at the current build/sales rate, it will take 2.5 years to get back to the historical number of homes and inventory.

Let's look at this with the assumption that foreclosures have to bottom out before the housing recovery begins. Option mortgage resets peak in two years, and foreclosures take about one year after house payments start to be missed. So that means that foreclosures will not bottom out for three years. And, with the number of upside-down mortgages, there are likely to be mortgage walkers in excess of those being hit by mortgage resets, adding to the foreclosure totals, which are estimated by Pew Research (www.pewtrusts.org) to be three to four million by the end of 2009.

So, our analysis says that it will be 2010 to 2012 before housing starts to recover. This is far different from the first quarter of 2009, which seems to be the predominant estimate being bandied about in the media. Note that two- to three-and-a-half years is a minimum, because, over the coming years, we will have reduced the number of buyers capable of buying homes because of the large number of people who will have lost their homes in foreclosures and the growing level of unemployment. Those people will not be able to get financing, reducing demand. Nor will owning a home be considered such a desirable investment. This will make it likely that homes will drop in price below their expected historical level, as they did in the Great Depression of the thirties. So the real housing bottom will not likely occur for three- to four-and-a-half years, consistent with this book's estimate that the depression won't bottom out until 2012 or 2013.

So, how bad is housing as I write? Construction of single-family homes is the lowest since 1991; 783,000 laborers, carpenters, plumbers, and so forth are looking for work. And, of course, that doesn't include people who work at stores and suppliers affected by the slowdown in building. By the end of 2008, 2.8 million people will face foreclosure or sell their homes for less than the value of their mortgage. As home prices continue to drop, the financial wisdom of walking away from an upside-down mortgage becomes more attractive, even for those with traditional mortgages. And, as we have mentioned, Alt-A, interest-only, and option loans are replacing subprime loans as the primary mortgage defaults.

How This Affects Homeowners

To better understand how all of this affects homeowners, let's look at a typical couple who got a one-year adjustable rate mortgage (ARM) of $150,000 in 2005. Assume that, based on the terms of their mortgage, they were paying 3 percent above the CMT rate, so they were paying 6 percent interest on the loan, which is $9,000 in interest per year. If the mortgage interest rate adjusted up 2 percent when the rates were reset after one year (see Figure 2.7), their payments would have increased by $3,000 per year in 2006. In fact, for many people, the increase would have been even higher because ARMs often had initial very low teaser interest rates, or they were interest-only loans. So the actual payment in many cases went up *more* than $3,000 per year. And, to make things worse, as the *New York Times* reported in 2006, wages had not been keeping up with inflation; in fact, "real" wages had gone down 2 percent since 1993, which reduced the amount of available disposable income.

Many people chose adjustable rate mortgages because that was the only way they could afford to buy their homes, and they did not have the extra funds to make the higher payments after the resets. Because of resets, mortgage payments began to jump dramatically in 2006. And since it often takes a year between the initial missed house payments until homes are actually foreclosed, the effect of ARM resets often carry into the year following the reset dates; thus the high level of foreclosures starting in 2007.

Even without foreclosures, some people will just walk away from their mortgages. This is especially true for people with homes now worth less than their mortgages, which is the case for 10,000,000 home-owners in 2008. In some cases, people make an economic decision that not making the house payment is their best and most logical action. Sometimes people choose between making a payment on a house worth less than the mortgage and making another payment which may be more important to them, like a college tuition payment for a child. In 2008, mortgage walkers are becoming so commonplace that Treasury Secretary Henry Paulson found it necessary to lecture people about the morality of not making a mortgage payment! Of course, it is hard to imagine that this lecture would influence anyone who just didn't have the money to make that house payment!

In Figure 2.10, we saw the dramatic rise in foreclosures starting in 2007. Now, if people could have survived their higher payments until 2008, they would have received some relief since interest rates dropped. But even the 2008 ARM rate would have been much higher than the initial teaser rates or interest-only payments that were offered on many ARM mortgages.

Since the resets on ARMs were programmed to happen on a given date, and teaser rates were only for a brief period, it was not difficult to predict the coming housing disaster when I wrote my earlier depression book in 2004. That is why it is very frustrating to hear people like former Fed chief Greenspan say that none of this was foreseeable. We have seen how housing prices just took off in 2002 when the Fed lowered their overnight funds rate below 2 percent and the financial institutions opened the creative mortgage floodgates. Not only should the government have seen this coming, but by lowering the interest rate they were knowingly pouring fuel on the fire to make it burn brighter!

Looking back at Figure 2.2, you can see that the debt obligation has been growing at approximately 1 percent every two years. In fact, Figure 2.3 shows that consumers have already spent the next one-and-a-third-years' worth of disposable income. But, we have only been looking at their current debt payments. As I write this book, inflation is running at a 6 percent annual rate. Much of the increase in prices is in food and energy, which are basic necessities. So the poorer elements of our society are hit much harder than the general inflation number indicates.

Food and energy are a larger proportion of a poor person's budget than is assumed in the government's inflation calculations, so a poor person's discretionary funds are reduced far more dramatically than for the average consumer.

The example couple I described earlier had an adjustable rate mortgage. So, how many people had risky mortgages? Well, in 2003, half of all the existing mortgages in the United States had been originated in that year, either because of new mortgages or through refinancing. This is $3.3 trillion dollars of mortgage debt, which represented approximately 24 million total mortgage loans: 28 percent of those 2003 mortgages were adjustable rate mortgages, so there were 6.7 million adjustable rate mortgages in 2003 alone. And two other types of mortgages started to become popular about that time: interest-only and payment-option loans. With a payment-option loan, payments could actually be less than the interest owed, resulting in an ever-increasing mortgage amount (negative amortization). The Joint Center for Housing Studies at Harvard University gives data showing that the incidence of these risky mortgages went from below 5 percent in the beginning of 2002 all the way up to 38 percent by the end of 2005. Even in 2006, when house prices were already starting to drop in many parts of the country, these high-risk loans still accounted for 32 percent of all mortgages.

As I write, more than 10,000,000 households are upside down on their mortgages. They owe more than their houses are worth. And Goldman Sachs predicts that there will be 15,000,000 upside-down mortgages by the end of 2008. The Pew Charitable Trust estimates that by the end of 2009, three to four million homes will be in foreclosure. Not since the Great Depression have we seen such severe housing losses! And looking at when resets are due on some of the option mortgages, the end of 2009 will *not* be the foreclosure peak. This is not likely to occur until 2011, so the number of foreclosures is likely to be even higher than the Pew forecast!

The Related Credit Crisis

Subprime, adjustable rate, interest-only, Alt-A, no-documentation, teaser-rate, and option mortgages! All are terms that have become part of our vernacular and are related to financial loan instruments that have contributed to the credit crisis. Subprime loans were generally given to people in low-income groups who had low credit ratings. These people often didn't understand the loans or the risk, and those giving these mortgages took advantage of this lack of understanding. The loans were primarily adjustable rate or had low initial teaser rates, which, when reset, could double the mortgage payment. Some of the people getting these loans were so over their heads that they never were able to make the first house payment, much less afford any adjustment. These subprime mortgages have had a high rate of foreclosures, and were the primary mortgage problem for 2007 and 2008. When you hear of the high foreclosure rates in cities like Cleveland and Detroit, these were generally the result of subprime loans. Alt-A loans are similar in nature, but they were given to people with somewhat better credit ratings than those people getting subprime loans. In 2008, Alt-A loans were just starting to have a high rate of foreclosures. In fact, the IndyMac bank failure in July 2008 was largely due to nonpayments on Alt-A mortgages.

Interest-only loans were generally given to borrowers with higher mortgage amounts. And their resets were often three to five years after the mortgage initiation. Their resets will occur in 2009 and 2010, so their effect has been minimal as I write in 2008. But they are coming! Option mortgages, which allow a payment less than the amount of interest, were originally designed for people with periodic incomes, such as annual bonuses. Initially, these loans had very tight qualification requirements because of the amount of freedom that was given the homeowner on when and how much they paid down the loan principle. However, as it turns out, most of the people who got these mortgages have only been paying the minimum, so their mortgages have been increasing as their home values have been going down. In addition, many of these mortgages were also no-documentation loans, with no required documentation of income. These mortgages became known as "liar loans," and in some cases the people applying for the loans were encouraged to exaggerate their incomes. Recent surveys show that approximately 80 percent of the people getting no-doc loans exaggerated their incomes, many dramatically! So the most risky loans were coupled with the least credit documentation. When option mortgage resets happen in 2009 and 2010, they could be the most problematic of all, since their payments are likely to go up the most. And, as we have said, since fore-closures often trail resets by a year, the foreclosure issue does not bottom out until 2011. And it will take some time after that before the excess homes on the market get absorbed and real estate starts to recover. That is one of the reasons why the depression won't bottom out until 2012 or 2013.

Now, people took these creative home mortgages largely on the expectation that home prices would continue to go up forever, even though data and logic said that this could not happen. Banks gave these foolish mortgages on the same expectations: that homes would go up in price forever. They convinced themselves that even if the person own-ing the home stopped making payments and were foreclosed upon, the banks' losses would be minimal because the financial institutions would just sell the homes to recover the mortgage amounts. At every step in the mortgage process, all the way up to the purchase of the securitized mortgages, people convinced themselves that the risk was minimal be-cause of this ability to sell the properties if required. Apparently no one realized, or wanted to realize, that the number of potential buyers would diminish such that the homes would have a much reduced value.

In the past, local banks gave mortgages to area home buyers, and the banks kept those mortgages. That was a big source of the bank's income, so they were careful about who got these mortgages. Banks verified income, employment, and past payment history. And they did their best to make sure that people did not get over their heads on the amount of their mortgages because they realized the high costs of foreclosures even if homes could be sold at their current market prices. There even seemed to be a morality involved, and bankers were looked up to in their communities as conservative protectors of wealth.

Recent mortgages were handled differently. The people selling the mortgages to the home buyer often had no tie to the area and little financial background. Their goal was to sell the mortgages immediately to a bank (for a profit.) These mortgage sellers were motivated to give the home buyer the largest mortgage possible at the highest possible rate. The well-being of the buyer was seldom a consideration. The bank would then package the mortgages and sell them (for a profit) to a financial institution that would then divide these mortgages into different risk groups (tranches), securitize these groups, and sell them as investments (for a profit). Note that all the profits were coming from the transfer and packaging of these mortgages, not from the actual servicing of the mortgages. The servicing of the mortgages was generally jobbed out to a separate firm that had no part in the earlier steps of the mortgage process. Therefore, the emphasis at every step of the mortgage process was the selling of mortgages, not concern for risk. And the final buyers of these securities weren't concerned because many of these securities were rated AAA, the highest safety level rating. This was especially true for the top tranches (slices) of mortgages. This rating was determined by a generalized computer program designed to streamline this whole process, and this program was used by most people involved in the mortgage industry. Only later did buyers (and sellers) realize that the computer program that was being utilized to determine risk had assumptions based on past times when mortgages were given to borrowers with much more review and care. Also, as time went on, to continue finding additional mortgage opportunities, the standards for the mortgages deteriorated such that even the highest level tranches contained a lot of problematic mortgages. Lenders had gotten used to the profits they were realizing in the mortgage process, and no one wanted the good times to end. So the requirement for mortgages just kept deteriorating until the point that it was said, only partially in jest, that all a borrower had to be able to do was fog a mirror! So the mortgages given just before the bubble burst will probably have the highest foreclosure rates. But it will be well into 2011 or 2012 before this story finally plays out with these terrible mortgages and we truly know if this is true!

But the chickens have started to come home to roost! The financial institutions that have been party to this greed are now hurting. They are *not* able to recover their mortgage amounts when homes foreclose. Nor do they have enough liquidity to cover all their losses. The Fed has had to come to the rescue of several financial institutions, private and public, to stop them from failing and putting the whole financial system at risk. In addition, the Fed has created all sorts of innovative ways of trading Treasury bonds for almost worthless mortgage-backed debt so that the banks' reserves have some real value. All of this is putting the value of the dollar at risk, and other countries' currencies are going up in value versus the dollar as the United States fights this credit crisis. In addition, many individuals, cities, and pension funds who have been hurt by this process are now suing everyone involved. In many cases the obvious misrepresentation of risk for both the mortgages and the resultant mortgage-backed securities approached the level of fraud, and victims want justice and compensation. Of course, many of these victims *chose* not to see the risk they were taking. Purchasers of the mortgage-backed securities never stopped to wonder how a no-risk security could be paying twice the rate of a similarly rated bond that was not related to the mortgage industry.

The liquidity problems resulting from the mortgage problems are exacerbating the housing issue. Banks have become very conservative in their lending practices because they have no idea of how much risk is still on their books related to earlier mortgages. They are holding on to their resources so that they can survive potential losses. This is slowing home building even more than it would have without the tightening of lending requirements. People who want to buy or build just can't get loans! And, financial institutions have every reason to be concerned. Subprime loan resets don't peak until late 2008, with related foreclosures a year later. Interest-only and option mortgages don't peak until 2009 and 2010, with related foreclosure peaking a year after that. So the financial crisis that started in 2007 and 2008 is far from over! And banks have no idea of the total amount of losses lurking out there!

The Energy and Food Crises

For many years, a few people have been predicting Peak Oil, which is the point when the oil being produced from existing oil wells is decreasing faster than new fields are coming on line. The U.S. Energy Information Administration data show that global crude production peaked in May 2005. Peak oil is now here! Other people, including me, have been sounding the warning that we are not building the required refineries and that the ones we have are being pushed to their limits. In fact, our whole oil infrastructure, including pipelines, is at capacity. And everyone has been watching China and India's thirst for oil skyrocket as their economies boom. Well, all the problems related to these events are

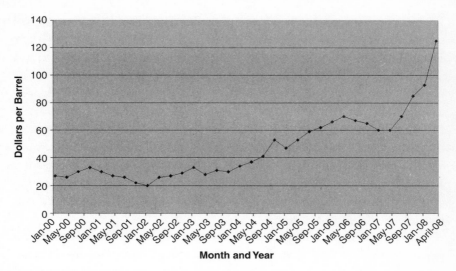

Figure 2.12   Oil Prices January 2000 to April 2008
SOURCE: The Financial Forecast Center, www.forecasts.org/oil.htm.

coming together even sooner than many people were predicting, and the price of oil is soaring, as is seen in Figure 2.12.

As I write, oil is $148 a barrel, more than double what it was a year ago. And gasoline is $4.09 per gallon. Economists at Goldman Sachs forecasted that oil would go to $200 a barrel in 2008, and economist Jeff Rubin predicted $7-a-gallon gas by 2010. Fed chief Bernanke is frustrated because oil is one of the things driving inflation, and his economic tools are worthless against this problem. A recent *USA Today* article was titled "Oil, the Wild Card in Predicting Stock Rebound." And Congress is really feeling the heat from their constituents over gas prices!

Trading in oil futures is being portrayed in the press as being similar to the past actions of Enron traders that led to the tight supply of California power. Four oil experts told the Energy and Commerce Committee that if the United States were to outlaw speculation in oil, the price of oil would drop to $65 a barrel within a month! Whether any of this is true or not, Congress is unable or unwilling to ignore the possibility that they could indeed affect oil prices and make the voters love them again!

So, in response, Congress has introduced nine bills addressing oil speculation, and several more are coming. And the Emergency Markets Energy Act passed the House by an overwhelming vote of 402 to 19. This act directs the Commodity Futures Trade Commission (CFTC) to use its emergency powers authority to curb excessive oil speculation. Speaker of the House Nancy Pelosi sent a letter to President Bush calling on him to "direct the CFTC to use its emergency powers to take immediate action to curb speculation in energy markets. They should act to investigate all energy contracts. This is an authority Congress has already given to the CFTC, but which they have not used." By the time you read this book, you will know the outcome of all this activity. But this gives a flavor of the times.

Now, I really don't know how much speculation has driven up oil prices, but I do know that the increased activity by hedge funds in oil futures is not being done for the betterment of mankind or for the purposes of providing liquidity. They are doing it to make money, and some of those hedge fund profits are likely to be reflected in the final price of oil. I believe that the underlying cause of the increase in oil prices is the limit of supply versus demand, which will not be addressed by any action to limit speculation. But I also believe that some limits will be put on oil speculation, given the pressures on Congress to *do something*, and the real possibility that restricting oil speculation may measurably lower gas prices. These limits could involve increasing margin requirements, limiting hedge funds (already portrayed as bad guys) in oil speculation, or prohibiting anyone without the ability to actually accept oil delivery from buying an oil futures contract. Note that since oil prices are a problem for all the world's economies, and OPEC says that speculation is what is driving up prices, that the CFTC may get cooperation from most other countries and their trading markets in restricting oil speculation.

All of these proposals have associated risks, but Congress may decide that the risks are worth the chance of lowering gas prices, especially before elections! And, it may not even take actual implementation. If the head of the CFTC would go public in declaring that they are going to limit speculation in the near future, and that could happen at any time, the response in the oil futures market would be instant, with demand and price dropping. How much would they drop? I have no idea. But the stock market is likely to act positively and jump dramatically. Just as the

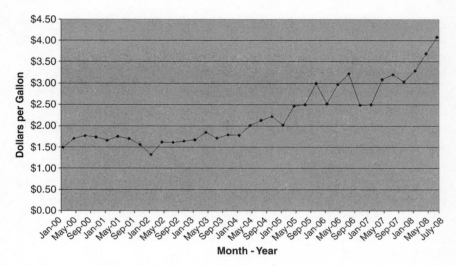

Figure 2.13 Gas Prices January 2000 through July 2008
SOURCE: www.randomuseless.info/gasprice/gasprice.html.

price of gas has been overly blamed for all of our economic ills, so will the response to some possible gas price relief be overzealous on the upside.

In the 1970s, the Hunt brothers attempted to corner the silver market, and by 1980 they had driven the price of silver from $10 to $130 an ounce (in 2007 dollars). When the Hunt brothers were fined and forbidden to trade in silver, the price of silver quickly went back to $10 an ounce. Some people feel that oil speculation is having an effect on oil prices that is similar to what the Hunt brothers did with silver, and such people want restrictions on oil speculation.

This increased oil cost is finding its way into our gas prices, as is seen in Figure 2.13.

Now, if consumers were not already at their discretionary spending limit, perhaps they could shrug off this increase in gas price. But, given the tightness of consumers' budgets, this gas cost increase is resulting in consumers having less to spend on other goods, further slowing the economy. Sure, the consumer is adjusting for some of the gas price increase by driving less, but there is no way for them to compensate for a doubling of gas prices in the last four years without reducing their spending in other areas. A worldwide depression may reduce the growing demand for oil, perhaps stabilizing oil prices. And perhaps the measures by Congress to restrict oil speculation may temporarily lower gas prices. But there is no sign that oil and gasoline will go back to the low prices they had before 2005.

Of course, the increased gas prices are not just being felt at the pump. Food costs are predicted to jump 5 percent in 2008, and oil prices are one of the factors contributing to this increased cost. The use of corn to make fuel has exacerbated the problem. Bad weather, including flooding in the Corn Belt, has caused corn to double in price in the last year. And egg prices are up 67 percent in the last year. But we continue to pay farmers not to plant, and the world's less prosperous populations are converting to inefficient meat eating rather than their traditional direct grain consumption. The world seems to be going out of its way to make this economic downturn as bad as possible!

Because of fuel costs, airlines have raised fares substantially while reducing manpower, giving the economy a double hit. They are even beginning to charge for each piece of luggage. GM is reducing their production of gas-guzzlers and the number of employees while raising prices. Again, a double whammy! Even Starbucks has announced the closing of 600 stores, affecting 12,000 employees. Not only are people reducing their purchase of luxury items like vanilla lattes, they are reducing their driving, which brought them to their favorite coffee house.

Companies are no longer able to absorb the higher energy costs, and they are passing them on to consumers. Even China recently raised their government-controlled cost of fuel 18 percent, which will be passed on to consumers in increased costs of goods, including those exported to the United States.

The solutions to the higher oil costs—which include drilling in environmentally sensitive areas; building nuclear plants; and developing solar, wind, and wave power—all will take many years. This is made worse by the infighting going on in our government. Bush and his fellow oil cronies want to emphasize additional oil drilling in currently prohibited areas, whereas others in Congress want more assistance for new energy sources. In fact, the way out of the coming depression, which will bottom out about 2013, will likely be led by some of the clean and renewable energy source industries. At least that is this author's opinion!

Our Economy Has Been on Life Support

Let's re-look at our GDP from 1950 to 2006. This is shown in Figure 2.14. It is shown in logarithmic scale to emphasize that the increase has been very uniform.

To show just how much zealous consumer spending and reduced savings since 1990 have carried the economy, let's go back and look at what the GDP would have looked like *without* the reduction of savings rate, money taken out of inflated homes, and increased credit card debt; in other words, what the GDP would have looked like if the consumer had kept saving at the 8 percent rate of 1990 and not built up excessive debt. We will assume that 70 percent of whatever extra the consumer spent due to the increasing debt eventually made its way into the GDP, because given the outflow of dollars from this country, not everything goes into our GDP. In Figure 2.15, I have also superimposed a straight line to make it easier to see the resultant change starting in 1990.

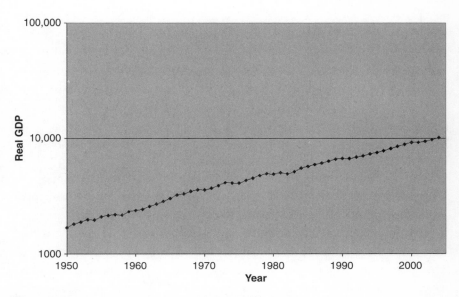

Figure 2.14   Real GDP Since 1950 (1996 Dollars)
Source: U.S. Department of Commerce, Bureau of Economic Analysis, www.measuringworth. com/uscompare/sourcegdp.php and www.bea.gov/national/nipaweb/TableView.asp?SelectedTable=6 &FirstYear=2006&LastYear=2008&Freq=Qtr.

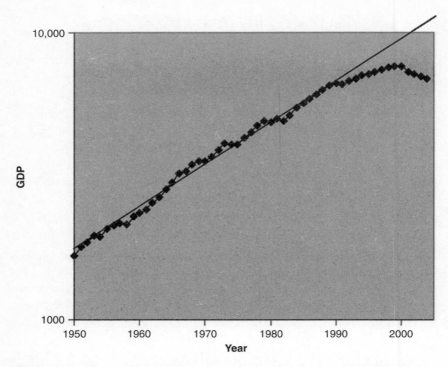

Figure 2.15 Adjusted GDP Without the Savings Drawdown and Added Debt
Source: U.S. Department of Commerce, Bureau of Economic Analysis, www.measuringworth.com/
uscompare/sourcegdp.php   and   www.bea.gov/national/nipaweb/TableView.asp?SelectedTable=6&
FirstYear=2006&LastYear=2008&Freq=Qtr.
Note: Modified to Remove Savings Reduction and Debt.

As you can see in Figure 2.15, without the drawdown of the consumers' savings rate and increased debt, the United States would have had a slowing economy since 1991. In fact, we would have been in a *depression* since 2001, with a dropping GDP. Why did I use the term *depression* rather than *recession*? Because in the last 108 years, there was only one other time the GDP dropped four years in a row, and that was during the 1929 to 1933 depression. So the economy, without all the temporary cover from the consumers' excessive spending and the reduced savings, has not been doing very well. What has been so gloriously touted as a great economy looks rather sick without the crutch of consumers going into debt and reducing their savings rate. And the consumer carrying the economy on debt is not sustainable!

What caused the *real* economy (the one without all the consumer debt cover) to be so sick? Could it have been due to all the money that flowed into the dot-com companies in the 1990s that would have traditionally gone to investments in "regular" industry and then grown the future economy? Sure, eBay survived, but not too many other dot-coms did. Historically, a large number of new businesses fail, but most of them just lose the entrepreneur's life savings in the failed venture. Many of the tech businesses of the nineties garnered huge inputs of money and intellectual capital to pursue ideas that were not challenged with traditional tests of merit, and many of these investments never generated any earnings.

Or maybe the sick economy is the result of our shipping all our manufacturing overseas, which then predetermined slower growth for the future. Or maybe it is because a disproportionate amount of wealth is in the wealthiest 1 percent of our society, restricting the ability of the rest of society to spend. The spending by the chosen few can not make up for the lack of money by the masses. There are many possible causes of our weak economy. But, no matter the cause, the data show that the underlying economy has been sick!

However, Figure 2.15 was just pretend. The consumer *did* draw down their savings and go into debt, so we didn't have the depression and the economy has *looked* okay. But now the savings rate is approaching zero, so consumers can't use this reduction of savings as a way of supporting their ever-increasing spending habits. And with home refinancing played out, the cash-out from the home ATM will no longer be dumping additional funds into the economy. And consumer debt is pretty much maxed out. The GDP for the last quarter of 2007 was negative, and, for the first quarter of 2008, the GDP was close to zero. Given that the government's inflation numbers are understated, which makes the GDP *overstated*, the real GDP was likely negative the first quarter of 2008 and our economy actually sunk into a recession that began in 2007.

Not only is the GDP showing negative growth, but the stock market is down 22 percent from its high in 2007. And a 20 percent drop from a market high is traditionally called a bear market. Unemployment is up, and inflation is rearing its ugly head. And the financial markets remain in turmoil, with potential huge losses related to housing just over the horizon.

Investors will eventually realize that they are not getting rich in the stock market and they had better start inputting extra funds into their savings if they want to have any chance of saving for their child's education or for retirement. They will also begin to see that paying down their 14 percent interest-per-year credit card debt, which averages $10,000 per household, will benefit them far more than being in the stock market. In either scenario, the economy slows, and the stock market goes down.

Summary

We have a huge debt bubble that cannot just keep growing. Governments can overspend for many years, with the inevitable bad effects delayed for years. But consumers hit a maximum debt limit that cannot be exceeded. They just aren't able to make their payments. Stimulus checks from the government can delay the inevitable for a few months by propping up the consumer, but the fall must come!

The bursting of the debt bubble is the trigger for this depression, and this downturn will affect many people. This is because the debt and housing bubbles are spread across all economic classes, whereas stock bubbles mostly affect the middle- and upper-income people. Few classes will escape the ravages of this depression.

Chapter 3

Why Are the Good Times Ending and the Bubbles Breaking?

In Chapters 1 and 2, we saw that both stock prices and debt reached outlandish levels in the nineties. Stock prices corrected some in 2000, but debt just kept soaring. So why won't stock prices return to their prior upward trend of the nineties—taking the Dow to 36,000 or even higher within several years—with this rising stock market then pulling the whole economy, including housing, with it?

In this chapter, I show that the combination of the reduced demand for stocks, debt being at its maximum, stagnant real incomes, and reduced consumer purchasing is causing an inevitable slowing of the economy and a drop in the stock market. I use Japan's recent economic slump and stock market drop as an example of what we can expect over the next several years.

I show how, by looking at the historical price/dividend ratio for stocks, we can see that the stock market is currently overpriced and make some estimate of how much it is likely to fall during this economic depression. I list some other books that, even if they don't predict a depression, show that future stock market gains are likely to be much lower than they have been since 1990.

In addition, this chapter discusses some historical bubbles and the current economic bubbles that are in the process of breaking. The stock market, debt, housing, and dollar bubbles are not unique. There is quite a history of economic bubbles, *all of which eventually broke. No exceptions!* In my earlier book on the depression I tried to show why this would happen. In this book I emphasize that the bubbles have a long way to go before they are fully deflated!

Our Economic Slump

First, we have seen that stock prices rose in the nineties due to the combined effects of an increase in the population of people in the stock–buying ages and the increased stock ownership of the general population. Let's look at both of these to see what is happening to each.

If you go back to Chapter 1 and look at Figure 1.2, you can see that the growth of the population of stock buyers aged 30 through 54 has leveled off, and it is now beginning to drop. Also, Figure 1.3 shows that the number of households holding mutual funds peeked in 2001. So there is no longer the strong demand for stocks facilitated by the growth in these two areas. Given a few more years, the reduction in the age 30 to 54 stock buyers will start having a negative effect on the market, causing it to drop. The effect of the debt bubble reaching maximum will likely cause the market drop to happen even sooner, but the reduced population of potential buyers will exacerbate the problem as the depression proceeds.

As shown in Figure 2.2, the Financial Obligations Ratio is at an all-time high, and many people have reached well beyond their highest sustainable debt ratio. But the Financial Obligations Ratio is not the only thing affecting disposable personal income. Energy costs related to the oil shortage will continue to put cost pressure on all fuel users, private and corporate. This will affect virtually every industry, especially the food industry. The value of the dollar against other currencies is falling, which makes imports more expensive. We are not just talking about big ticket items here. Look at how many everyday items—from clothes, to appliances, to electronics—are imported. The weaker dollar is beginning to make all of these things more expensive. As imports become more expensive, domestic companies, no longer restrained by lower-priced import competition and affected by oil prices, are starting to raise prices. This is fueling inflation.

Sure, if the prices of imports go high enough, it may again become economical to make more products here in the United States. This will help reverse the current drop in manufacturing jobs in the United States. However, the product price rises would have to be substantial, and the net affect on the consumer will be much higher prices. All of this will put cost pressure on the consumer, who is already spending beyond his means.

Real incomes are not going up, and the reduction of manufacturing jobs is making the overall average pay of the remaining jobs lower than in the recent past. So people are reducing spending and starting to draw from their existing savings, including selling stocks. Let's look at the effect of both.

As people reduce spending, industries are seeing reduced sales. To maintain profits and to match production demand, companies are raising prices and reducing their workforces, driving up unemployment and further reducing demand. This can be seen in many industries, especially automotive. Since many of those who are unemployed have little ready savings, they have to start selling stocks from their retirement savings. This selling pressure on stocks, along with the downward pressure on profits caused by the lower sales demands for goods, is one of the reasons stock prices are dropping. This spiral will continue until stock prices and the business level have dropped to levels matched by earlier severe downturns or depressions.

The above scenario had people reducing their spending as their first response to their maxed-out debt level. If, instead, they continue to spend and sell their stocks to continue their spending habits, then the stock-selling pressure on stocks will cause a related drop in the market, which will then lead the economic downturn rather than follow it. Withdrawals from 401(k) savings plans have already reached historical highs. The net effect, however, is the same as that of the reduction in spending in that the stock market will go down dramatically along with the economy.

Some people do not believe that this scenario is possible. They believe that the Fed has learned how to minimize downturns by controlling interest rates or that the government can "print money" as a last resort. However, former Fed chief Alan Greenspan stated in 2002 that the Fed does *not* have the ability to stop bubbles or recessions. Extended downturns are either psychological or caused by some specific factor, like the debt bubble, and are little affected by any action of the Fed. The Fed can *delay* a downturn, but not stop it. In an economic downturn, people become very negative on the economy and the stock market, and then they retrench. The more the government attempts to reverse this negativity, the more people sense that things are *really* bad and are likely to get even worse. And, even though Ben Bernanke, the current Fed chief, has emphasized that the government owns the printing presses and is willing to use them, printing excess money to solve the current problem will cause rampant inflation, hurting those on fixed incomes. Those on fixed incomes will then have to reduce *their* spending, which again causes a resultant market drop.

Japan's Economic Slump

This inability of government policy to stop or reverse an economic downturn is evident if one looks at Japan since 1990. At that time, the Japanese economy went into a funk, which Figure 3.1 shows continues, with mediocre 2 percent growth to this day. In fact, the latest quarterly GDP results are negative.

In response to this slowdown, the Japanese government cut interest rates to zero and initiated massive spending programs, to no avail other than to create a huge debt versus its GDP (see Figure 3.2).

Note that the measures implemented to reverse Japan's slump were done in conjunction with the expertise of American economists, who were thought to have the formula to fight recessions. None of these steps has helped resolve the mediocre growth of Japan's economy.

Lest any of you forget, Japan was the economy that the United States was trying to emulate before Japan's downturn began in the 1990s. Japan

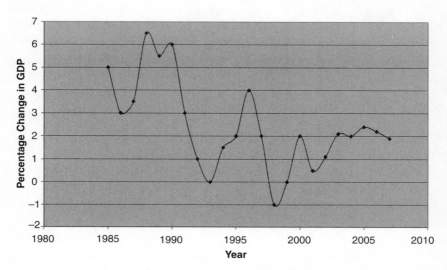

Figure 3.1   Japan's Real GDP Percentage Change Year-to-Year
SOURCE: www.imes.boj.or.jp/english/publication/mes/2002/me20-3-2.pdf.

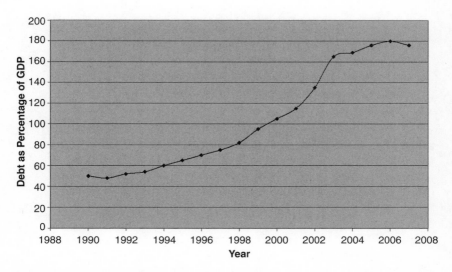

Figure 3.2   Japan's Total Debt as a Percentage of GDP
SOURCE: EconStats: Govt. Debt in Percent of GDP, www.econstats.com/weo/V029.htm.

had the computer expertise to use all of the information technology that has been so broadly advertised as the positive driver for the American economy. So if information technology was the positive driver for the American economy, how come it didn't help the Japanese economy spurt ahead?

Nothing stopped the Japanese consumer from entrenching and contributing to Japan's continuing economic slowdown. It is worthwhile to look at what happened to the Japanese stock market as all this was going on. The Nikkei 225 Stock Index is shown in Figure 3.3.

Note that the 71 percent drop in the Japanese stock market took about 13 years, from 1989 to 2003, and it had a plateau on its way down. The first drop was approximately 50 percent over a three-year interval, and then it recovered some and stayed at a general level 40 percent below its high for five years. It then proceeded to drop 50 percent from that plateau. Since 2004 it has recovered slightly, but only to its 1985 level. In real terms (without inflation), it isn't even close to its 1985 level.

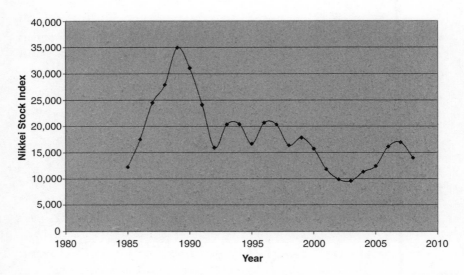

Figure 3.3 Japan's Nikkei 225 Stock Index (2008 Midyear)
Source: Japan—Equity/Index, www.sdw.ecb.europa.eu/quickview.do?SERIES_KEY=143.FM.A.JP. JPY.4F.EI.JAPDOWA.HSTA.

In 2000, the United States stock market dropped about 44 percent and then recovered to 85 percent of its 2000 high (in real values). In 2007, the market again began to drop, and if it matches the Japan Nikkei 225 total loss, this drop will continue until the S&P 500 reaches 450 in the year 2013.

Much of the troubles of the Japanese economy of the nineties is now being mirrored in the current United States economy, just with a delay. Some people attribute the drop in the Japanese market to an aging of their population, and the United States is now entering a similar era. What has happened in Japan should not be dismissed lightly as not being applicable to the United States. In 1989, the Japanese didn't believe that their stock market could crash, any more than people now do in the United States.

Remember, in the eighties Japan's economy was the envy of the world. The Japanese are in many ways more educated than Americans, and they have a very stable government. They certainly had the technical expertise to use the advantages of the new-era information systems, if that was the solution to their economic doldrums. It wasn't; nor was it the reason *our* stock market flourished in the nineties. It is important to remember that it was the increased demand for stocks that drove up stock market prices in the United States, not any real improvement in the U.S. economy. And it was extremely low interest rates and foolish loans that fueled the housing bubble that began bursting in 2006.

Note that the debt chart in Figure 3.2 was for Japanese *government* debt. The debt problem of the individual Japanese consumer was never as severe as that of the American consumer, because the Japanese people never reduced their savings rate below 11 percent. The debt spending by the Americans has been the driver for the U.S. economy since 1990, and low interest rates and the housing bubble have enabled this overspending to go on longer than it would have otherwise. But this debt bubble just delayed the inevitable American economic downturn, which has now begun. Due to this long delay, and the size of the personal debt bubble, by every measure the downturn in the American economy will be worse than the one experienced by Japan. This is because American consumers must both reduce their debts and begin to save before they can even *start* to become again a positive influence on the economy.

Likely U.S. Stock Market Drop

Getting back to the stock market, how far will the United States' stock market drop in the predicted depression? The stock market has always had a tendency to regress to the level such that stock prices are justified by competitive investments. It has sometimes taken many years, but the market has *always* regressed from overly high levels. In Figure 3.4, let's relook at an earlier chart showing the price/dividend ratio for the S&P 500 stocks.

Note that a price/dividend ratio of 20, with the exception of the last 20 years, was pretty much the norm for the last 100 years. In the sixties, the ratio temporarily increased to about 35. But in the seventies, it had again returned to the general ratio of 20. The reason for this regression tendency is that stocks must eventually compete with other investments. When stock prices are high, and if dividends have not increased proportionally, the price/dividend ratio becomes too high, and stocks are no longer competitive as a true investment. Stocks can continue rising in price for many years, but at some point a stock

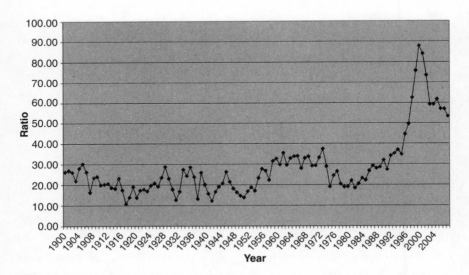

Figure 3.4   Year-End Price/Dividend Ratio
SOURCE: Stock Market Data Used in Robert J. Shiller, *Irrational Exuberance* (Princeton, N.J.: Princeton University Press, 2005), updated at www.econ.yale.edu/~shiller/data/ie_data.htm.

purchase is not investing. It is just gambling that some bigger fool will pay an even higher price for the stock in the future.

Why won't dividends increase in future years, thus making the current stock prices justifiable? First, the dividends would have to be 250 percent of current levels to justify current prices. Presumably, *real* corporate earnings would also have to be 250 percent of current levels for companies to afford such a dividend jump. Since even the continuance of current corporate earnings is at risk because of past operating costs being postponed to the future and higher energy costs, such an increase of earnings is highly unlikely. Nor is it likely that real corporate earnings will be going up at all, given that consumers are curtailing their spending because they have reached their debt limits.

At the beginning of 2000, the dividend yield on the S&P 500 stocks was only slightly higher than 1 percent, versus the historical dividend yield of over 4 percent. In 2007, it was approximately 1.5 percent. This is still well below its historical level. Obviously, people have been speculating on stock prices in the expectation of asset appreciation—the bigger fool issue; they have *not* been investing for dividend income. As stock price speculation ends, which is already starting, stock prices will again drop sufficiently to put the dividend yield in line with other competing investment opportunities. In later chapters, we will discuss some rather sophisticated methods of determining the real (correct) value of stocks; but just using Figure 3.4 to monitor the price/dividend ratio will give you almost as good a tool.

2000 Stock Market Drop

Early in 2000 it appears that some investors decided to take their money and run. No one knows for sure why they did this, but we have already mentioned that the demand for stocks had flattened due to the leveling off of the number of potential buyers. Also, most people were aware that stocks were outrageously overpriced, and some investors were just waiting for the slightest hesitation in the upward price trend to sell their stocks. However, the stock market did *not* drop far enough to lower the price/dividend ratio to its historical level. And by 2007, the stock market had returned to 85 percent of its 2000 value, in real terms.

Why did the market stop dropping before it got down to historical price levels? One reason is the very effective campaign by brokers and mutual funds that has convinced people that the stock market is the wisest place to invest, no matter what the cost. Another probable reason is the effect of the continuing influx of money from the pension 401(k)s. This continuing influx of funds into the market due to these savings plans is a relatively new phenomenon. Earlier downturns in the market did not have this stabilizing effect. People saving in their 401(k) plans do not make daily decisions as to their investments; their money is automatically invested in whatever their investment choice was when they set up their savings plan, and they don't change their investment choices often.

If people take money out of a 401(k) savings before they are 59½ years of age, they pay a substantial tax penalty. So people are hesitant to remove funds from their IRAs. The effect of the continuing 401(k) stock investments puts a damper on any extended market drop. However, continuing weakness in the economy accompanied by periods of poor market performance *will* eventually cause people to *change* their 401(k) investment choices to other investments, like treasury bonds. Switching investment options within a 401(k) plan does not garner a tax penalty but will cause the market to drop. And the increase in unemployment is causing early withdrawals of 401(k) savings, regardless of tax consequences.

Stock Market Predictions by Other Books and Articles

There are many books and articles on the stock market. However, most of these assume that the world will repeat itself, at least in regard to the perceived nineties' stock market performance. They blindly assume that the stock market has always been the best long-term investment, disregarding the fact that in the last century there were several extended periods of 20 years or so when stocks were *not* the best investment. This blind assumption makes the conclusions and advice in many of these books and articles questionable.

One thing seems to stand out in most of the books on the stock market that I have used for reference. Even those pushing stocks for long-term investments indicate that, in the future, stocks will not be as profitable as they were in the past. They tend to almost hide this conclusion and immediately go back to examples of buying stocks for the long term. Assuming historical 3.5 percent inflation, here is a summary of the predictions of real stock performance from those reference books that *did* choose to make a prediction. Note that in many cases, the values shown required some interpretation on my part, partly because the authors often gave alternate scenarios of a sudden drop in market prices or a level market for many years, and partly because inflation was included in some estimates.

In addition to the listed reference books, investment manager Robert Arnott and Vanguard's retired founder John Bogle have both stated in articles and interviews that they expect future returns to equal 7 percent to 7.5 percent (including inflation). I have included their predictions.

Books/Articles	Future Stock Yield without Inflation
Winning with the Dow's Losers	3.5%
Yes, You Can Time the Market	0%
Empire of Debt	Negative
The Trillion Dollar Meltdown	Negative
The Collapse of the Dollar	Negative
Ahead of the Curve	Negative
Conquer the Crash	Negative
The Four Pillars of Investing	3.5%
Valuing Wall Street	2.5%
Winning the Loser's Game	4.0%
Financial Reckoning Day	Negative
Irrational Exuberance	1%
Robert Arnott and John Bogle Articles	3.5 to 4%

NOTE: See the References at the end of this book for further publication information.

Reiterating, the above estimates are for "real" gains, which do not include inflation.

The median (middle value) of these predictions is zero percent, versus the historical 6.5 percent real stock performance. The baseline TIPS (Treasury Inflation Protected Securities) we used as a baseline in a prior chapter were assumed to be paying 3 percent, with basically no risk and in addition to any inflation. The median prediction made by the reference books for future yields is less than the assumed yield for TIPS. Even if TIPS are only paying 1 percent base interest, when the market is priced extremely high, TIPS may very well be a wiser investment than the market because of market downside risk.

None of these books or articles precludes stocks as a possible great investment in the future. Once the market takes a *huge* dive and prices drop, and if you are not already invested, the market would then again be viable. You want to be in a position of having capital available to take advantage of this opportunity. All of the books just listed allow for this scenario.

History of Bubbles

When listing past bubbles, many books on the economy start out detailing the Tulip–Bulb craze affecting Holland in 1635. Another major bubble was the South Sea Bubble that occurred in the United Kingdom in 1711. These events were so long ago, and the related economies were so different, that few people can equate them with current events. However, we have had our share of bubbles within the last 100 years, which are instructive, at least as far as seeing how they are natural happenings that seem to occur periodically, not unlike earthquakes or hurricanes. Nor do we seem any better at preventing them than the other natural disasters. Mother Nature creates earthquakes and hurricanes, whereas *human* nature creates economic bubbles. Human greed drives the creation of bubbles.

The Florida Bubble

In the early 1920s, people began to relocate to Florida in droves, causing property values to skyrocket. Property values would sometimes quadruple within a year. This went on for several years, with some people making huge profits. Of course, these profits attracted ever greater numbers of people "investing" in Florida property, causing the price bubble to swell bigger and bigger. Finally, in 1926, as the number of buyers willing to pay the now outrageous prices began to shrink, panic selling ensued, and prices dropped precipitously. The bubble burst!

The Great Depression of the Thirties

The Great Depression of the thirties actually started in 1929, with the stock market drop in October of that year. In the summer just prior to the October market drop, Professor Lawrence of Princeton University had declared that the judgment of those buying stocks was that stocks were *not* overpriced. After all, almost everyone investing in the stock market was getting more affluent every day. Prices just kept going up, and there seemed to be no reason why this would ever end. People bought stock on margin so that they could leverage their market gains by buying even more stocks. Why not? The United States was booming, and people were reaping the benefits of industrialization and the new technologies. This was a new era. Things were good!

But, as everyone knows, the market crash *did* come. Just as investors so blindly entered the market with no other knowledge than the observation that others seemed to be getting rich, they just as quickly panicked, without having any other specific reason than that the market was beginning to falter, which then triggered panic selling. The bubble had burst. The market drop was then followed by the most costly depression in the history of this country.

The Market Drop of October 19, 1987: Black Monday

On October 19, 1987, the stock market lost more than 22 percent of its value, the largest one-day percentage loss ever. There is a lot written on the underlying reasons why this happened. Certainly, some stocks were overpriced, and there were shenanigans going on in the market, like insider trading, that spooked investors. But the reason for the *huge* drop was that computer programs, triggered by stop-loss limits, automatically kicked in and started selling. As prices dropped, additional computer programs kicked in, creating panic selling of a new, automated nature. Without those computer programs, which are now required to cut out if the market drops too fast, the huge drop would probably not have occurred. In this case, people had programmed "panic selling" into the computer programs.

The Market Crash of 2000, 2001, and 2002

As was noted earlier in the book, some call this the Dot-Com Crash; but it affected almost *all* companies, not just the new technology companies. Granted, the dot-com companies were part of the outrageous stock price rise in the nineties, but other stocks, including those of most of the largest corporations in the country, had also climbed to price levels that made no sense.

I think history will decide that this market drop was the first stage of the depression that has now started. Two things stopped the market from dropping even further and the economy from completely going into the dumper in 2002. First was the continuing influx of 401(k) pension money coming into the stock market. This ongoing input of money into the market stopped the panic selling that would probably have ensued if investors were making their own active decisions on whether to invest in the market on a daily basis. If they were making such a decision, they probably would not have invested, and panic selling would have followed.

The second thing that delayed an economic downturn was the dramatic lowering of interest rates, which allowed investors to refinance and switch some of their credit card debt to a lower mortgage-based rate. This also contributed to the current housing bubble.

The Current Debt, Stock Market, Housing, and Dollar Bubbles

As I write, we have four bubbles breaking simultaneously. There is the Consumer Debt Bubble, the Stock Market Bubble, the Housing Bubble, and the Dollar Bubble. I don't believe that the United States has had such a perfect storm in its history! And it will take a severe depression to cleanse our economy of the misuse that has gone on in these four areas since the early nineties.

The Housing Bubble is just beginning to break. As I write, homes are predicted to drop an additional 30 percent in price. This continuing drop will encourage more people to walk away from their mortgages, drastically devaluing many mortgage-backed securities. This will not only devastate financial institutions; but it will also hurt pension funds, municipalities, and others that invested in these securities. Many municipalities will take a double hit, because much of their tax income is based on home values.

Consumers are finally at their debt limit and are cutting back on spending. This is slowing our entire economy and driving up unemployment.

The stock market is still historically high. But company earnings are dropping because consumers are slowing their purchases!

And the Dollar Bubble is already crashing. The value of the dollar is decreasing compared to most other currencies, especially the euro. And this drop in the dollar makes commodities like oil increasingly expensive, further limiting the consumer's ability to spend.

The current bubbles may be more costly than any of the earlier bubbles mentioned in this chapter because they affect a broader span of the population. Most of the earlier bubbles affected primarily the wealthy, with the exception of the Great Depression which also devastated the poor and unemployed. But the middle classes survived with minimal hurt. *All* classes will be hurt in the current depression. Many of the middle class will be ruined because they are active in the stock market, in debt, and leveraged in their home mortgages.

And there may be one additional bubble: energy. There is much disagreement on how much of the recent oil price rise is due to speculation. Although there is a real issue of peaked oil supply versus a growing demand, especially due to increased usage by China and India, there is also much speculative buying coming from hedge funds, pension funds, and so on. This increased buying activity exaggerates the demand side since there are a lot more buyers bidding up oil futures.

Summary
Some people interpret the limited market drop in 2000 and its recovery as verification that things are "different this time." However, former market drops after bubbles often came in several spaced and delayed downward steps. This was also true in the recent Japanese market drop. Everyone is aware of the October 1929 market drop in the United States, but not everyone

(Continued)

is aware that the market recovered most of this drop in the months following. The total large market drop following the initial 1929 drop actually took years, with several partial recoveries along the way.

I am predicting that the market price/dividend ratio, which is at 47 as I write this book, will eventually drop below its historical 20 level in a severe downturn of the economy. This would be at least a 64 percent stock price reduction versus 2008 stock prices, which will lower the S&P 500 to 423.

This chapter discussed some historical bubbles and the current economic bubbles that are in the process of breaking. The stock market, debt, housing, and dollar bubbles are not unique. There is quite a history of economic bubbles, *all of which eventually broke. No exceptions!*

Chapter 4

Current Times Compared to 1929–1930

Comparisons of the Great Depression to this Depression

Economists disagree on the causes of the Great Depression and even on whether the actions by the government helped or hurt. But we can still compare the current economy to the economy of the years immediately before and at the start of the Great Depression. And since I wrote my first depression book in 2004, the housing mess has made these comparisons even more valid.

The 1920s were a time of easy money and low interest rates, enabling speculation in the stock market and the wild times generally called the Roaring Twenties. But on Black Tuesday, October 24, 1929, the stock market crashed, and everything began to change.

There certainly was less involvement of the government in economic matters before the Great Depression versus now. But, starting in 1929, the government's involvement grew immensely, even under Hoover. To address a slowing economy, the 1930 Smoot-Hawley Tariff Act was passed. The intent of this act was to reduce imports so that consumers would be forced to buy goods made in the U.S., which, it was hoped, should have stimulated the economy. However, in response, other countries implemented retaliatory tariffs, dramatically slowing international trade and slowing economies around the world.

Even though the historical image of Hoover is one of a hands-off president, besides the Smoot-Hawley Tariff Act, he implemented many relief and subsidy programs that increased government spending. In fact, the New Deal, so often associated with President Franklin Roosevelt, was actually just an extension and expansion of many programs started under President Hoover.

In this chapter, I compare current times to the early years of the depression of the thirties. These comparisons include wealth distribution, leveraging by individuals and banks, real wages, consumer debt, inflation/deflation, government involvement, unemployment levels, depression length, housing issues, consumer spending, tariffs, money supply, and free markets.

Wealth

Unequal distribution of wealth was one of the probable causes of the Great Depression and is a problem now. The wealthiest 1 percent of people currently own 40 percent to 50 percent of the country's wealth. This level of wealth disparity inevitably leads to underconsumption by the masses. The accumulation of wealth by the top 1 percent was exacerbated by the tax changes early in George W. Bush's administration. These tax changes are now up for renewal, and readers of this book will know whether they were extended.

There has been a lot of push-back from those who are in the lower 90 percent of income and wealth, and this could lead to more active protests if the wealth disparity continues to grow. This wealth disparity is pushing many people who were previously in the middle class into the ranks of poverty.

Leverage

In the Great Depression, stocks were heavily speculated and leveraged; this time the speculation and leveraging was in housing. And the breaking of the housing bubble with its risky mortgages is affecting many banks and individuals. Currently over 10 million people owe more on their houses than what they are worth, and this number increases daily as home values drop. Foreclosures have already exceeded historical levels. The current leveraging includes hedge funds that borrowed low-cost money from Japan and then leveraged it to buy large amounts of mortgage-backed securities.

Wages

In the 1920s, productivity was rising dramatically while average manufacturing wages were nearly flat. All the profits were going to corporations. Currently, real wages are flat or falling while productivity has been rising; and costs for energy, food, and medical care are soaring. And most of the profits in this depression are going to both corporations and the wealthy few. So the situation is similar!

Debt

In the 1920s, credit sales and luxury spending were carrying the economy. Credit sales eventually caused consumers to build up payments to the point where they had to slow purchases. And the stock market crash of 1929 put an end to luxury spending, which had been excessive and very visible.

In recent years, it is skyrocketing consumer debt that has been carrying the economy, and that debt is now backfiring with homes worth less than what is owed on them and monthly credit payments too high to be manageable. Just as in the Great Depression, consumers are beginning to cut current spending to keep up with payments, lowering the demand for new products. Some people just won't be able to make their payments no matter what they do.

In the Great Depression, in response to bad loans, banks tightened credit, slowing growth. And many people lost their homes, creating Hoovervilles of the homeless. This is also happening now, and it remains to be seen if the actions of the Fed can encourage banks to start lending again and get people back into homes. It seems unlikely! Small communities of homeless are already starting, with a tent community outside Los Angeles already having 350 residents with six port-a-potties and two hoses for water.

Inflation/Deflation

The Great Depression was deflationary, with prices dropping. This caused consumers to slow spending even further in expectation of lower future prices, making the depression worse. In the current slowdown, dropping home prices are also causing consumers to delay purchasing a home in expectation of future lower prices. In addition, stock prices are deflating as industries slow and profits drop. Both housing and stock market prices are in bubbles, so their situation is unique, with prices dropping on both as their bubbles break. Almost everything else is inflating, as is currently being seen in energy and food prices.

One of the reasons why these things are inflating is that we now have a world economy driving demand, not just the U.S. consumer. Increasing oil prices influence the cost of most things. And of course, India and China are strong influences that are out of our control. Finally, our Fed chief Ben Bernanke has made it very clear that he will not allow deflation. He will print and inflate money if need be, and he has already demonstrated an expertise in this area.

Government Involvement

Fed chief Bernanke has commented that, in the early years of the Great Depression, the government was too slow in taking required action to minimize the effects of the downturn. Part of the reason for this delay was that the United States was on the gold standard, which limited government action. Also, President Hoover felt, to some degree, that the economic problems had to resolve themselves: that excessive government involvement would just delay a recovery.

The United States is no longer on the gold standard, and in the coming depression the government will be creating jobs, rebuilding our infrastructure, and funding new energy sources early on. This will prevent unemployment from rising as high as it did in the Great Depression. However, the government's actions will require money creation, causing high inflation, which creates its own set of problems.

Unemployment

Unemployment will be less than the 30 percent of the Great Depression; but it will rise to higher than 15 percent. And the only reason it will be limited to 15 percent is the government's quicker action on job creation.

Length of Depression

The Great Depression lasted at least 11 years, ending with World War II. Similarly, the coming depression will bottom out in 2012 or 2013; but our country won't fully recover until 2020. The United States will come out of this second depression with less arrogance and wealth. We will also no longer be the world's number one power or number one policeman.

Housing

On April 16, 2008, the Pew Charitable Trust came out with an estimate that by the end of 2009, 4 million households will be in foreclosure. And by 2011 this number is likely to be higher, because that is when the foreclosures will peak. According to Nouriel Roubini, an economist who is outspoken on the economy, this is going to be the "worst

housing recession since the Great Depression." (www.housingdoom.
com/2008/04/18/roubini-on-housing/)

Consumer Spending

Early in the Great Depression, people lost confidence and reduced
spending by 10 percent. Car sales plummeted. We can see the same
thing happening now. Not only are car sales plummeting, but U.S. automakers are shutting plants because there no longer is a market for the
big gas-guzzlers that Detroit loved to make. Almost all consumers' purchases have taken a hit, and retailers are seeing signs of a further slowing.
And, of course, as unemployment grows, there will be a continuing
cycle of slower consumer spending.

Smoot-Hawley Tariff Act

In 1930, the Smoot-Hawley Tariff Act was passed to reduce imports.
In response, other countries implemented retaliatory tariffs, dramatically
slowing international trade and slowing economies around the world.
Similar measures are being discussed in Congress to help reduce Chinese
imports. We also see efforts to reduce illegal labor from Mexico, with the
stated goal to open up jobs for more Americans. These recent measures
are likely to elicit negative responses from affected countries.

Expansion of the Money Supply

Both in the twenties (especially in 1927 in response to a slowdown) and
in recent years, the money supply has expanded, increasing the likelihood
of inflation and hurting the value of the dollar against other currencies.
The M3 measure of money supply is no longer published, giving rise to
many conspiracy theories. But the M2 money supply, which is simply
more limited in scope than the M3 measure, has been expanding at a
10.7 percent annual rate early in 2008.

Free Market versus Government Role

There is much disagreement about whether government actions made the Great Depression worse, especially with respect to liquidity. However, in this slowdown, Fed chief Ben Bernanke has made it very clear that liquidity will be maintained at all costs, even if it weakens the dollar. Bernanke even took the controversial step of rescuing Bear Stearns, a private investment firm. Such an action had not been done since the Great Depression.

Summary

Wealth, both before the thirties' depression and now, is disproportionally in the hands of the very wealthy. Leveraging in the Great Depression was largely in stocks; whereas the current leveraging is by both individuals and banks, putting both at great risk. In both depressions, real wages are flat and consumer debt at its maximum. The earlier depression was deflationary; this depression is likely to be inflationary, with the exception of housing and the stock market.

Unemployment exceeded 30 percent in the earlier depression but is unlikely to be that high in the current depression because of more active job creation. The thirties' depression lasted about 12 years, which is the prediction for this depression. Many people lost their homes in the Great Depression, and the foreclosures in this depression are rapidly approaching the same level. By necessity, consumer spending is being reduced as it was in the Great Depression. Protective tariffs are being discussed to stimulate production in this country. The Smoot-Hawley Tariff Act was implemented in 1930 for the same reason. Money supply growth was evident in both depressions, and free markets are being reined in by federal bailouts.

Chapter 5

What This Depression Will Be Like

This chapter attempts to glimpse into the future. And that future may not be what people want to see! Investors really *want* the stock market and the economy to go up! If *willing* the stock market to go up worked, the resulting market gain would be dramatic. And obviously no one wants the country to sink into a severe depression. This positive desire is blinding people to economic realities. But the excesses of the last 17 years have a severe and inevitable price that must be paid. Neither individuals nor the country could keep spending beyond their means forever. House prices could not keep rising faster than the rate of inflation, becoming more and more unaffordable. *Everybody* knows that this is true, but few wanted to face the reality of what was needed to correct for prior overspending.

Because individual debt has reached the maximum point, because the savings rate is close to zero, and because houses are beginning to regress to their mean price, the depression has started. People can argue about the timing or severity, but a slowdown *had* to happen. Some will think this chapter is like Chicken Little. So be it!

Stocks can stay overpriced for many years, as they have in past periods. Overpriced stocks alone will not *cause* a downturn in the economy. Many economists were burned in the middle nineties because they predicted an economic slowdown based on overly high stock prices. Even Fed chief Greenspan came out and told everyone that stocks were overpriced. But the slowdown didn't happen, so economists looked bad. Something other than excessive market prices had to trigger the downturn, but the degree that the stock market is overpriced *will* determine how far the market will fall.

Let's walk through what is likely to happen in the next several years. Don't write me letters about specific details in these predictions, pointing out that what actually happened didn't follow the examples in this chapter precisely. The predictions made in my earlier book on the depression have so far been largely correct. But the intent of any prediction is to show what type of things are likely, not that everything will happen exactly as or when forecasted. My predictions lay out a frightening scenario, but similar things have happened in our country and in other countries during past periods of severe economic stress. People can act very irrationally when their economic world comes crashing down around them, which is exactly what happens to those severely hurt in a depression. And the people likely to be hurt in this depression, because it will include a large number of the middle class, will have far more potential to do real damage than those hurt in the Great Depression.

The Inevitable Slowdown

Consumers are cutting back on spending, and the resulting slowdown of the economy started to be seen in the economy late in 2007. The consumers' general living costs have been raised by outside forces, and this hastened the point at which they hit their maximum debt. In fact, even if consumers had started reducing their spending in 2005, it would have been too late to prevent a depression. Their other costs—like food, energy, medical costs, and all imported goods—have gone up so much that consumers would not have been able to sustain payments on their debts.

In response to the 2001 terrorists' attacks, America has gone to war several times and has implemented costly procedures to protect our "homeland." Rather than funding these wars and their related costs with tax increases and a general tightening of the belt on spending, which is what has happened historically in times of war, instead the United States lowered taxes, and consumers went on a spending spree. You don't need a doctorate in economics to see the folly in this. This is akin to someone responding to a family financial crisis by having the wife quit her job and taking out a loan to buy a 7-series BMW. You may be able to get by temporarily, and even appear to be doing very well, but going further in debt is not a viable long-term solution.

In addition to the consumer debt hitting maximum, the continuing excessive *government* debt, even though it does not have the defined maximum of an individual's debt, is nevertheless starting to contribute to a financial slowdown. The people who have been loaning money to the U.S. government are primarily the Chinese, Japanese, and Europeans. Since the value of the dollar versus their currencies keeps dropping, the Japanese and Europeans are actually losing on their investments. They are therefore likely to start insisting on higher interest on these loans. Fed chief Greenspan warned of this way back in November 2004. The resulting expected higher interest rates will cause everyone in America to have higher loan payments, because the higher rates will make both the United States' and the individual debtors' interest payments higher. The increased debt burden will cause the consumer to further reduce spending, which will further slow the economy. The government will either have to raise taxes or borrow even more money to stay solvent. If the government tries to reduce spending by shrinking the size of the government bureaucracy, the resultant increase of people out of work will also slow the economy.

As interest rates go up on Treasury bills and other debt instruments, these investments will become more attractive; and some money will flow out of the stock market to these other securities. In the long run, the stock market must compete with other investment options, so the stock market will go down in price due to lower demand. This will be happening the same time that dividends are dropping due to low profits, causing a spiral of lower stock prices.

Company Innovations Won't Save Us

Companies have been optimizing bottom lines rather than investing for future businesses, so it seems less likely that there are any great new technologies that are in the wings ready to rescue us. In the last century, we had world-changing inventions that were consumer and industry game-changers, such as telephones, radios, automobiles, airplanes, televisions, transistors, microchips, computers, and such. The continuing increase in computer speed may allow people to download high-resolution videos of their grandchildren at faster speeds, and to accumulate even more data; but the higher speeds have no obvious big advantage for most industries or consumers. There are no apparent breakthrough technologies ready to reignite our economy. That doesn't mean there won't be great innovations in the future, but invention has not been the recent priority of industry; its priority has been making profits look good.

Companies will respond to any slowdown with layoffs to lower their expenses, and they will implement price increases in an attempt to maintain profits (and their executives' salaries). They are already starting to do this. They will not expand to go after new business because, even in the recent relatively good times, companies have found that it is easier and less risky just to push harder on current people and businesses, using creative accounting when required. They hadn't believed the government's economic data that we had turned the corner on the economy, so they have been conservative on any expansion plans. And, of course, with current economic numbers starting to look very bad, they are even less likely to expand.

The Perfect Storm

If this sounds like the makings of a perfect storm, it is. None of the above is new information, but it is now coming to a head because the savings rate is zero and consumer debt is maxed out. Debt is the trigger that is causing it all to crash. All the evils we have fed on for the last

15 years are beginning to feed on us. Some will blame the government, and some will blame the terrorists. Some will blame the mortgage lenders and some will blame President Bush. But *we* are the villains here. Few have not participated in the excesses, and few will be spared the hurt the country is starting to go through.

There will be several apparent *recoveries* as the depression marches down its path, with glimmers of hope led by those who have not yet given up on the stock market or the economy. The TV stock analysts will continue to ask "experts" if the market has now bottomed out, and the experts will assure everyone that it has and that those who are maintaining their buy-and-hold investment philosophies will be rewarded. Perhaps they will, but not in *this* life!

Over the last several years, economists related to the housing industry assured us multiple times that the bottom had been reached. Fed chief Bernanke had said that the second half of 2008 would be better. President Bush assured us that this is just a temporary slowdown and that the stimulus checks that were sent out early in 2008 were all that was needed to turn the economy around. Predictably, none of this was borne out!

The problem with any depression scenario is that it is self-energizing. As unemployment goes up, the economy becomes weaker; causing companies to downsize further and therefore adding to the rolls of the unemployed. As sales go down, profits also go down. Dividends will have to be cut, since there will be no earnings to support the current dividends. Slowly, people are losing faith in the market, selling some stocks, and driving stock prices down.

The Current Situation

The number of people giving up on making house payments is skyrocketing! Since many of the recent mortgage loans were adjustable rate, or had little or no collateral, banks have been forced to foreclose on homes and sell them, causing a glut of homes on the market and a deflation of home values. In the 2000 market drop, almost no banks went belly up because people had not bought stocks on leverage. This is not true in housing, where both people and banks were leveraged. As the inflated home values went down, more and more people had mortgages greater than the value of their homes, and some of these people are willingly giving their homes back to the banks rather than fight their mortgage payments, despite lectures by Treasury Secretary Paulsen that this is not the moral thing to do! In 2008, 2.8 million people are facing foreclosure or having to sell their homes for less than the amount of their mortgages. And these numbers are expected to climb dramatically in the coming years.

Unless the federal government continues to come to their rescue, as they did for Bear Stearns, many banks and investment firms will fail. IndyMac and The Columbian Bank of Topeka were the eighth and ninth banks shut down by the government in 2008. And, in September of 2008, Washington Mutual became the tenth bank to collapse and the largest bank to fail by far in the country's history. Banks became too confident and optimized bottom line results, with little consideration for the risks they were taking with marginal mortgage loans. And if the Fed continues to rescue banks, private and public, they will weaken the dollar against other currencies. Every rescue involves some deterioration of the dollar. At the time of writing, 116 additional banks were identified by the Fed as being in financial trouble, so this problem is just beginning. In response, the Bush Administration is orchestrating a controversial $700 billion rescue package to calm the world's financial markets that are on the verge of freezing up.

In 2008, you can get a great deal on a used SUV, especially a Hummer! The automotive market is for cars getting great gas mileage, and Detroit was caught off guard and all geared up for the gas-guzzlers. Sound familiar? This is causing massive layoffs at Detroit carmakers. Millions of Japanese high-mileage cars with new technologies, like hybrid engines, have been on the road for many years. But the American automakers, with little on-road experience with these new technologies, are a car-generation or two behind. And hydrogen cars, despite Detroit's hype, are far from ready for production. GM is trying to catch up with its plug-in Volt hybrid that is due out in 2010. This car will go 40 miles on a charge, and its energy costs will be less than half of the best current automobile for that first 40 miles. But, even if this innovative car is successful, it will be many years after 2010 before GM can introduce this technology across its product line. In the meantime, some are wondering whether GM will have to declare bankruptcy!

The war in Iraq has calmed somewhat, with violence down. But the Iraqi government has yet to show that it can get cooperation between the Sunnis, Shiites, and Kurds. Shiites are in control, and the Sunnis and Kurds don't like it. Electricity in Iraq is spotty, and everyday services like garbage pickup are often not being performed. Deaths and high monetary costs continue.

President Bush and Israel may decide to bomb Iran's nuclear facilities before Bush leaves office. This is consistent with Bush's "strike first" policy with rogue states. But the world's image of America's military might have been hurt by our being tied up in Iraq. Russia's foray into Georgia shows that they had no fear of any military response from the United States.

McCain or Obama Will Face Huge Economic Problems

The two presidential candidates have differing views on how soon America can withdraw troops from Iraq. Obama says in 16 months; McCain makes no commitment! With the U.S. economy weakening, tolerance of the war is very low. Yet there seems to be no easy way for the United States to leave without having a huge risk of a civil war within Iraq, or a wider conflict in the whole Middle East. If McCain is elected, he will keep us heavily engaged for an extended period of time. After all, if he is elected it will be in part because of his steadfastness on the war on terror, in which he includes the Iraq war. But Congress will have had it. In a very open and heated battle between the White House and the likely Democratic Congress, Congress will, in 2009 or 2010, refuse further war funding, bringing the soldiers home. If Obama is elected, he will bring the troops home sooner than McCain, but withdrawal may take longer than he plans.

In any case, once we leave Iraq, a ruthless Iranian-type religious anti-American government may take over Iraq. And we will no longer have the motivation to stop them, unless they interrupt our oil supply!

By 2011 the Economy Will Be in Big Trouble!

By 2011, the United States government will be in huge trouble. They will try government make-work programs to stimulate the economy (similar to the massive programs Japan initiated), but the United States will have entered this depression with so much debt that we will have trouble getting the money to support these make-work programs, even with high interest rates being offered on Treasury bonds. The government will eventually resort to printing money, because that is the only economic trick that has not been tried in Japan. This will cause worldwide turmoil in the financial markets. Unemployment will be well over 10 percent, and protest marches on Washington by various groups will start to become commonplace.

Congress will likely be Democratic, but they will find themselves having to take actions very alien to the traditions of the Democratic Party. Sure, they will increase taxes on the wealthy and collect windfall taxes from the large oil corporations, but this will not be enough income to support the needed public programs necessitated by the growing unemployment. Because of reduced tax income caused by a slowing economy, the Democrats will have to reduce spending across the board, including spending for social programs. Government will have to be downsized, with massive layoffs. Foreign countries will require a balanced budget plan before they will loan us any more money. We will protest but give in, having no choice. We will be treated with disdain, just as *we* previously treated third world countries with out-of-control economies.

Retirement age will be changed in 2011 to age 70, since this will reduce Social Security retirement costs starting the following year. A law will be passed that companies cannot lay off any more people due to reduced sales; companies *will* be allowed, however, to reduce salaries or work hours.

The birth rate will go to zero; and, much to the consternation of the Right to Life people, the rate of abortions will increase. No one will want to bring a child into the very tenuous economy that will be gripping the United States.

The Depression Will Bottom Out in 2012 or 2013

In 2012, China may start pressuring Taiwan to rejoin China, and the United States will only be able to rant and rave. The world will no

longer take the military threats from the United States seriously because Congress will not be ready to take on another war. China and
India will start to be the dominant forces in the world, politically and
militarily.

By 2013, people in the United States will have given up. Unemployment will be over 15 percent, and the stock market will be down by
more than 60 percent from its early 2008 price level. With everything
looking so glum, at last this country will slowly start to rebuild. This
will also be the time to get back into the stock market.

The debt problem will begin to slowly diminish because, with inflated dollars, both the consumer debt and the government debt will
seem smaller, and they will be paid down with dollars worth far less
than they are now. The winners in this exchange will be the debtors.
The losers will be all the countries that loaned money to the United
States, everyone who bought non-inflation-adjusted bonds or saved
money in a bank, and those who are on fixed incomes, like retirees on
a pension.

It will be a simpler country that comes out of the depression. Perhaps
looking back at England in the 1960s can give some hints. The United
States consumer will no longer be trying to buy whatever is new and
cool. They will just be trying to get by, getting their pleasures from
more simple things, like a walk in the park or playing cards. Plasma
TVs and such will no longer be affordable, nor will they be a priority.
Foodstuffs and a comfortable survival will be the goal. High school
students, poor dears, will have to take the bus to school, rather than
drive their family's third car. The joys of sex will again have to be learned
in the back seat of the family car rather than in the teenager's own car.
Of course, this is only after teenagers convince their parents that they
need the car to go to the library. Some things just seem predestined to
go around.

Car pooling will again become popular. The stock market will
be akin to poison for most people. We will no longer be the world's
policeman or act so morally superior in our dealings with other countries. Perhaps the terrorists will then no longer consider us their number
one target. We will withdraw from many trade relationships with other
countries, having set up trade barriers in response to our country's huge
financial and unemployment problems. Equally, the world will withdraw

from us. They will be looking at us as another world power has-been. We will have paid back debts with dollars that had lost much of their worth, and the world will be in turmoil, since so much of the global economy previously revolved around a stable dollar.

There will be cries to go back to a gold-backed dollar. Young people will rebel en masse against the debt that is being left them. There will be much negativity toward recent immigrants because they will be blamed for some of the unemployment. Immigration will be stopped.

Shareholders will force down the often obscene salaries of corporate managers and directors. Everyone living in wealthy developments will feel vulnerable, and private security businesses will be one of the few businesses prospering. Alcohol sales will jump, as they do in most downturns.

Environmental concerns will take a back seat to getting industry running. The exception will be the heavy government support of green renewable energy sources. The Democrats, much to their own dismay, will temporarily weaken pollution limits to promote industrial growth. The number of people attending college will drop dramatically because of the costs, and those attending will often have to work part-time to help make expenses. Some colleges will fold. Government loans for education will be long gone. When job openings occur in industry, the lines of applicants will be long, with people having doctorates competing with high school dropouts even for manual labor jobs.

Automobiles will become extremely small, and many families will only be able to afford one. Plug-in hybrids will be the norm for new cars. Multiple TVs and video games will become things of the past. Books will go up in sales. Religion will become even stronger, and some of these religious folks will use the economic downturn as a way of "proving" their "God's wrath" theories. Communists, socialists, revolutionaries, fascists, Nazis, skinheads, white-power groups, black-power groups, and other fanatics will come out of the walls; and they will all get an inordinate amount of support from the populace. This will *not* be a very happy country!

Protest groups will have a new and powerful means to rally forces against the government. The Internet will be used to coordinate protest marches and other mischief. This will enable quick and, at times, violent reaction to any event that some group finds distasteful. Mob mentality will be easier to excite and riots easier to incite, because large numbers of people can be rallied on very short notice when an event is still at an emotional high. Since no one can verify the veracity of items posted, half-truths and pure fabrications will sometimes trigger mass reactions. The quickness of this digital communication will often preclude the real truth from interceding.

The care of the aged, which is now thought of as a looming problem for the future, will be less of a problem because it will be literally un-funded. People will have to care for their elderly parents at home, rather than hiding them away in a nursing home. With the scarcity of jobs, few families will have two wage earners, so this home care will be possible, even if not desired. No longer will most of our medical expenses be spent on the last year of life, keeping someone alive who often has minimal quality of life. When the elderly get sick, the government will support only minimal care. Talk of euthanasia will become commonplace, even though the practice won't be implemented, at least not openly. The care of the increasing number of elderly with Alzheimer's will trigger many of these discussions.

As for other medical costs that are currently paid by Medicare and Medicaid, forget it. Hospitalization and medicines will be tightly ra-tioned and given only to those with prospects for a quick and com-plete recovery. Other than for the very wealthy, who, as always, can survive any downturn, the remaining nursing homes will be sorry affairs indeed.

Some people who thought they had retired well, with comfortable fixed pensions, will be close to poverty. Their pensions will be small compared to the cost of everything in now-inflated dollars. Many pen-sion plans will have failed because the parent companies could no longer afford their costs.

Few people will fly anywhere, even on business. Energy costs and the costs of making flights terrorist-resistant will have made flying too expensive. Many airlines will have failed. Few people will be able to afford distant vacations. People will be closing up parts of their large houses to save energy. To save energy costs, houses will be cold in the winter and hot in the summer. People won't be able to downsize because the market for large houses will have tanked. They will go the way of the SUVs!

Is the Aforementioned Scenario Too Negative?

Some readers may think that I am being too negative. Not so! Here is *negative*: Terrorists attack the oil facilities in Saudi Arabia in 2009–2010. Now *that* would be negative because all of the world's economies would be put in turmoil. And I won't even go into the type of terrorist attacks on the United States that could cause massive disruption.

More negative: The dollar could become so devalued by our government using its printing presses with abandon that our whole monetary system fails. A dictatorial government will then be voted in that restricts freedoms in order to get our country back on a firm financial footing. Remember, Germany *elected* Hitler in the midst of an economic crisis. And despite what we want to believe, the Germans were just as civilized and educated as Americans are now. Now *that* is being negative!

Sadly, I think I was being realistic and rather optimistic in my earlier predictions.

Summary

The depression started in late 2007 to 2008, with housing and debt issues causing our economy to start slowing. Obama or McCain will inherit a sick economy with no easy solution. Unemployment will be rising, and the GDP will be negative, with no good financial news on the horizon. The war will still be draining resources, and we will have to leave Iraq without any confidence that we are leaving a stable government. Inflation will be increasing as the economy continues slowing, putting the Fed in an impossible situation with regard to adjusting interest rates.

By 2010 or 2011, unemployment will be so high, and the general economy so slow, that the government will be forced to create jobs. The emphasis will be on jobs in self-sustaining energy industries that will help free us from foreign oil. But the U.S. government will be so much in debt that they will have to print money to pay for these programs. This will cause double-digit inflation.

By 2012 or 2013, the depression will be bottoming out, and the slow recovery will begin. This will be the time to reenter the stock market. The history of earlier severe downturns, both in the United States and in Japan, makes it likely that recovery will not be complete until 2020. And we will be a simpler and more humble nation at the end of the depression. India and China are likely to inherit the world leadership role.

Chapter 6

What Else May Deepen the Depression

When someone is working on an industrial process or a system, either to fix a problem or to find out what is critical, they try to identify the Key Process Input Variables (KPIVs). These are the things that are most likely to influence a change. Note that it is the *key* input variables that are of interest, *not* all the sundry input variables that, although theoretically possible influences, do not generally play a critical role. If you analyze every theoretically possible influence, you become inundated with detail and data. Similarly, in this case, we want to know the KPIVs likely to exacerbate an economic depression and whether any of these identified KPIVs are at a state, or a condition, such that they could indeed already be doing their damage. I used KPIVs successfully in my earlier book on the depression, and I have continued using this approach here.

The KPIV that we have identified as the most likely cause of this depression is consumer debt. This key process input variable was identified as most critical because it is already blowing by its sustainable maximum. Because this is happening, only bad things can follow. Those bad things are a slowdown in spending, the selling of stocks, the foreclosure of houses, an increase in unemployment, and/or the declaring of individual bankruptcy. These, indeed, are all already happening.

We have discussed that overpriced stocks were *not* a KPIV, at least as far as triggering a depression. Stocks can be overpriced for many years, as they were in the late nineties, without triggering much of an economic slowdown at all. Even with the market drop in 2000, no great economic downturn occurred. In fact, consumers just kept spending and waiting for the stock market to recover. However, once the depression actually is in full bloom, the degree to which stocks are overpriced *will* determine how far the stock market will fall. And the fall of the stock market will worsen the depression.

There *are*, however, additional KPIVs whose effects could aggravate this depression. Although the timing of these other KPIVs is likely to be later than the effect of consumer debt, events can happen that will increase their urgency and cause one or more of them to happen sooner or be worse than expected. The additional KPIVs are the wars in Iraq and Afghanistan, terrorists, energy prices, a drop in the dollar's value, the deficit, the balance of payments, inflation, and interest rates. These KPIVs are not all independent, and many are likely to act in concert. The fact that there are so many other KPIVs just about ready to explode, or actually beginning to explode, makes it very difficult not to believe that a severe depression is on the way. We will discuss each of the aforementioned additional KPIVs throughout this chapter.

Wars in Iraq and Afghanistan

Even those who supported the war in Iraq do not see an easy ending. It appears possible, especially if McCain gets elected, that we will be in Iraq for many years. Our military is very tight on personnel, a problem that will have to be addressed to support McCain's extended commitment. To get additional personnel to join the military, or even to keep manpower at the current level, the military is offering greater incentives, both in sign-on bonuses and salaries. And some in Congress are pushing for a World War II–type GI Bill. Both of these will be very costly. People are becoming discouraged about the cost and length of the war, but the war costs will go on for many years even if we do eventually bring our troops home. Estimates for the long-term care of our injured veterans run into the trillions of dollars, which is going to be a continuing drag on our economy well into the next generation or two. In addition, if we try to remove our troops before Iraq is stable, which could be what Obama is planning, we risk further instability in the Middle East. This could greatly increase the cost of oil in the United States. So, no matter what we do in Iraq, future costs are likely to be high and continuing.

Afghanistan superficially looks more promising than Iraq, but the people really in control of the country are the drug lords. The amount of poppy being grown in Afghanistan is feeding 70 percent to 80 percent of the world market for poppy-related drugs. Opiates come from the seed pod of the poppy, which is then converted to opium. Codeine and morphine are derived from opium; and other drugs, such as heroin, are processed from morphine or codeine. The profit these drug lords are making will make it very difficult for the government of Afghanistan to stop this trade, especially since growing poppy is the main income source for the country. Stopping the drug lords may require a substantial increase in military backup from the United States, and it will have to be a long-term commitment because the minute we look away the drug lords will again reassert their control.

There are 20,000 drug-induced deaths every year in the United States, and the UN estimates 100,000 drug-induced deaths per year worldwide. If America leaves the current situation in Afghanistan in place, an argument can be made that far more lives will be lost in America every year due to increased drug problems than were lost in the terrorist attacks on the Twin Towers and Pentagon. The United States will be *forced* to get more aggressively involved in stopping the drug war lords.

Besides the drug problem, Al Qaeda in Afghanistan is again becoming powerful, especially along the Pakistan border. And there is a real question on whether the Pakistani government, especially with its recent change in leadership, wants to take on this terror group, given the support that Al Qaeda has in some border areas. Afghanistan will continue to be a costly issue for the United States and the international community for the foreseeable future.

All of these conflicts will eventually wear down America's confidence, affecting both the economy and the stock market. It may take several years, but eventually the cost of these military adventures will not be tolerated, given the sorry state of the U.S. economy. The United States will have to minimize its worldwide military presence. But we will still have the continuing high costs of war-related health care.

Terrorists

Terrorists are a great unknown. The terrorists have learned a dangerous lesson in Iraq—that they can make and use homemade bombs almost with impunity. There is no need to go for the sophistication of weapons of mass destruction. If they go after the Saudi oil fields and refineries with these homemade bombs, they will bring America and the world to its knees. Also, there are many oil refineries in the United States with only rudimentary protection. Even a reasonably short interval of oil interruption will have huge negative affects on the American economy, and an extended oil interruption will be devastating. An example of the power of these groups is a recent attack on a drilling platform in Nigeria. They literally shut down the platform, and this reduction in oil supply cancelled out the effect of a Saudi increase of oil production.

In general, American industry is not geared up to protect their facilities. Nuclear storage sites may have some degree of protection, but chemical plants, water-treatment facilities, refineries, and other vulnerable areas often only have rudimentary protections, like six-foot fences surrounding the facilities.

Terrorists are the wild card in the economy because they are so unpredictable, and their acts are potentially so disastrous. The timing of another major attack on the United States is just unknown.

There is some thought that our war activities in Iraq have only magnified the terrorist problem. Even though our intent of going into this war may have been noble, some Moslem nations read our actions as religious persecution. This is being used as a means of stirring up Muslim youth throughout the world against America, which, if it continues out of control, could affect our economic well-being in many countries.

By every measure, since the Iraq war we have become more despised around the world. We have lost the moral high ground and are now thought of as aggressors and torturers. This puts us more at risk, because it not only encourages terrorist acts but also makes the populace of other countries less likely to warn us.

Energy Prices

As discussed earlier in this book, energy prices are increasing faster than anyone imagined. Some say it is because demand has now exceeded supply. Some say it is speculation that is driving up prices. Others look at the Middle East oil producers as the problem, because they won't increase output. Whatever the cause, oil prices and related gasoline prices are driving up the costs of just about everything we buy. There is a real potential of double-digit inflation due to the oil price effect. And with India and China's growing thirst for oil, no end of price increases is in sight, at least until the United States develops alternative energy sources. And we have no one to blame for this but ourselves. OPEC gave the United States headaches many years ago, and in response, for a few years after the OPEC oil embargo, the United States made real progress on becoming less dependent on foreign oil. Our cars began to get decent gas mileage, people insulated their homes and replaced inefficient windows, and some people even carpooled. Industry made great strides on energy efficiency, and we were beginning to wean ourselves, at least a little, from foreign oil. Alternative energy sources, such as windmills and solar panels, even received government financial support.

Then, almost everything related to energy efficiency stopped. OPEC started to act friendlier, and their lobby in Washington assured us that everything was now okay. We no longer felt at risk from the oil-producing countries. We stopped requiring ever-higher gas mileage from cars; and, in fact, SUVs and big pickups began to dominate the market. Federal funding of new energy sources was either reduced or eliminated. And, for better or worse, environmentalists effectively blocked oil drilling in many ecologically sensitive areas. We are now firmly back in the grip of foreign oil.

It was mentioned that terrorists may attack the Saudi oil refineries. Equally possible is an overthrow of the Saudi government because of unrest within their country. President Bush has made no secret that he wants to sow the seeds of discontent through all the dictatorships that are in the Middle East. However, one of the worst dictatorships is the Saudi government, and the United States may get more than it bargained for if the people in Saudi Arabia decide to get rid of the Saudi family. There is a good chance that whatever government replaces the Saudi's would not have as chummy of a relationship with the United States, and they may even take great satisfaction in reducing the availability of oil to the United States.

The likelihood of a global slowdown is causing oil prices to temporarily retreat. But, once economies start to recover, oil prices will start rising as demand increases.

Drop in Dollar Value

The value of the dollar has dropped dramatically against most of the world's currencies. This issue is interwoven with all the other KPIVs that may affect a depression. As mentioned earlier in the book, this could eventually sour foreign investors on buying Treasury bonds at their current yields, forcing those yields to rise. Those with adjustable rate mortgages, which are generally tied to the Treasury security yields, could find their monthly payments almost doubling, eventually leading to even more foreclosures on their homes.

One of the reasons oil prices are going up has nothing to do with the availability of oil. It is because oil is priced in dollars. As those dollars lose purchasing power in Europe, the Saudi family can no longer afford as many European products, so they raise oil prices. They are looking to keep their purchasing power the same in Europe; so as the dollar goes down in value, the price of oil will continue to go up.

Imports continue to be more expensive. Go into Wal-Mart and see how many things are imported. Then you can understand what is happening to the cost of living as the prices on these items are increasing. Of course, if imports become expensive enough, at some point it will become economically viable for U.S. companies to again produce the goods, and that would theoretically help the employment picture in the United States. However, it will take many years of higher import costs before American industry will take the risk of adding capacity. A higher cost of living will come much quicker. And this higher cost of living will cause people to reduce their spending, reducing demand, and thus removing the motivation for industry to add capacity. This is the kind of death spiral that is taking us into a depression.

As the price of imports goes up, the industries in the United States no longer have to price-compete against low-cost imports. The American industries then feel free to raise prices to help their bottom lines, which is already happening. Here comes double-digit inflation!

Record Budget Gap

As of June 2008, according to the U.S. Treasury Department, the national debt is $9.4 trillion and growing at $1.33 billion per day. And to pay for the recent stimulus package, the government borrowed an additional $160 billion. The government is doing pretty much what the consumers are doing: spending much more than their income. Now, this problem started well before Bush came into office, although his administration did make it worse. The Clinton administration received a lot of positive press for running a surplus, but to some degree that is part of the price we are paying now. If Greenspan had followed through on his concern in December 1996, when, at a speech to the American Enterprise Institute, he made his now famous "irrational exuberance" comment regarding the stock market, he would have raised interest rates at that time or done other things to slow the economy. We probably would have had a mild recession in the late nineties; and Clinton would not have had budget surpluses, since those surpluses were caused by the exorbitant taxes raised from those who cashed in on the overheated stock market. But the consumer spending spree would probably not have occurred, and we would not be listing consumer debt as the cause of this depression.

Certainly, some of the government overspending was going to occur in any case. When we went into the war with Iraq, the administration ignored those who said it would cost $200 billion. The administration said $50 billion. But at the time I am writing this, the dollar costs are well over $500 billion (with long-term costs estimated to be in excess of $2 trillion). There is no end in sight to this war spending and related future costs.

In 2001, the government sent out $38 billion in stimulus checks to help stimulate the economy. In 2003, our government gave tax relief to many of its people, especially the wealthy. And, in 2008, Uncle Sam again sent out checks! Now, if these stimulus checks and tax reductions had been matched with similar cuts in government spending, it truly would have been a boon to the consumers. However, the government reduced no costs and instead took out loans to pay for the stimulus money and the tax relief, because the government was already spending more than it had. This would be like having an uncle, who you were quite sure was in debt, sending you a $1,000 check through the mail with a nice note saying that he liked you and just wanted you to have it because he thought you could use it. Then, sometime later, you find that somehow he had taken out a loan in your name, and you or your children will have to repay it someday with interest. You *then* find out that this uncle *also* sent a similar note to a wealthy cousin, who you never really liked, and that this uncle had given *him $5,000* that you and your children will *also* have to help repay. Would you really feel good about these "presents" from your uncle? The taxpayers in the United States seemed to like *their* presents from their Uncle Sam!

In the past, when this country went to war, the populace was expected to carry part of the load. In World War II, women went to work in factories, production of automobiles was pretty much put on hold, critical things were rationed, and ordinary people were drafted. The two recent wars in the Middle East, however, were accompanied by a lowering of interest rates and taxes, and resulted in a spending spree by consumers. The cost of the wars will be paid by future generations. However, the idea is apparently that the future generations won't *have* any more wars because the Middle East will be democratic, peaceful, and maybe even converting to Christianity. So, presumably the future generations will be more than happy to pay the debt for this latest war-to-end-all-wars.

People who live in the United States either think that our government is immune to the possibility of a complete meltdown of our money system, or they are totally unaware that a currency not backed by gold has always succumbed to an overspending situation followed by the printing of money, thereby destroying the currency. They seem unaware that our currency has been without at least some gold backing for less than forty years. Nor do people seem aware that, in an earlier life, their former Fed chief Alan Greenspan was a currency-backed-by-gold fanatic, and many years ago he wrote a paper saying that the very things that are currently happening in our economy were inevitable for a currency not backed by gold. Maybe Greenspan was just trying to prove the points he made in his earlier paper! And our current Fed chief Bernanke has made it clear that he will create money rather than allow the country to get into a liquidity problem or have the currency deflate.

Now, I don't think that our monetary system will collapse. But I do think that our currency is going to be terribly hurt by the creation of money that will be required to stimulate new industry. When this depression is over, the dollar will no longer be the world's currency.

Balance of Payments

In 2007, the United States imported more goods than we exported, and the account deficit for the United States was $700 billion. This deficit was financed by foreigners, mostly the Japanese, the Chinese, and the Europeans. This causes multiple problems, certainly not the least of which is that the money we send to other countries to buy *their* goods could be better used to supply employment to our citizens.

Why do people in the United States buy foreign goods? Well, obviously one reason is status. Many people would much rather drive a German or English luxury automobile than a Cadillac because of the image thing. But there are also some very real reasons people buy foreign goods. With very few exceptions, if someone wants a performance sedan that is fun to drive, they have to go to Germany. If they want the smell of fine leather and the richness of real hand-rubbed wood in an automobile with classic styling, they buy a Jaguar. If they want great gas mileage in a reasonably priced and superbly built automobile, they go to Japan. And the mileage economy issue was made worse by the overwhelming number of American vehicles that were SUVs and large pickup trucks. Of course, there are exceptions to this, and some of this attitude is left over from the sixties when American automobiles had real quality issues. But those negative attitudes were based on real experiences, which take years to forget. Every year automobiles are rated for quality by various consumer groups, and, to this day, few American automobiles are generally very high on that list. So the problem has not completely vanished.

Of course, the other reason people buy imported goods is low cost. People can put American flags on their automobiles and support foreign wars that have little justification, but when it comes to buying an item made in the good-old-USA or a less-expensive one made overseas or by a foreign-owned company, we know which one wins.

Just like high stock prices, the trade deficit alone was not the trigger for this depression. But the trade deficit *will* contribute to how bad the depression will be. And, since in many cases we no longer even have the industries that make what the American consumer wants to buy, it will be difficult to climb out of this depression.

Inflation

Inflation is the 700-pound gorilla, and it is wreaking havoc by driving prices to untenable levels, which will make the depression even worse by having higher prices. This will be stagflation squared! The declining value of the dollar against foreign currencies is making imports more expensive. Everything points to inflation. Even the government's understated inflation numbers indicate a 6 percent level of inflation. As we have mentioned earlier, in the seventies we had high inflation for many years, so this is more than an intellectual exercise. And inflation can be devastating, especially to people on fixed incomes. Let's look at the actual inflation numbers from the 1970s and early 1980s.

Year	Inflation
1973	6.2%
1974	11.0%
1975	9.2%
1976	5.8%
1977	6.5%
1978	7.6%
1979	11.2%
1980	13.6%
1981	10.4%
1982	6.2%

SOURCE: Stock Data, www.econ.yale. edu/~shiller/data/ie_data.htm.

With this degree of inflation over the 10-year period, $100 at the beginning of 1973 was only worth $40 by the end of 1982. We will refer to this time period later in the book because it looks as though we may be entering a similar inflationary period.

Even when businesses are slowing, they are often causing inflation. We see that airlines are reducing flights. But they are making sure that they make money on the remaining flights by substantially raising prices and charging for everything possible. GM is announcing shutdowns of some manufacturing plants while announcing price increases on its remaining vehicles. And this is while real wages are flat or falling.

Now, the flip side of inflation is deflation. From 1930 through 1932, prices deflated approximately 25 percent, and it wasn't until the forties that this was reversed. However, in the current depression this is unlikely to happen for two reasons. First, in 2002, the Fed, through its governor Benjamin Bernanke, announced to the world that it would print money before allowing deflation to happen. That certainly would stop deflation, but just like chemotherapy on many types of cancers, the side effects may not be trivial. In fact, the cure could indeed weaken the patient by lessening the viability of the U.S. currency. Currency maintains its value only by its relative scarcity. This is especially true for any currency without gold backing, which has been the case with the U.S. currency since 1968 when Nixon pulled the final plug on gold. Too much currency in the market makes its value go down, which leads to inflation. Now that Bernanke is our Fed chief, the chances of inflation rather than deflation are quite high.

The other reason that deflation is less likely than it was in the 1929 depression is that industry has not increased capacity or hired additional workers for many years. Industry has not been convinced that there truly has been an economic recovery, so their response to any increase in orders has been to work their current employees additional hours or to outsource to other countries. Industry didn't add excess capacity. Also, there has been no great buildup of inventory. So when the depression comes, industry will not be forced to lower prices to keep excess capacity utilized or to get rid of excess inventories. They *will* downsize their labor force, but since they are already at a lean level, the effect will not be as dramatic as in the 1929 depression.

Two exceptions to the no-deflation statement are housing and the stock market. In this century, home building has been rampant, and prices inflated dramatically. There truly has been a housing price bubble, but it is now breaking. And, as previously stated, the stock market is also in a breaking bubble. Deflation will probably be limited to housing and the stock market. Most things will inflate.

Again, inflation or deflation didn't cause the depression that is now starting. But inflation is slowing consumer spending by making goods more expensive.

Interest Rates

Low interest rates were one of the contributors to the housing problem. Rates have at times been less than the inflation rate, making money basically "free." But, with the banks now in problems due to defaults and foreclosures on past loans, lending criteria have tightened up, making mortgages and other loans very difficult to get. So, low interest rates are not stimulating the economy.

Interest rates have not been high enough to cause a depression. But, the interest that must be paid on consumer debts, credit cards, home equity loans, and mortgages are pushing people from being economically borderline to being in deep financial trouble. Also, interest rates are not independent of inflation. Sometimes there is a response delay from one to the other, but they generally track together. So, as inflation rises, interest rates are likely to follow, further slowing the economy.

Summary

Besides consumer debt, there are other issues that can trigger a major slowdown or depression. These are the costs of the wars in Iraq and Afghanistan, possible extreme and costly terrorist attacks, a huge jump in energy prices, a continuing drop in the dollar's value, the deficit continuing to grow, the balance of payments getting worse, hyperinflation, and high interest rates. These issues are not all independent, and many are starting to act in concert.

With all these problems just about ready to explode, or already beginning to explode, it is very difficult not to believe that a severe depression has not already started.

Chapter 7

Could the Fed Have Stopped This Depression?

U nder the leadership of Alan Greenspan, the Fed built up an almost godlike reputation for being able to guide the economy. Greenspan had been able to respond to every blip in the economy with seemingly just the right amount of finesse, generally with adjustments to the funds rate, the overnight interest rate charged to banks. The economy had gone without a severe slowdown for so long that many people began to believe that severe jolts to the economy were a thing of the past: that with periodic interest adjustments by the Fed and the additional freedoms given to the financial institutions to keep liquidity in the economy, our economy would just continue to grow.

This chapter examines the past actions by the Fed to see if its mystique was well earned, or whether the Fed just delayed a series of minor recessions for the big depression that has now started.

103

What Is the Fed?

The Fed (Federal Reserve System) was established by Congress in 1913 as a means to foster a sound money and financial system. It basically is the central bank of the United States.

The Fed has 12 regional Reserve Banks and a Board of Governors appointed by the president. They have a Federal Open Market Committee, with 12 members that set the overnight Fed funds rate. They also influence how much money is in the market, and therefore the interest rates, by buying and selling government bonds. When they buy bonds they are injecting more money into the economy, which tends to make money available for borrowing at lower rates, stimulating the economy. When the Fed sells bonds, it does the opposite.

Alan Greenspan was the chairman of the Board of Governors in the years just before the current financial problems surfaced. And when Alan spoke, the world listened! A negative comment from Chairman Greenspan—for instance, when he made his infamous comment on "irrational exuberance" at a dinner at the American Enterprise Institute in 1996—could cause a tremor in stock markets around the world. His almost godlike reputation made it difficult for others to question his policies. He was regularly on magazine covers and even had books written about him.

The Fed is technically not a branch of the federal government and can operate independently. But since all of the members of the Board of Governors are appointed by the president and confirmed by the Senate, they *are* influenced by political pressure, especially when a considered action by the Fed may slow the economy. Also, they are not immune to their star status when the economy seems to be humming.

The Fed's Power and Limitations

As mentioned earlier, the Fed influences interest rates by adjusting the Fed funds rate and by buying or selling government bonds. Current Fed chief Ben Bernanke and his team expanded their power when they rescued the private investment firm Bear Stearns and created innovative ways of assisting banks. Starting in 2008, the Fed began accepting largely worthless mortgage-backed securities in exchange for Treasury Bonds. This gave the banks much more liquidity, but put the government (the taxpayer) at risk of owning worthless securities.

But there are powerful outside influences beyond the Fed's control that also affect interest rates. One of the biggest risks on current Treasury security yields, which Greenspan warned of, is that the Europeans, Japanese, and Chinese, who are buying many of these securities, will start to demand higher rates to balance out the huge losses they are experiencing through the value drop of the dollar against their currencies. The Fed has little control over this. And perhaps an even bigger risk is that these countries will start to sell back their current holdings in our stocks and bonds. Where would the United States get the money? And the stock market would crash because of the sell pressure. The government would have to print money to put liquidity in the market, causing inflation and leading to worldwide panic about the dollar. Again, these events are largely out of the Fed's control.

Bob Woodward's *Maestro: Greenspan's Fed and the American Boom* gives an insider's look at the workings of the Fed, and it does not always create a warm, fuzzy feeling. There was much dissention within the Board of Governors when action was needed, with other members of the Board often having to dissuade Greenspan from following his first reactions to a problem. Also, the Fed's actions often seemed to be very shortsighted, just delaying a problem into the future, when it later worsened.

With Benjamin Bernanke now running the Fed, people have less faith that the Fed can do what is required to keep the economy healthy. He has not yet earned the respect that Greenspan had throughout the world. Of course, Dr. Bernanke has to deal with problems that are largely the result of Greenspan's readiness to lower interest rates in response to any perceived risk to the economy.

The Fed's Past Actions

The Fed's actions since the early nineties are indicative. They lowered the Fed's fund rate to 3 percent in 1992, overstimulating the economy, especially the stock market. This is what eventually triggered Greenspan's comment on "irrational exuberance" at a dinner at the American

Enterprise Institute in 1996. He knew that stock prices were becoming outrageously high, and Alan warned that "we should not underestimate or become complacent about the complexity of the interactions of the asset markets and the economy." Yet, while he was making this statement, the Fed was allowing the M3 money supply, which had been reasonably stable for five years, to start rising dramatically. This was like pouring gasoline on a fire that was already burning out of control. Apparently due to political pressure and despite Greenspan's publicly expressed concern, the Fed did nothing to dampen the "irrational exuberance" on stock prices, and the stock market continued to rise for another four years. This certainly felt fine to everybody during those years, but it is like someone overindulging on rich meals for years—a price would eventually have to be paid.

In 2000, the market made a downward correction. Some like to refer to this as the Dot-Com Crash, but that is an oversimplification. Almost all stocks were affected, not just the new technology stocks. Stock prices had just risen so high that some investors decided to cut and run.

The stock market drop in 2000 did not trigger much of an economic slowdown because it had nothing to do with the basic economy. Even the September 11 terrorist attacks, which came shortly after the market drop began, did not trigger much of a recession. But to make *sure* it didn't, the Fed lowered interest rates dramatically. This was supposed to encourage spending by consumers (who were already spending too much), which would then cause industry to expand and begin hiring more employees and bring the economy back to the high growth of the past. But this strategy did not work. Yes, it got the consumers to refinance their homes and go even further in debt. But this influx of consumer money did nothing but keep the GDP growing at its prior rate. It did not stimulate the economy to expand. Nor did the tax reductions put in place by Congress.

So the Fed, by first overstimulating the economy in 1992, and then by not slowing it in 1996 when they saw it was spinning out of control, avoided a probable minor recession in the mid-nineties. And then, by lowering interest rates dramatically early in this century, they again avoided a recession, but triggered the housing bubble.

Consumer debt, money drawn out of homes with inflated bubble values, and the reduction in the savings rate were the only things keeping the economy afloat. Since these sources of additional money have now run dry, the economy is spinning into a depression. The moves by the Fed to continuously encourage consumers to get over their heads in debt set the United States up for the current depression.

In 2008, the Fed expanded its powers in its rescue of Bear Stearns. Since Bear Stearns was a private organization and normally not covered by government protection and oversight, the Fed had to use a provision in their charter not used since the 1930s. The Fed justified their action by claiming that Bear Stearns was so large that its failure would upset the whole world's economic stability. But the downside of this action is that it is increasing the likelihood of high inflation as the government puts more money, directly or indirectly, into the system. And, large financial institutions may be more likely to take future risks because they are confident that the Fed will come to their rescue if they get in trouble.

Summary

The Fed lowered the funds rate to 3 percent in 1992, overstimulating the economy, especially the stock market. Starting in 1996, the Fed allowed the M3 money supply, which had been reasonably stable for five years, to start rising dramatically, and the stock market continued to rise for another four years. In 2000, the market made a downward correction. Some like to refer to this as the Dot-Com Crash.

The stock market drop in 2000 did not trigger much of an economic slowdown because it had nothing to do with the basic economy. Even the September 11 terrorist attacks, which came shortly after the market drop began, did not trigger much of a recession. But to make *sure* we didn't head toward a recession, the Fed lowered interest rates dramatically. This started the housing bubble and got consumers to refinance their homes and go even further in debt.

(Continued)

Consumer debt, money drawn out of homes with inflated bubble values, and the reduction in the savings rate were the only things keeping the economy afloat for 15 years. Since these sources of additional money have now run dry, the economy is spinning into a depression. The moves by the Fed to continuously encourage consumers to get over their heads in debt have set the United States up for the current depression.

Chapter 8

Now That It Has Started, How Are We Going to Work Our Way Out of This Depression?

S ince we haven't had a true economic depression for over 60 years, and the last one ended with a world war, which is not a great way to solve economic problems, we need to look at what it will take to end this depression. In this chapter we will look at the recovery steps our country took in the depression of the thirties, and what other countries have done in severe downturns in an attempt to turn an economy around. Then we will look at which of these actions are applicable to our current economy, given our massive government and consumer debt.

Traditional Steps to Fight Economic Downturns

Looking back to the Great Depression for hints on how to get out of a depression has only limited value. Although our country was making strides toward recovery in the late 1930s, it was World War II that finally took us out of the depression. Many people wonder whether our recovery would have taken even longer without this war. And we would rather find some alternative to war as a means of escaping the depression that has started.

For a few years, traditional actions by the Fed and government will be tried to reverse the slowing of our economy. But, the Fed will be torn between lowering interest rates to stimulate the economy, which risks inflation, or keeping inflation under control with higher interest rates, which risks an even steeper slowing of the economy. And the reality is that the depression will come in either case because it is consumer debt that is driving the depression, and interest rates will not resolve that debt. Yes, high inflation will slowly diminish the "real" value of the debt, but that will take many years and will greatly reduce the value of the dollar.

Japan has tried massive stimulus programs to try and get their economy going. Because their economy again slipped back into a negative GDP in 2008, they have unveiled another stimulus package costing $18 billion. However, since Japan has continued to pour money into their economy with only limited success, they are now facing high inflation. Their 2008 inflation has spiked to its highest level in 11 years! But the United States doesn't have the financial resources even to try what Japan is doing because we have no money! We would either have to borrow more, and that is becoming costly since other countries are starting to worry about the size of our debt and the continuing fall of the dollar's value, or we will have to create money, which is very inflationary.

As we fall deeper and deeper into this depression, massive amounts of government intervention will be required to make sure that unemployment doesn't spike to 30 percent, as it did in the Great Depression. In fact, government action will be required to prevent severe rebellion of the masses, which came close to a reality in the thirties' depression.

What the government must *not* do is continue to send out stimulus checks as it did in early 2008. To give the consumer money to spend, with no expectations of doing anything but give a temporary jolt to the economy, will do no more than delay the depression for a few months. The government must be sure that any money it hands out has the potential to magnify its effect through job creation. Otherwise, no long-term benefits result.

Where possible, government money given to industry should be accompanied by matching funds from the receiving company. In this way, the involved company has a vested interest in success. And the areas identified for investment should be measured by how effectively they can affect future well-being for the country and how likely they are to create good, well-paying jobs.

It will be very tempting to invest money on rebuilding our infrastructure, like roads, bridges, dikes, and so on. This was done in the thirties depression, and we are still enjoying the benefits of this work in our parks and in our infrastructure. But, as desirable as this is, funds invested in infrastructure will not lead to self-sustaining additional jobs. Sure, we must repair bridges that are in imminent danger of collapsing, fix dikes that are at immediate risk of failure, and repair roads needed to transport goods. But parks and various good-but-not-required-now areas should not be funded for repair or upgrades. We must stay focused on meaningful job creation.

Funding of Renewable and Clean Energy Sources Should be a Priority!

Areas of critical need should be identified for special attention. The first priority is to build self-sustaining clean energy sources. Alternative energy companies should have to compete for government funds. The candidates that should be chosen are those that are most likely to succeed in creating jobs and meaningful products, at least to a level that assures continued progress in this area. Funding should be prioritized to companies that are willing to self-fund a reasonable portion of the required investment.

To persuade manufacturers to commit to investing hundreds of millions of dollars in new energy processes, these industries will need some guarantee that their energy production will sell above some minimum price. Otherwise, the oil companies can periodically lower oil prices and bring development of alternative energy sources to a standstill. Also, if taxpayer money is used on this development, some assurance must come from the companies that the manufacturing will occur in this country. The intent of all this investment should not be to allow some CEO and his marketing team to make a fortune manufacturing energy devices overseas with low-cost labor and then importing them to the United States!

Along with the clean and self-sustaining energy sources, we need electric cars so that we can wean ourselves completely from the shackles of oil. The electric car is likely to go through several stages of development, the first stage being a fuel-efficient plug-in that has a gas auxiliary engine. But, eventually the goal must be to develop completely electric vehicles. Only in this way can we push our oil independence to the maximum. Planes may still need oil, but most products, processes, and vehicles should be transitioned to electric power, which can come from alternative energy sources.

Besides alternative energy sources and cars, we will need additional electric infrastructure to support the electric vehicle conversion. We need massive underground power cables crisscrossing this country so that excessive power availability in one area of the country can supply the needs of a neighboring state that is having a power shortage, such as one that is caused by an extended cloudy or windless period. We need storage devices to level out the intrinsic variability of many of the alternative energy sources. These devices are currently expensive, but economies of scale will drive down their costs as volumes go up. We will also need quick-charging stations for the electric vehicles so battery capacity will not limit their range.

All of the technology for these projects already exists. No technical breakthroughs are needed. Sure, as we progress through this massive undertaking, innovations will surface. But these will just make the projects more cost-effective and will likely lead to another round of replacement/expansion with improved devices.

When economically justifying alternative energy products, a broader view must be applied. How many dollars have we sent to other countries to buy oil, and how much of that money was then used to finance terrorists and others who then forced us to spend money for defense? How much have we spent on our military and on wars that had at least some oil-protection motivation? What are the health and environmental costs related to the burning of fossil fuels? What will be the dollar cost if global warming is even partially true, with ocean levels rising and weather changes across our country? What are the costs of the unemployment that occurs when labor is used in other countries to supply us with oil when we have neglected our own energy industries? How much have we subsidized our own oil companies over the years? What are the costs of the pollution that has resulted from oil spills and pollutants coming from oil refining? And, let's not forget the costs of the pollutants from vehicles!

When people have attempted to put values on the above items, alternative energy becomes not only viable but an economic gain. We have become blind to the real costs of our oil addiction! So, the investments in clean and renewable energy sources, although requiring money creation because we have no available funds, will truly pay off in building a stronger economy for the future!

Of equal importance as the alternative energy programs is the training of technicians for the return of manufacturing. When we shipped manufacturing out to low-cost countries, we no longer had the need for such skills; the skills of electricians, welders, mechanics, and so on have been lost. People have to be trained to step into these jobs as needs develop.

This chapter was the most rewarding chapter to write in the book. Like the mythical phoenix that dies in flames and is then reborn out of its own ashes, the United States will also be reborn, with more self-sufficiency and ability to control its own destiny. No longer will we be victims of oil-producing countries that often don't like us and who often finance people who are actively trying to hurt us. Yes, we will be poorer and more humble after this depression. But we will survive and be stronger after the ordeal.

Summary

The government will be forced to take unconventional measures to take us out of this depression. And those measures will require money creation, with resulting high levels of inflation. What the government must *not* do is continue sending out stimulus checks as it did in early 2008. To give the consumer money to spend,

(Continued)

with no expectations of doing anything but give a temporary jolt to the economy, will do no more than delay the depression for a few months. The government must be sure that any money it hands out has the potential to magnify its effect through job creation. Otherwise, no long-term benefits result.

The first priority is to build self-sustaining clean energy sources. To persuade manufacturers to commit to investing hundreds of millions of dollars in new energy processes, these industries will need some guarantee that their energy production will sell above some minimum price. Otherwise, the oil companies can periodically lower oil prices and bring development of alternative energy sources to a standstill. Also, if taxpayer money is used on this development, some assurance must come from the companies that the manufacturing will occur in this country.

All of the technology needed for these projects already exists. No technical breakthroughs are needed. When economically justifying alternative energy products, a broader view must be applied. All the costs of oil, including pollution and wars, must be included in any financial evaluation. The investments in clean and renewable energy sources, although requiring money creation because we have no available funds, will truly pay off in building a stronger economy for the future! And it will eventually take us out of the depression!

Part II

THE MARKET IS BAD NOW, BUT IT COULD BE GOOD IN THE FUTURE

Investors have been inundated by brokers and investment firms telling them that the stock market is always the place to be, no matter what its price, no matter what the condition of the economy. Part II shows that, when the market is dramatically overpriced in comparison to historical values, the stock market is not the best place to have your investments. Also, we look at when it is time to get back into the market and the best investment options.

Chapter 9, Why the Stock Market Is Currently a Bad Investment: Even without the current depression that is now starting, at current stock prices, TIPS would be a better investment than the stock market.

Chapter 10, When to Get Back Into the Stock Market: The stock market becomes reasonably priced when the S&P 500 price/dividend ratio is 17.2 or less.

Chapter 11, Once You Are Back in the Stock Market: Index funds are a better investment than actively managed mutual funds. But buying the most recent stocks added to the Dow, when the S&P 500 price/dividend is 17.2 or below, may be even better than index funds.

Chapter 9

Why the Stock Market Is Currently a Bad Investment

A s I was writing and discussing this subject with others, it seemed as though I had little trouble getting people to believe that a depression was starting. They knew that they or their acquaintances had been living beyond their means and had been borrowing to their maximum limits. They also knew people whose homes had been foreclosed or who had lost their jobs. They also were aware that there would be a price to be paid for excessive spending, although I don't think they fully appreciated how high that price will be.

The thing I had the most trouble with was convincing people that the stock market is currently a very bad investment. And that is the subject of this chapter. The media has done phenomenally well at convincing people that a buy-and-hold strategy in the market is the best and only way that people should invest long term. The old saw of buying low and selling high is apparently felt to be invalid. The investment gurus have convinced people that this approach might cause people to miss the biggest market jumps because they may be out of the market.

In this chapter, I will try to dispel popular market myths. Using the data analyzed, I will show why, even if we weren't beginning a depression, the stock market would still be a bad investment at this time. Because of the belief that the stock market is always best, this chapter will go into some detail on why the market is sometimes just overpriced, and, like anything else in the world when it is dramatically overpriced, it is then a very bad buy!

Stock Market Myths

Market Myth 1: The stock market has always been the best place for the long-term investor.

Between 1982 and 2000, the stock market had an unusually large and sustained upward trend. Those recent 18 years are *not* typical of most market time periods! Within the last 100 years, there have been several periods of 20 years when the market was *not* the best investment.

Market Myth 2: The stock market is a long-term investment vehicle, with most investors getting the benefits of many years of accumulated capital appreciation through compounding and reinvestment.

Intentionally or not, few investors leave their money in the stock market for extended periods. They usually have some reason to withdraw funds. Even if a savings program does endure for a large number of years, since investment input is spread throughout the time period, only a small portion of the invested funds enjoy the full benefits of long-term appreciation and reinvestment.

Market Myth 3: Although the risk due to market volatility is high for short-term investors, longer-term investors are not affected by this risk.

Although longer-term investors are *less* affected by market risk (price variability) than short-term investors, the investment horizon for most investors is not long enough to discount the risk completely. This is especially an issue for retirees living off their savings.

Treasury Inflation Protected Securities (TIPS) as an Investment Option

Before we go into any more detail on the stock market, it is time to further define TIPS, the Treasury Inflation Protected Securities we alluded to in several earlier chapters.

It is important for readers to know that I am aware that the government's inflation numbers are understated, so that the inflation adjustment on TIPS will not completely keep up with real inflation. I will address this further as we consider TIPS as a possible investment.

TIPS have only been available since 1997. TIPS can be bought and sold through a broker or bank, but they will charge a fee. They can be bought directly from the government for no fee. For information you can call 800-722-2678, or log onto www.publicdebt.treas.gov. They can be purchased in minimum denominations of $1,000, in $1,000 multiples.

The rate of interest to be paid on a TIPS investment is established at the time of purchase and stays constant for the life of the security. However, every six months the face value of the security is indexed with inflation, and the interest rate is then paid on this adjusted security value. This insulates the effective rate of interest on the security from inflation, at least the inflation reported by the government.

TIPS are also available as a stock security. (TIP is the stock symbol of one of several of these ETFs) or in mutual funds. An ETF is an Exchange-Traded Fund which tracks an index, but can be traded just like a stock. Buying TIPS as a stock security does increase volatility somewhat because the fund in which the security is held can decide to sell the security rather than hold it to maturity. Holding a security to maturity is the only way to guarantee the principal. Also, the value of the ETF can vary based on whether the most recent TIPS have a different base interest versus prior TIPS that the ETF holds.

TIPS have a base interest rate assigned at time of purchase, which, since their introduction, has varied anywhere from below 1 percent to 4 percent based on the auction results that determine this interest rate; 3 percent is the assumed interest rate for most calculations in this book because that interest rate was the most prevalent in the study period.

The base purchase value of the TIPS is adjusted semiannually based on the inflation rate. So, if you purchase a TIPS for $1,000 and inflation goes up 4 percent the first six months, then the security base value becomes $1,040 for the next six months to adjust for inflation. The next six months' interest rate will then be calculated using $1,040 as a base, not $1,000. This semiannual adjustment goes on for the life of the TIPS, and after maturity you get the accumulated inflated value of the TIPS. TIPS are exempt from state and local income taxes. In the unlikely event that there is deflation during the term of the security, the U.S. Treasury guarantees the full original principal at maturity.

There can be some negatives; for instance, you are taxed annually on any gain in the inflated value of the TIPS. But this negative is cancelled if you have them in a Roth IRA (which will be discussed in a later chapter) or in any other tax shelter. For now, know that these are a low risk, conservative saving means, and TIPS will be used for baseline comparisons throughout the book.

There is another similar government savings instrument that offers identical inflation protection. They are Series I Savings Bonds. These have some advantages over TIPS if someone is saving outside of an IRA or Roth tax-sheltered mode, in that the interest and inflation adjustments on the Series I Savings Bonds are accumulated tax free as the bond builds to maturity. Also, some people may qualify for tax relief if the gains are used for college expenses. The Series I Savings Bonds have no secondary market such as TIPS, but they can be "put" back (sorry, a government term) into the U.S. Treasury with some possible loss of interest if someone needs to get the money out before maturity.

There are subtle individual advantages for both TIPS and Series I Savings Bonds. A case can be made that the Series I Savings Bonds are best for the period of time when you are saving for retirement, since no regular payout of interest occurs; whereas TIPS may be best for the years of actual retirement when you are counting on using the interest for income purposes. However, the differences between the two are small enough that both can be considered equivalent as far as their effect on the savings analysis being done here. Know that Series I Savings Bonds are considered an equivalent investment wherever TIPS are referred to in this text; it is for simplicity only that I refer to TIPS throughout the book.

Going back to the concern that the government reported inflation is understated, it is the author's opinion that the average base interest on TIPS, which has ranged from below 1 percent to about 4 percent, will largely make up for the understatement of inflation. So the sum of the base interest plus the inflation adjustment will largely keep up with real inflation. I am aware that some people think that reported inflation is so much less than real inflation that the addition of the base interest will not help enough. Let's look a little closer at the Consumer Price Index, on which the government's inflation numbers are based.

Consumer Price Index

One economic indicator used by most investors is the CPI (Consumer Price Index), which is a measure of the cost of goods purchased by an average U.S. family. This is one of the key measurements for price inflation, which affects the value and prices of stocks dramatically. Note that I am talking about the government's total inflation number: that is, the number used to adjust the TIPS inflation rate. The government also calculates a "core" rate that doesn't include food or energy. That number does not affect the TIPS interest calculation.

As I am writing this, the government is showing a CPI of 3.3 percent. Some people maintain that if our government still calculated inflation the way it did in 1990, the CPI would be about 6.3 percent. They also claim that if the CPI were calculated the same as in 1980, then the CPI would actually be over 10 percent! These are *huge* differences! So, are the much larger CPI numbers correct, or are the government's current and lower numbers the right ones?

It is important to know that the government acknowledges that it has made substantial changes in the way it calculates CPI. If someone looks at the government's U.S. Bureau of Labor Statistics web site, all of this is explained. There is no attempt by the government to keep these changes secret.

Let's look more closely as to why the government chose to change its method of calculating CPI. The government changed its manner of calculating CPI in two ways. First, it now uses a variable market basket, rather than a fixed market basket, to calculate CPI. For example, if the price of green beans were to suddenly double because of some temporary cost related to the growing of beans, the current way of calculating CPI assumes that the purchaser will switch to some more affordable vegetable, such as broccoli or asparagus. This assumption of purchase change bothers some people because they think that you should not change the comparison baseline. But the government did large surveys that showed that the consumer *does indeed do product substitution.* Consumers adjust what they buy based on cost, so their effective cost of living is somewhat leveled. This is the basis of the "real" CPI as determined by the government!

The other change in calculating CPI involves what the government calls a "hedonistic" adjustment of price data. For example, if someone buys a current automobile, it is likely to have safety features like antilock brakes and multiple air bags. If the government were to compare the cost of that current automobile to one that was purchased perhaps 20 years ago, the government would make some allowance for the cost of these safety features that were not on the earlier automobile. In other words, the government's inflation assumption would be less than it would be if the two automobiles were assumed to be comparable. The government would adjust current prices downward in an attempt to make the automobile price comparisons more equivalent. Note that this is done even though in most cases it is impossible to buy a new car without the safety features. This same kind of cost adjustment is made on products like computers and other consumer goods. For example, if the computer you buy has higher speed, memory, and so on compared to a similar computer purchased for the same price a year ago, the government's way of calculating inflation assumes that the price on the new computer actually went down because you are now getting much more computer for the same money. It doesn't matter whether you really needed the increased speed and memory, or if it is even used.

Because of the hedonistic adjustments, many economists, and this author, think that *the CPI is understated by 1 percent to 2 percent.* They believe that the previous CPI calculation method *overstated* inflation. I therefore believe that the base interest largely makes up for the understatement of the CPI.

Inflation has to be a big concern. That is why we have chosen to use TIPS as our baseline savings. Inflation has been relatively low in recent years, but, as we saw earlier, in the years 1973 through 1982, inflation averaged 9 percent per year. That means that in those 10 years, a fixed amount of money lost 60 percent of its value. There is no reason to take that kind of risk on savings when TIPS will largely protect you from such a devastating loss.

Note that although TIPS are *almost* a zero-risk investment, they are not totally without risk. Let's assume you buy a TIPS paying 3 percent interest, and for some reason immediately after you bought this security the stock market and the economy just started to take off, with real earnings and dividends rising dramatically while inflation remained low. As we have noted in this book, we find this scenario unlikely, but it is possible. In this situation, the value of the TIPS security, if you had to sell before maturity, would likely have gone down because of the higher gains being realized in the stock market. Also, if the interest rates on more recent TIPS are dramatically higher than on the TIPS you purchased, the value on the earlier TIPS will be reduced if you have to sell. Holding them until maturity would still guarantee the principal, but you would have been getting a lower interest rate during that hold period versus the later TIPS.

Gold

Some investors protest that gold is a far better hedge against inflation than TIPS, with much more upside potential. Let's look at the history of inflation-adjusted gold prices to see if this is true (see Figure 9.1).

As you can see in Figure 9.1, in real terms gold actually went down in price from 1933 (when the United States went off the gold standard) to 1968. It also generally lost money after its peak in 1978. So, it appears that for most periods between 1933 and 2007, the real value of gold did *not* keep up with inflation. In fact, referring to Figure 9.1, in real terms, gold cost less in 1998 than it did in 1933! Although gold *may* be a good crisis hedge (what people buy when they have lost faith in the world's economies or their fiat currencies), gold has generally *not* been a good inflation hedge.

Now, let's get back to the stock market.

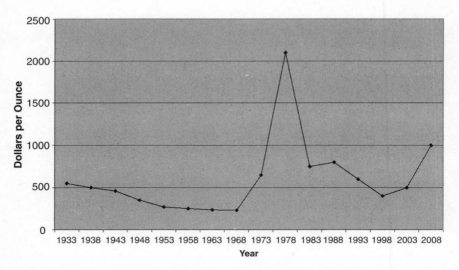

Figure 9.1   Inflation-Adjusted Gold Prices, 1933–2008 (2008 Dollars)
SOURCE: www.finfacts.com/Private/curency/goldmarketprice.htm.

Modeling the Past Stock Market Performance at Current Dividend Yields

When one looks at the gains that were made on the stock market in the last 100 years, we find that roughly one-third of the gains came from inflation, one-third came from the stock prices going up *in excess of* inflation, and one-third came from dividends. Since the percent dividend is now substantially lower than it was in the past, this means that if the market price continues at its current level, the dividend portion of future gains will be much less than in the past. So let's look at a stock performance similar to what we have had in the last 100 years, but at our current lower dividend rate. How would a stock market investment look versus a 3 percent TIPS alternative investment? After all, we are starting at the lower dividend baseline if we enter the stock market at this time, and a repeat performance on the stock market is a fairly optimistic outlook. For our model, we will use the last 50 years.

In Tables 9.1 through 9.3, we are going to do "pretend" models of the stock market since 1957. In doing these models, we are going to do a "replay" of the exact S&P 500 performance, including the same inflation

Table 9.1   5-Year Replayed "Buy-and-Hold" with 1.56 Percent Dividend Yields

Replay Year	5-Year TIPS	5-Year S&P	Replay Year	5-Year TIPS	5-Year S&P
1957	1.231	1.626	1983	1.715	1.854
1958	1.243	2.404	1984	1.577	1.674
1959	1.273	1.798	1985	1.458	1.682
1960	1.285	1.381	1986	1.356	2.135
1961	1.257	1.656	1987	1.364	1.898
1962	1.238	1.705	1988	1.372	1.820
1963	1.237	1.468	1989	1.381	2.283
1964	1.228	1.529	1990	1.411	1.689
1965	1.235	1.719	1991	1.438	1.861
1966	1.268	**1.213**	1992	1.417	1.905
1967	1.289	1.652	1993	1.395	1.815
1968	1.327	1.496	1994	1.370	1.404
1969	1.393	**1.174**	1995	1.325	2.015
1970	1.442	**1.077**	1996	1.328	1.919
1971	1.439	1.373	1997	1.313	2.407
1972	1.444	1.322	1998	1.299	2.848
1973	1.497	**1.015**	1999	1.299	3.457
1974	1.582	**0.805**	2000	1.309	2.316
1975	1.602	**1.058**	2001	1.292	1.675
1976	1.626	**1.137**	2002	1.290	**0.980**
1977	1.676	**0.870**	2003	1.297	**0.977**
1978	1.681	**1.065**	2004	1.288	**0.891**
1979	1.695	1.701	2005	1.281	**1.021**
1980	1.781	1.627	2006	1.270	1.335
1981	1.848	1.232	2007	1.265	1.803
1982	1.799	1.598			

numbers as the last 50 years, but *at current dividend rates*. The dividend yield for the last 10 years has been 1.56 percent, which is far less than historical dividend yields. This is mostly a reflection of the extremely high price of stocks, rather than some dramatic change in dividend policy. Without a *dramatic* drop in stock prices, this dividend ratio is likely to stay the same for the immediate future. When we "replay" the last 50 years' S&P 500 performance, we are going to assume this 1.56 percent dividend yield, then compare the stock market performance versus the almost zero risk 3 percent TIPS performance, assuming that they were available at that time. Again, the only difference from the prior market performance is to incorporate recent dividend yields onto the past 50 years' stock market performance.

Five-Year Buy-and-Hold

The numbers within Table 9.1 are the total gains on an investment held for five years. Assume that you are going to invest $100 and leave it invested for five years. The first number under "5-Year TIPS" is 1.231. That means that if you bought TIPS at the beginning of 1953, and they were paying an assumed 3 percent interest, the total principal, including inflation, at the end of 1957, would have been $123.10. Equally, the first number under "5-Year S&P" is 1.626. That means that the total value of your $100 invested in 1953 on the S&P 500 would be $162.60 in 1957.

The bold numbers, representing the 13 lowest prior five-year results, are all with S&P 500 stocks. Now, since the stock market is supposed to be the best place to invest, this should be surprising. In fact, if TIPS were equally likely to give superior yields, the random odds of the lowest 13 yield results being exclusively from the S&P 500 would be less than one in ten thousand! So, this does not seem to be random. There must be an assignable cause! Let's relook at the real S&P 500 values in Figure 9.2 for the periods five years before the earlier Table 9.1 results, because that is when the five-year periods started. We especially want to look at the two groupings of low yields. Five years prior to the 1969–1978 grouping will be the years 1965 through 1974. Five years before the most recent low result grouping will be 1998 through 2002.

Looking at Figure 9.2 for both the period 1965–1974 and the period 1998–2002, we note that both represented unusually high-priced S&P 500 periods. So, buying during these times when the market was historically high priced generated very low 5-year yields that were lower than the lowest TIPS yields over the total 50-year period.

Let's also look at these same years on the Figure 9.3 Price/Dividend Ratio graph.

Again, looking at Figure 9.3 for both the period 1965–1974 and the period 1998–2002, we note that both represented unusually high price/dividend ratio periods. So, buying during these times when the

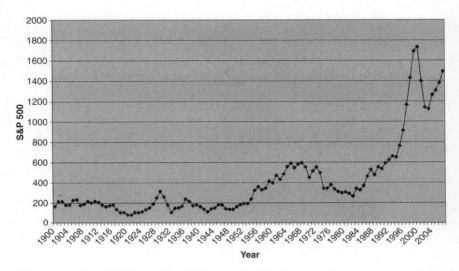

Figure 9.2   Real (Without Inflation) S&P 500 Value History (2007 Dollars)
SOURCE: Stock Data, www.econ.yale.edu/~shiller/data/ie_data.htm.

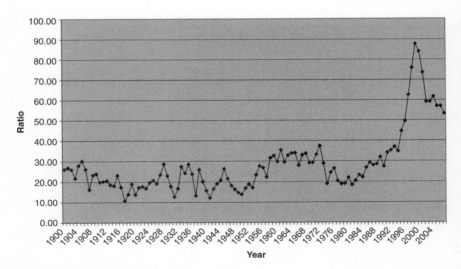

Figure 9.3   Year-End Price/Dividend Ratio
SOURCE: Stock Data, www.econ.yale.edu/~shiller/data/ie_data.htm.

ratio was historically high generated very low 5-year yields that were lower than the lowest TIPS yields over the total 50-year period.

I believe that the price/dividend ratio shown in Figure 9.3 is a better way of evaluating whether the market is overpriced than looking at the S&P 500 prices. But, in this case, both comparisons worked!

If you take the average yield for both TIPS and the S&P 500 over the 50 years shown in Table 9.1, the S&P 500 average yield easily beat TIPS. But, the average yields for the S&P 500 would have been even higher without the 13 low-yield periods shown in bold in Table 9.1. And, even more important, if someone had invested in the S&P 500 in those low-yield periods and suddenly needed to withdraw her money, she would be forced to take a loss versus her potential TIPS gains, often withdrawing funds that didn't even keep up with inflation. Even though people may invest with the intent of keeping their money invested for 20 or more years, emergencies or just plain human nature often causes them to withdraw their money early. We will be discussing this further, including formulas that help in giving guidelines on when the market is just too high to be a good investment.

10-Year Buy-and-Hold

Let's look at 10-year holds and see if we get similar results as we did on the 5-year holds. The numbers in Table 9.2 are the total gains on an investment held for 10 years. Assume that you are going to invest $100 and leave it invested for 10 years. The first number under "10-Year TIPS" is 1.622. That means that if you bought TIPS at the beginning of 1948, and they were paying an assumed 3 percent interest, the total principal, including inflation, at the end of 1957, would have been $162.20. Equally, the first number under "10-Year S&P" is 3.051. That means that the total value of your $100 invested in 1948 on the S&P 500 would be $305.10 in 1957.

The bold numbers, representing the seven lowest prior 10-year results, are all with S&P 500 stocks. This is fewer than in the 5-year hold example, but it does not mean that things are better. Since the second problem grouping in the 5-year holds represented the investment years 1998–2002, we would not expect to see the results of those investment years until 2007–2011, and we don't have the results for most of those

Table 9.2   10-Year Replayed "Buy-and-Hold" with 1.56 Percent Dividend Yields

Replay Year	10-Year TIPS	10-Year S&P	Replay Year	10-Year TIPS	10-Year S&P
1957	1.622	3.051	1983	2.883	1.974
1958	1.603	4.241	1984	2.673	2.848
1959	1.664	4.173	1985	2.597	2.735
1960	1.594	3.324	1986	2.506	2.631
1961	1.516	3.515	1987	2.454	3.034
1962	1.524	2.772	1988	2.354	3.374
1963	1.538	3.530	1989	2.179	3.823
1964	1.563	2.750	1990	2.058	2.840
1965	1.587	2.373	1991	1.950	3.974
1966	1.594	2.010	1992	1.933	3.617
1967	1.596	2.817	1993	1.914	3.302
1968	1.641	2.197	1994	1.891	3.207
1969	1.711	1.795	1995	1.869	3.404
1970	1.780	1.852	1996	1.909	3.572
1971	1.825	1.666	1997	1.861	4.586
1972	1.861	2.185	1998	1.812	5.168
1973	1.987	1.518	1999	1.779	4.855
1974	2.204	**0.945**	2000	1.735	4.669
1975	2.309	**1.139**	2001	1.715	3.214
1976	2.339	1.562	2002	1.694	2.358
1977	2.420	**1.151**	2003	1.685	2.783
1978	2.517	**1.081**	2004	1.679	3.081
1979	2.680	**1.369**	2005	1.673	2.366
1980	2.852	1.720	2006	1.658	2.235
1981	3.004	**1.402**	2007	1.652	1.766
1982	3.016	**1.391**			

years. However, for 2007 you can already see that the S&P 500 results are quite disappointing. But let's relook at the real S&P 500 values in Figure 9.3 for the periods 10 years before the Table 9.2 low results of years 1974 through 1982. The 10 years before, when the investment started, were the years 1965 through 1973.

These are the exact same problem years that were identified in the five-year holds, so the effect of investing when the market was high had not gone away after 10 years. We now want to see if the problem years are still apparent after a 20-year investment period.

Table 9.3 20-Year Replayed "Buy-and-Hold" with 1.56 Percent Dividend Yields

Replay Year	20-Year TIPS	20-Year S&P	Replay Year	20-Year TIPS	20-Year S&P
1957	3.495	5.172	1983	5.727	2.997
1958	3.654	5.697	1984	5.891	2.690
1959	3.715	6.535	1985	5.996	3.116
1960	3.738	7.489	1986	5.863	4.110
1961	3.432	11.225	1987	5.940	3.492
1962	3.196	8.805	1988	5.924	3.646
1963	3.156	8.764	1989	5.840	5.234
1964	3.116	8.701	1990	5.869	4.886
1965	3.107	7.259	1991	5.857	5.570
1966	2.730	7.157	1992	5.830	5.032
1967	2.589	8.595	1993	5.519	6.519
1968	2.631	9.315	1994	5.056	9.133
1969	2.847	7.489	1995	4.854	9.311
1970	2.837	6.155	1996	4.785	9.398
1971	2.766	5.855	1997	4.567	13.912
1972	2.837	6.055	1998	4.265	17.437
1973	3.054	5.360	1999	3.876	18.557
1974	3.445	2.597	2000	3.569	13.259
1975	3.664	2.704	2001	3.345	12.772
1976	3.729	3.139	2002	3.275	8.529
1977	3.863	3.242	2003	3.225	9.191
1978	4.130	**2.373**	2004	3.203	9.880
1979	4.586	**2.457**	2005	3.191	8.053
1980	5.077	3.185	2006	3.256	7.983
1981	5.481	**2.335**	2007	3.207	8.100
1982	5.612	3.039			

20-Year Buy-and-Hold

Let's look at 20-year holds and see if we get similar results as we did on the 5-year and 10-year holds. The numbers in Table 9.3 are the total gains on an investment held for 20 years. Assume that you are going to invest $100 and leave it invested for 20 years. The first number under "20-Year TIPS" is 3.495. That means that if you bought TIPS at the beginning of 1938, and they were paying an assumed 3 percent interest, the total principal, including inflation, at the end of 1957, would have been $349.50. Equally, the first number under "20-Year S&P" is 5.172.

That means that the total value of your $100 invested in 1938 on the S&P 500 would be $517.20 in 1957.

The bold numbers, representing the three lowest prior 20-year results, are all with S&P 500 stocks. This is fewer than in the 5-year hold and 10-year hold examples, so it appears that after 20 years the negatives on investing when the market is historically high priced are minimized. This is consistent with the general observation that over a period of 20 or more years, the market is probably the best investment regardless of the price of the market when you buy. However, as we have stated, relatively few investors leave their investments untouched for that number of years, no matter what their intentions. So, later in the book we will be identifying a way to get the higher long-term yields of the market while utilizing TIPS to minimize the risks related to early withdrawals.

Other Methods for Determining Whether the Market Is Overpriced

In an earlier chapter, we used the price/dividend ratio to determine that the current stock market is dramatically overpriced, at least versus historical values. There are other more esoteric ways to evaluate the fair-market value of the stock market, which we will now review. These other methods are being shown only to emphasize that, no matter what method we use for this evaluation, we find that the stock market is currently priced too high! As we already stated, the price/dividend ratio is a fully acceptable way of determining the correct market price, and it is the key measurement we use in this book. So those of you without a keen interest in the other methods can just quickly gloss over the details of the other techniques discussed in this chapter.

One way to estimate the correct stock market value is based on an expected Future Discounted Dividend Stream. Two of the reference books, Smithers and Wright's *Valuing Wall Street* and Bernstein's *The Four Pillars of Investing,* use this method. The other method is to estimate the stock market's value by determining the stock market companies' replacement value. Both Smithers and Wright and Stein and DeMuth use similar methods related to fundamental values. You can refer to these books for more detail. I will briefly review both methods. I will also show the regression to the mean way of evaluating whether stocks are overpriced.

Irving Fisher Formula

Seventy-five years ago, Irving Fisher, former professor at Yale, came up with a way to evaluate individual stocks, or in our case, the S&P 500 Index. It is similar to what we discussed earlier, that a company is worth its Future Discounted Dividend Stream. The formula derived by Irving Fisher is:

$$\text{Market Value} = \text{Current Dividend} / (\text{DR} - \text{Dividend Rate of Growth})$$

Let me explain each of the terms in this formula.

Market Value is, in this case, the fair-market price of the S&P 500 stock index. Once we calculate this value, we can then compare it to the actual price of the S&P 500 that is announced daily. In this case, we are trying to calculate what the price, or Market Value, *should* be, based on the Current Dividends being paid by the companies in the S&P 500, and how much those dividends are increasing every year, which is the Dividend Rate of Growth.

The DR is the yield we expect from the stock market to make it a viable investment. Because the stock market is generally thought to have more risk and variation than many alternate investments, people won't normally invest in the stock market unless its expected yield is higher than more conservative investments, like government bonds. In very positive investment time periods, where people feel very good about the stock market's likelihood to go up, they may assume a small amount of stock market risk and therefore a smaller DR. In hard times, such as in the midst of a depression, when investors are sour on the market, investors may demand a very large market risk adjustment, which makes the DR higher. We will evaluate the Market Value with two extremes of DR, which includes the assumed market risk.

First, let's see how the market is priced if we assume a positive investor attitude. We have assumed throughout this book that, besides inflation, we can get 3 percent from TIPS, a very low-risk investment. The actual base interest rate has ranged from below 1 percent to 4 percent; but 3 percent has been the norm. We will assume for this analysis that future inflation will be 3.5 percent (the same as historical), and we want an added 1.5 percent for stock market risk. This sums to 8.0 percent. This is our DR. This is a very low DR because it assumes that people *want* to invest in the stock market and are not requiring it to pay more than 1.5 percent over a conservative investment like TIPS. When the stock market is very popular, as it was in the nineties, the DR is small. Let's now calculate what the price of the S&P 500 should be under a positive investment attitude.

Using the data from Robert Shiller's Real S&P Stock Price Index (www.econ.yale.edu/~shiller/data/ie_data.htm), we calculate that historical average dividend growth (Dividend Rate of Growth) has been 4.2 percent. Current dividends on the S&P 500 are $28.00. Plugging these values into the previous equation we get:

Market Value = Current Dividend/(DR − Dividend Rate of Growth)

Market Value = $28.00/(0.08 − 0.042)

Market Value = $737, versus the $1,278 S&P 500
                          price as of mid-2008

On the basis shown here, the market was 73 percent overpriced at mid-2008, even when assuming a very positive investor attitude.

If investors become sour on the stock market, which will happen if investors begin to accept that we are at the beginning of a depression, then they will not want to invest in the market unless they foresee profits far in excess of what they could get on a more conservative investment such as TIPS. We will now recalculate the Irving Fisher formula for Market Value with a negative attitude toward the market.

With a negative attitude on the stock market, the investor will demand more than an added 1.5 percent premium for market risk. Let's assume that the investor demands an extra 4 percent. This means that the new DR will be 3 percent TIPS, plus 3.5 percent inflation, plus 4 percent extra for stock market risk. This sums to 10.5 percent, or 0.105.

The other values in the equation stay the same as in the earlier chapter.

Market Value = Current Dividend/(DR − Dividend Rate of Growth)

Market Value = $28.00/(0.105 − 0.042).

Market Value = $444, versus the $1,278 S&P 500 price at mid-2008

On this basis, the market, as of mid-2008, was 188 percent over-priced. This is more likely to be the value of interest because we want to know how far the market will drop in the midst of this depression, when the investors will truly be negative.

Note that there have been periods in the past where investors have demanded a DR value *far greater* than the 0.105 we used in the above calculation.

Replacement Cost versus Selling Price

Another way to evaluate an investment is to determine its replacement cost versus its selling price. In the case of the S&P 500, the assumed replacement price would be either the internal book value of all the companies in the S&P 500 or the government's value on what these companies are worth. Both methods give similar results.

In *Valuing Wall Street*, using the government's estimates on company values, Andrew Smithers and Stephen Wright concluded that the market was approximately 2.25 times overpriced at the end of 1998. Adjusting these numbers to the S&P 500 price as of 2008, we conclude that the market was 203 percent overpriced as of mid-2008, which is close to the 188 percent overpriced market value we found using Fisher's Future Discounted Dividend Stream method with a more negative-market DR.

Regression to the Mean

One other very simple way of evaluating the market is to use a concept called regression to the price mean. As stated earlier, the real gain on the stock market (not including inflation) for the first half of the last century was 5 percent. Between 1951 and 1982, it was 6 percent. So, for the first 82 years of the last century, the average real gain on the stock market was 5.4 percent per year. For the last 25 years, the real stock market gain has been 6.6 percent per year. Since we have seen nothing that justified the excess rise in stock prices since 1982, this means that the price of stocks has been growing in excess of 1.2 percent (6.6%–5.4%) for each of the last 25 years and would now be expected to regress to the price mean.

Let's see how much it should regress. Given that the market price has been increasing excessively at a 1.2 percent rate for 25 years, if we take 1.02 to the 25th power, we get 1.64. This means that the market is overpriced by 64 percent.

Summary of Analyses

Let's summarize all the methods we used in this chapter to evaluate whether the market was overpriced at mid-2008:

METHOD	AMOUNT OVERPRICED
Market Value via Future Discounted Dividend	73% (positive attitude)
Market Value via Future Discounted Dividend	188% (negative attitude)
Replacement cost versus its S&P 500 selling price	203%
Regression to the price mean	64%

The above results show that the market is anywhere from 64 percent to 203 percent overpriced at the 1278 price of the S&P 500 at mid-2008. This can be compared to our price/dividend ratio analysis in Chapter 3 that showed the market as being 135 percent overpriced, which is just about the same as the 132 percent average of the numbers in this summary.

Just for reference, we saw earlier that, using the Japanese stock market as an example, the market is 184 percent overpriced. Also, we saw that, calculating the Future Discounted Dividend Stream with a sour investor attitude, the market is 188 percent overpriced, almost identical to the Japanese example. Both of these numbers reflect the investor attitude that will prevail near the bottom of the depression. These numbers indicate that an extremely conservative investor could wait until the market drops even lower than our earlier price/dividend numbers suggest. We will be calculating a more exact price/dividend ratio that does indeed come close to the 184 percent overpriced number.

The important thing to glean from all the methods used here is that all of them show the stock market to be greatly overpriced!

Summary

Even if we weren't beginning a depression, the stock market would still be a bad investment at this time. But investors have a difficult time believing this because of three market myths:

Market Myth 1: The stock market has always been the best place for the long-term investor.

Market Myth 2: The stock market is a long-term investment vehicle, with most investors getting the benefits of many years of accumulated capital appreciation through compounding and reinvestment.

Market Myth 3: Although the risk due to market volatility is high for short-term investors, longer-term investors are not affected by this risk.

This chapter showed that none of these myths are true.

Treasury Inflation Protected Securities (TIPS) are a viable investment option, especially when the stock market is historically overpriced, even though the interest rate adjustment on TIPS is somewhat understated. Some investors protest that gold is a far better hedge against inflation than TIPS, with much more upside potential. But historical data questions this assumption.

The current stock market is dramatically overpriced when compared to the historical price/dividend ratio. We get a similar conclusion using the Irving Fisher Formula, which assumes that a stock, or the stock market, is worth its Future Discounted Dividend Stream. Another method is to determine the market's replacement cost versus its selling price. And Regression to the Mean can be used to determine the market's value. These methods show that the market price as of the middle of 2008 is 132 percent above the average value determined by the above methods. For reference, we saw that, using the Japanese stock market as an example, the market is 184 percent overpriced. We also saw that, calculating the Future Discounted Dividend Stream with a sour investor attitude, the market is 188 percent overpriced.

Chapter 10

When to Get Back Into the Stock Market

As we concluded in earlier chapters, all analyses indicate that the market is dramatically overpriced, and TIPS (Treasury Inflation Protected Securities) are currently a much better investment choice than the stock market. As we have noted, the idea of owning TIPS is to generally maintain the real value of your money until the market drops enough to make it a good buy. The author doesn't suggest that TIPS are the preferred investment vehicle for long-term growth, especially if you don't feel that inflation is an issue. However, if someone started buying $100 worth of the ETF TIPS every month for 36 months starting when my first depression book was published in the middle of 2005, 36 months later, in 2008, he would be 11 percent ahead compared to the purchasing of $100 per month of an S&P 500 ETF at the same time!

For the price of the stock market to get down low enough to be back into its historical price/dividend range, we will see in this chapter that the market would have to drop 62 percent from its mid–2008 S&P 500 level of 1278. This conservative investment approach is based on not getting back into the market until the price/dividend ratio is 17.2 or less, which was determined by examining historical data. Once you are back in the stock market and it starts to rise, the sell trigger when the market again becomes too high is a price/dividend ratio of 28. This sell trigger, and how it was quantified, is discussed later in this chapter.

Approximate S&P 500 Trigger Points to Get In and Out of the Stock Market

Since dividends have historically risen at a 4.2 percent rate, we can extrapolate the likely S&P 500 price equivalence for the 17.2 and 28 price/dividend buy and sell triggers. These values are shown in Table 10.1. These extrapolated prices can be used as a trigger that you are getting close to an entry or exit point on the stock market. Because of inflation and probable dividend changes, you will then want to calculate the actual price/dividend value at the time. Table 10.1 is only a rough estimate of the future S&P values at the trigger points.

We noted in an earlier chapter that, if our stock market follows the Japanese example, in 2007 the U.S. market began a drop that will continue until the S&P 500 reaches 450 in year 2013. In Table 10.1, we identified a 572 target for year 2013, using a totally independent approach. These aren't very far apart, given the difference in the logic paths to get to these numbers.

Table 10.1   Approximate S&P 500 Trigger Prices to Get into the Market and Also to Get Back Out

Year	S&P 500 Buy Price	S&P 500 Sell Price
2008	482	784
2009	498	811
2010	516	840
2011	534	869
2012	553	900
2013	572	931
2014	592	964
2015	613	997
2016	634	1032

Using the numbers in Table 10.1, if the market drops far enough in 2009 that the S&P 500 stock index is below 498, it would be time to consider reentering the stock market. You would first want to calculate the actual price/dividend value to verify this decision. This additional calculation is needed in case companies are doing so poorly that they reduce their dividends. Then, suppose that in early 2010 the market rises above 840; it would be time to consider getting out of the market and back into TIPS. It is very possible that, in late 2010, the market could then drop below 516 and you would again reenter the market, selling in year 2011 if the S&P 500 Index goes over 869. During the turmoil of the coming depression, these kinds of wild market swings could very well happen; but you only want to participate when the market drops to a historically acceptable level, using the values in Table 10.1 as a guide. Again, as the stock prices approach the values in Table 10.1, it would be wise to calculate the *actual* price/dividend ratio to verify the 17.2 price/dividend ratio to buy, or to verify the 28 price/dividend ratio to sell, since some companies may have been forced to reduce dividends, making the actual trigger prices of the S&P 500 lower than what are indicated in Table 10.1.

Does Market Timing Work?

What was just shown is a form of market timing, which many books say can't be done. Certainly in the nineties you would have done well with the S&P 500 versus other investments at most buy dates. But those who bought the S&P 500 in year 2000 at a value of over 1550 may be in for a long wait to get their money back when inflation is included.

Part of the reasoning for people saying that market timing doesn't work is that no one knows how to sell at the *absolute top* or buy at the market's *absolute bottom*. In this book we are only talking about buying when stocks *are at a relative low, not an absolute low*. And we use historical data and logic on the market's real worth to determine these buy and sell values.

Why don't more people invest this way? Well, the very effective marketing campaigns put on by stock brokers encourage a buy-and-hold strategy. They obviously are *not* going to support any method that would keep someone out of the market for almost 20 years, which a relative price/dividend strategy would have done several times in the last 108 years. Brokers do not make money when people are not in the stock market.

The other reason people don't invest this way is that mutual funds control 90 percent of the stocks traded. And as we discussed earlier, the mutual funds managers are only interested in short term profits. They cannot keep their investors' money out of the stock market for multiple years because mutual fund managers are measured on how they play the market each year, which requires them to be *in* the market.

Let's use the price/dividend ratio, which we discussed earlier in the book, to see if buying stocks when they are at a relatively low price is better than buying them at a relatively high price. The answer to this may seem obvious, but the buy-and-hold philosophy says that there is no difference—that you cannot time the market using market price or any other tool, and therefore you would be better off just ignoring price when you are considering investing in the market. Just buy at any price!

Table 10.2 shows the "ordered" end-of-year price/dividend ratios since 1900, listing them from the highest price/dividend ratio down to the lowest. I highlighted in bold the lowest 16 price/dividend ratios since 1900 with their related year, which is the range in which I would think that stocks would be a relatively good buy. For those statistically oriented, this represents price/dividend ratios lower than one sigma below the mean.

So, we would buy stocks if the price/dividend ratio was 17.2 or below.

But this presents a problem! If we look at the dates that represent the price/dividend values of Table 10.2, the most recent date is 1953. That means we would have been out of the stock market for 55 years, which may reduce risk but also precludes many potential gains from being in the stock market.

However, the dates shown in Table 10.2 need some clarification. The data shown in Table 10.2 are end-of-year values (we couldn't show all 26,780 daily values in the table), and we know that there is much price variation of the market within each year. Indeed, when we look at individual day data for the last 59 years, we see many additional years when the price/dividend ratio *was* below 17.2 at some time during the year. We don't have the daily data for the years of 1900 to 1949, but we

Table 10.2   "Ordered" Price/Dividend Ratios Since 1900

Price/Dividend	Price/Dividend	Year	Price/Dividend
87.72	28.01		20.2
84.03	28.01		20.16
75.76	27.7		19.88
73.53	28.57		20.37
64.3	28.57		19.69
62.5	28.01		19.27
59.9	27.4		19.12
59.17	27.32		19.12
59.17	26.88		19.05
57	26.81		19.01
56.8	26.74		18.94
49.75	26.53		18.83
44.64	26.32		18.59
37.45	26.18		18.48
37.04	26.18		18.21
35.46	26.04		18.18
35.21	25.91		17.79
34.84	24.51		17.76
34.13	24.27		17.45
34.01	23.98		17.33
33.9	23.87	1953	**17.12**
33.78	23.53	1951	**16.86**
33.22	23.42	1923	**16.86**
33	23.36	1932	**16.72**
32.89	23.26	1942	**16.56**
32.68	23.15	1948	**16.34**
31.95	22.99	1907	**16.31**
31.55	22.32	1940	**15.8**
30.21	22.22	1949	**14.71**
29.76	22.03	1918	**13.97**
29.59	21.88	1950	**13.89**
29.33	21.55	1920	**13.76**
29.24	20.75	1937	**13.19**
29.15	20.7	1931	**12.69**
28.9	20.62	1941	**12.24**
28.74	20.49	1917	**10.75**

SOURCE: Stock Data, www.econ.yale.edu/~shiller/data/ie_data.htm.

extrapolated the same price variation we saw in the most recent 59 years and used this for our assumptions on the 1900 to 1949 data as to the likely full range of data. With the daily data, we see that by using a price/dividend buy trigger of 17.2, we would have been able to invest in the market right up to the 1986 jump in stock prices.

Earlier in the book, we estimated that the stock market would drop anywhere from 40 percent to 67 percent from its mid-2008 level. Using the 17.2 price/dividend ratio, the stock market drop will be 62 percent. However, if dividends go down substantially, which is likely given the severity of the depression we are facing, then the market will drop more than 62 percent. In the Great Depression the stock market dropped 80 percent.

We have already determined that TIPS are the best investment when compared to the current overpriced stock market. Now we want to find some savings formula that allows us to get some of the greater stock market yields when the market is reasonably priced, but gets us out of the market in higher-priced market periods. The goal is to see if we can come up with a way to match the earlier stock market yields (even with their former higher dividends), but with the lower risk of being out of the market much of the time. The savings formula must take us out of the market whenever the market is overpriced, putting the investment into TIPS during these periods.

We have determined that a price/dividend ratio of 17.2 is a reasonable low level that we want to test as to when the market is a good buy. We now need to identify a high level at which we would want to sell our stocks. Let's look at Figure 10.1, showing year-end price/dividend levels.

The "relative high" on the price/dividend ratio has had three different general levels within the last 108 years. By looking at Figure 10.1, through the fifties, and again from 1975 through the eighties, it appears that the relative high was close to 30. In the sixties, the relative high was about 35. Then, in the nineties, it just took off, with the price/dividend ratio in 2000 being almost 300 percent of the relative high for the first 55 years.

However, we have already discussed that the stock market has recently been extremely overpriced, so we don't want to use recent highs as sell criteria. Just looking at the chart, it appears that a value of 28 may be a good test number. Since this is 63 percent higher than our buy

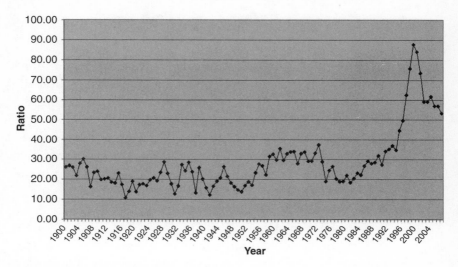

Figure 10.1   Year-End Price Dividend Ratio
SOURCE: Stock Data, www.econ.yale.edu/~shiller/data/ie_data.htm.

value of 17.2, it would certainly represent a reasonable gain. We also are aware that, due to the daily price variation we discussed earlier, we will be hitting the 28 price/dividend sell value more often than the year-end values in Figure 10.1 indicate.

So, here is the savings formula we want to test.

Formula: Determining When You Should Buy Stocks or TIPS

We will buy stocks whenever the price/dividend ratio on the S&P 500 is at or below 17.2. We will not only be putting new investment money into buying these stocks, but we will also sell all the TIPS we have accumulated and use those funds to buy stocks. When the price/dividend again goes above 17.2, we will stop buying stocks with new investment money and start buying TIPS. If the price/dividend goes above 28, we will sell all the stocks we have accumulated and use the funds from the sale to buy TIPS.

Let's look at the results of using this formula on investment periods of 5, 10, and 20 years. The detailed data on these investment scenarios are shown in Appendix A.

5-Year Investing, with a Constant Amount Invested Each Year, 3 Percent TIPS

Investing a constant real-dollar amount every year when our time period is five years, the formula-based investment equaled or beat the straight S&P 500 investment 67 percent of the time. In addition, the formula method averaged 10.1 percent greater returns for the five-year period. On this basis, the market timing per the formula is superior to just blindly investing in the S&P 500 when the investment period is five years. In addition, since the formula investment method was out of the stock market half the time, this is a far lower-risk method than being in the market continuously.

Note that nothing about this method involves any trick of beating the market. The only reason the formula method beats the straight S&P 500 investment is because it stays out of the market when the market is historically overpriced, instead investing in TIPS. This method works strictly because of market timing.

The fact that the five-year investment period works so well is of special interest because many people start out with the intent of saving for a longer period, but, because of some unforeseen reason, they have to withdraw their savings early. The formula method reduces the risk that they will lose substantial amounts of money if they have to cut their investment window short.

Now let's look at a similar comparison when the investment window is 10 years.

10-Year Investing, with a Constant Amount Invested Each Year, 3 Percent TIPS

Investing a constant real-dollar amount every year when the time period is 10 years, the formula-based investment beat the straight S&P 500 investment 66 percent of the time. In addition, the formula method averaged 11.7 percent greater returns per 10-year period. On this basis, the market timing per the formula is superior to just blindly investing in the S&P 500 when the investment period is 10 years. In addition, since the formula investment method was out of the stock market over half the time, this is a far lower risk method than being in the market continuously.

Now let's look at a 20-year investment window and see if the formula method is still superior.

20-Year Investing, with a Constant Amount Invested Each Year, 3 Percent TIPS

Investing a constant real-dollar amount every year when the time period is 20 years, the formula-based investment beat the straight S&P 500 investment 63 percent of the time. In addition, the formula method averaged 17.0 percent greater returns per 20-year period. On this basis, the market timing per the formula is superior to just blindly investing in the S&P 500 when the investment period is 20 years. In addition, since the formula investment method was out of the stock market almost half the time, this is a far lower-risk method than being in the market continuously.

In Smithers and Wright's *Valuing Wall Street*, the authors state that, when using a buy-and-hold strategy, investors never lost money when they were invested in stocks for 20 years. I agree with that. But the problem is that most investors don't leave their investments untouched for 20 or more years. And if you bought stocks when the market happened to be relatively high, the losses on getting out in less than 20 years can be very large. The use of the formula to keep you out of the market when it is relatively high priced minimizes the losses if you have to use your long-term investment money for shorter-term needs. And it is even superior at *any* investment time period, including as long as 20 years!

Assuming 1.5 Percent Base Interest on TIPS

One of the concerns on TIPS is that its base interest can vary based on auction results. Recently, because of concerns about inflation, TIPS have become so popular that the government has been able to sell TIPS with a lower base interest. So here are the comparisons of the formula method versus the straight S&P 500 investment assuming an average 1.5 percent TIPS base interest rather than the earlier 3 percent TIPS assumption.

5-Year Investing, with a Constant Amount Invested Each Year, 1.5 Percent TIPS.
Investing a constant real-dollar amount every year when our time period is five years, the formula-based investment equaled or

beat the straight S&P 500 investment 67 percent of the time. In addition, the formula method averaged 8.4 percent greater returns for the five-year period. On this basis, the market timing per the formula is superior to just blindly investing in the S&P 500 when the investment period is five years. In addition, since the formula investment method was out of the stock market almost half the time, this is a far lower-risk method than being in the market continuously.

10-Year Investing, with a Constant Amount Invested Each Year, 1.5 Percent TIPS.
Investing a constant real-dollar amount every year when the time period is 10 years, the formula-based investment beat the straight S&P 500 investment 63 percent of the time. In addition, the formula method averaged 8.3 percent greater returns per 10-year period. On this basis, the market timing per the formula is superior to just blindly investing in the S&P 500 when the investment period is 10 years. In addition, since the formula investment method was out of the stock market almost half the time, this is a far lower-risk method than being in the market continuously.

Now let's look at a 20-year investment window and see if the formula method is still superior.

20-Year Investing, with a Constant Amount Invested Each Year, 1.5 Percent TIPS.
Investing a constant real-dollar amount every year when the time period is 20 years, the formula-based investment beat the straight S&P 500 investment 59 percent of the time. In addition, the formula method averaged 9.0 percent greater returns per 20-year period. On this basis, the market timing per the formula is superior to just blindly investing in the S&P 500 when the investment period is 20 years. In addition, since the formula investment method was out of the stock market almost half the time, this is a far lower-risk method than being in the market continuously.

So, Does the Base Interest Rate of TIPS Matter?

In order to determine if the base interest rate of TIPS matters, let's summarize the previous results.

5-Year Investment Period—Percentage Gain of Formula versus Straight S&P 500

3% TIPS   Formula Gain 10.1%

1.5% TIPS Formula Gain 8.4%

10-Year Investment Period—Percentage Gain of Formula versus Straight S&P 500

3% TIPS   Formula Gain 11.7%

1.5% TIPS Formula Gain 8.3%

20-Year Investment Period—Percentage Gain of Formula versus Straight S&P 500

3% TIPS   Formula Gain 17.0%

1.5% TIPS Formula Gain 9.0%

Although the lower base interest on TIPS *did* reduce the gains over the various savings periods, its effect was quite small. This is because the gains from using the formula largely come from being out of the stock market when it is historically high. Also, the interest that TIPS contribute are generally mostly due to their inflation adjustment rather than their base interest rate.

A concern for any superior method of investing is that once the method is published it will no longer be effective because everyone will use it, canceling its advantage. Well, in this case, not to worry. Mutual funds will never buy into any method that would keep someone out of the stock market for as long as 20 years, which the formula method does. Even for individual investors, very few people would be able to stand being out of the market as it was in the nineties, when it looked as though everybody was making a killing!

In Smithers and Wright's *Valuing Wall Street*, it is emphasized that people nearing retirement age or who are already in retirement are at high risk using stock market yields as a source of retirement income. The potential upside gain for a retiree who is drawing down his principal is small compared to the downside risk of a market drop. Again, *Valuing Wall Street* states that, as you get close to retirement, you should only be invested in stocks if you are sure that the market isn't overpriced. I take that concept further and propose that near or during retirement someone should only consider investing *extra* funds in the stock market, and then only when the market is relatively *undervalued per the above formula!*

We have been using the price/dividend ratio as a trigger to buy or sell stocks. Here is a source for dividend information: http://www. indexarb.com/dividendYieldSortedsp.html.

Go to the bottom of the table at that web site and read the value opposite "Average Dividend Yield (%) of All S&P 500 Stocks." Then take the inverse of this value times 100 to get the price/dividend. For example, as I write this, the Average Dividend Yield percent of All S&P 500 Stocks is 2.08. Taking the inverse of that value times 100, which is 100 divided by 2.08, I get 48.2. Now, this is still much higher than the 17.2 target to buy, but it is lower than the 59 value for the price/dividend at the time I wrote my first book on the coming depression.

Summary

All analyses indicate that the market is dramatically overpriced and TIPS (Treasury Inflation Protected Securities) are currently a much better investment choice than the stock market. The idea of owning TIPS is to maintain the real value of your money until the market drops enough to make it a good buy.

For the price of the stock market to move low enough to be back into its historical price/dividend range, the market will have to drop 62 percent from its mid-2008 S&P 500 level of 1278. This conservative investment approach is based on not getting back into the market until the price/dividend ratio is 17.2 or less, which was determined by examining historical data. Once you are back in the stock market and it starts to rise, the sell trigger when the market again becomes too high is a price/dividend ratio of 28.

Chapter 11

Once You Are Back in the Stock Market

I n the previous chapter, we determined that once the market drops we could use the price/dividend ratio to determine *when* to buy and *when* to sell stocks. In this chapter we discuss very briefly some general knowledge related to the stock market. Subjects covered include index funds versus mutual funds, the Random Walk and Efficient Market Theories, buying individual stocks versus index funds, and buying recent additions to the Dow. Also, several theories about beating the market espoused by various books are discussed. This information will help you decide *how* to get back into the market.

Index Funds versus Actively Managed Mutual Funds

A stock index is a measure of the stock performance of a select group of companies that are supposed to be representative of the total stock market. For example, the Dow Jones Industrial Average Stock Index is a group of 30 company stocks picked by journalists at the *Wall Street*

Journal. A stock index is just a score card on how well that particular group of stocks is doing at any given moment. A stock index *fund* allows someone to buy stocks in the same balance as the stocks represented by that particular index. For example, if investors buy an index fund based on the Dow Jones, they are buying shares in all the companies in the Dow Jones index and in the same proportion. An index fund makes no attempt to evaluate the individual merits of each stock within the index, so the management costs of running an index fund are very low compared to an actively managed mutual fund.

Actively managed mutual funds, where fund managers evaluate the merits of each stock, and the buying or selling of them accordingly, generally charge between 1.5 percent and 2 percent for this service. What do the shareholders of a mutual fund get in return? On the average, they get *worse* performance than the overall market average! Even for those actively managed funds that happen, *by chance*, to beat the market in a given year, those *lucky* mutual funds are unlikely to do it the following year. There have been countless studies that confirm these findings. In the long run, actively managed mutual funds just do not perform as well as the general market!

More than a few books speak quite disparagingly about the relatively poor performance of actively managed funds and question the analytical skills of the active-fund managers, since a nonmanaged stock index fund can so readily beat them. But the relatively poor performance of actively managed mutual funds compared to index funds shouldn't be surprising. An index fund is indirectly using the average judgment of *all* the active fund managers, since the active fund managers, as a group, determine the prices of most stocks on the market. Any time a stock's price is felt to be out of line, at least compared to other stock prices at the time, some mutual fund buys (or sells) that stock until the price is again neutral in their collective judgment. They buy if the stock is seen as underpriced and sell if they feel the stock is overpriced.

So it's not luck, nor is it a mystery, why index funds do so well compared to actively managed mutual funds. An index fund's stocks are bought and sold at the collective (market) price, in balance with the index's stock loading, and the index fund shareholders get the service of price determination by mutual fund managers for free.

In fact, if all the investors got wise together and bought index funds rather than actively managed mutual funds, the field of active fund manager "experts" would no longer exist, and the stock market prices would become more chaotic. Only the individual investors would be determining a stock's current price, without the detailed analysis currently being done by professionals. Not to worry, though! The marketing skills of people selling actively managed mutual funds far exceed any book's ability to get the message across to people that they are wasting their money buying actively managed mutual funds. There are currently more actively managed mutual funds than there are individual company stocks listed on the major exchanges, and that is unlikely to change anytime soon.

Newspapers are happy to report the names of the current crop of successful (that is, who beat the average mutual fund) actively managed mutual funds, especially if they were better than the average fund several years in a row. It doesn't matter that this performance of "successful" mutual funds can easily be explained by simple probability. If a lot of actively managed mutual funds are playing the market, statistically some are bound to do better than the others, even sometimes for multiple years. In fact, with the large number of actively managed mutual funds, it is likely that some fund will beat the average fund 10 years in a row due to chance alone. After all, the odds of getting 10 heads in a row on 10 flips of a coin are one-in-1,024, and there are more than 1,024 actively managed mutual funds. Since each mutual fund has an approximate 50 percent chance of beating the average mutual fund in any given year, one is likely to beat the average fund 10 times in a row by chance alone.

The fund managers of the "better-than-average" mutual funds receive millions of dollars in bonuses. Many of the mutual funds that are unlucky enough to be below average several years in a row will just sort of vanish, so their results will no longer be seen as a blemish on the brokerage firm's mutual fund list. *Sweet game!*

As we have shown, an alternative to buying an actively managed mutual fund is buying an index fund that matches its stock mix to an index. Some of the indexes from which you can choose to match are the Dow Jones Industrial, the S&P 500, the Russell 3000, and the Wilshire

5000. So if you want to buy into the general stock market, choose an index fund, not an actively managed mutual fund.

Random Walk

The term "random walk," made famous by Burton Malkiel's *A Random Walk Down Wall Street*, which was published over 30 years ago, basically means that a stock's price movement is truly random, and that any prior change in a stock's price has no influence on whether its future price will be higher, lower, or the same. This is analogous to the concept of each flip of a coin being truly independent of the results of any previous coin flip.

The Efficient Market Theory

The Efficient Market Theory assumes that all stocks are perfectly priced at all times, based on all information available and that all information is instantly known by all. The effect of this theory is that no stock is more of a bargain than any other stock, since any difference between stocks related to current or future performance, perceived or real, is already incorporated instantly adjusted for. The Efficient Market Theory assumes that *everyone* becomes aware of any important piece of knowledge affecting the company at the same time, and the price instantly corrects without any individual being able to gain from the knowledge.

In the earlier discussion on index funds, it was stated that "any time a stock's price is felt to be out of line, at least compared to other stock prices at the time, some mutual fund buys (or sells) that stock until the price is again neutral in their collective judgment." This process is preassumed in an Efficient Market.

The effect of the Random Walk and the Efficient Market Theories is that the price of a stock is always correct. If both of these theories are 100 percent correct, then there is never a good buy or bad buy on a stock or on the market in general; nor is there a good time or bad time to buy stocks. Indeed, throwing darts at a financial page on random days would be just as effective as any other investment method!

The Random Walk and Efficient Market Theories may be generally valid; but, at times, nonrandom events seem to drive stock prices. On October 19, 1987, Black Monday, the market dropped 23 percent! Were the stocks properly priced per the Efficient Market Theory before or after the drop? Once the market started this severe drop, was every "next price" during the following hours truly as random as the Random Walk Theory maintains?

The Efficient Market Theory seems valid in keeping individual stock prices in line with each other at any given point in time. But it does not seem effective in keeping the *total* market "logically" priced at all times.

Most methods that attempt to beat the market violate the Random Walk Theory and/or the Efficient Market Theory, since they attempt to time the market or make some judgment on stock prices being over- or underpriced.

Figure 11.1 shows the S&P 500 total return for the last 107 years. Total return means that dividends and inflation are included.

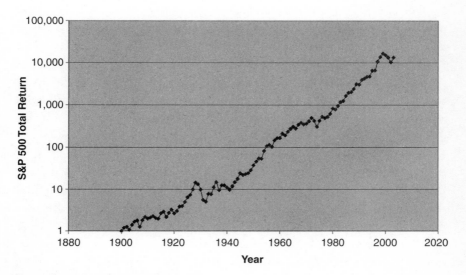

Figure 11.1   S&P 500 Total Return

SOURCE: Stock Data, www.econ.yale.edu/~shiller/data/ie_data.htm.

These results of the S&P 500 total return, shown on a semi-log plot (Figure 11.1), certainly don't look random. The chart appears to have a long-term upward trend. This graph and the other observations made here call into question the validity of both the Random Walk and Efficient Market Theories.

Buying Individual Stocks versus Buying an Index Fund

Even though index funds readily beat actively managed mutual fund performance, index funds may not be your best investment strategy once the market becomes reasonably priced. First, index funds still have some degree of stock turnover since companies are moved into and out of the fund portfolio. Since 1931, 40 stocks have moved in and out of the Dow, and the Dow is by far the most stable of the indexed funds. This stock movement does add to fund management costs.

With index funds, you will be buying many stocks that you would never consider buying as individual stocks. I will discuss several stocks included in the Dow Jones Index Fund as examples because then the stocks I mention will be familiar to most of you.

Periodically, companies are taken off the Dow. This is because people at the *Wall Street Journal*, who decide the makeup of the Dow, no longer feel that these companies are indicative of the general market. In 2008, Altria and Honeywell were removed, replaced by Bank of America and Chevron. Now, data shows that historically the stocks of removed companies don't necessarily perform worse than companies added, so the removal doesn't automatically indicate a sell situation for those stocks. But it should make one wonder how long they were on the Dow with questionable futures before they were removed. For example, in 2004 Eastman Kodak was removed. This company had been primarily in the photographic film business, which was largely being replaced by digital technology. Although Kodak has since attempted to enter the digital market with its own line of digital cameras, it was behind the development curve and does not lead the market. The company was too slow to react to the realities of the marketplace. However, this problem with Kodak was obvious for years before they were finally removed from the Dow, and anyone buying a Dow-based index fund was getting Kodak!

Here are some stocks I would be concerned about even if we weren't heading into a depression, where almost all stocks are likely to fall. Note that these are only *my* concerns, and no one should use these observations other than as one of many reference points and research sources. Nor do these concerns mean that I believe that the companies' stocks will go down. It's just my view that other stocks may be *more likely* to rise!

Boeing Co.: If airlines don't have customers or profits, they don't buy new planes. And airlines' profits are certainly hurting as I write! The United States military airpower is clearly superior to everyone in the world, so future plane purchases by the military will be at risk of budget pressures. Especially if our financial issues cause the United States to back off being the world's policeman.

General Motors: GM is close to bankruptcy. They judged the market incorrectly, continuing to make gas-guzzlers despite what the market was telling them. Gas prices were going up dramatically, but they ignored the warnings. They have a technically advanced plug-in hybrid, the Volt, coming out in 2010; but by the time that technology can be broadened to other product lines, GM will be hurting in a major way!

IBM: Another former powerhouse, IBM has trouble growing revenues. They are growing profits by cost cutting, but somewhere along the way this well will dry up, and the fact that their business is not growing will catch up.

McDonald's: No one can go into a McDonald's restaurant and not see that their star has faded. What was once a dynamic restaurant chain, clean, with uniformly hot food, with people smiling and working very hard, has now become mediocre by any measure. They keep searching for the new Big Mac that will make their business take off, but they haven't found it. Their expansions overseas have not met expectations, and they are slowing growth in that direction. Competitors have managed to give the public a perceived healthier and better product, served in a cleaner environment. McDonalds' long-term future just doesn't look that great. And with people cutting back on going out to eat in general to save money, all restaurants are at risk.

There is another problem with buying an index fund. There is one area where mutual fund managers may *not* be the primary element determining stock price. This concerns stocks that become fad stocks. AOL was an example of this during the recent bubble. Its price was bid up to levels that could never be justified by *any* future business forecast. Again, index funds may have some fad stocks included, which you buy automatically with the index fund.

Buying Individual Stocks

An alternative to index funds is buying individual stocks. Most books on investing stress diversification. So if you choose to buy individual stocks, purchase a different stock each time. Don't become enamored with one or two stocks. Once your portfolio has six or more stocks, you are getting sufficiently diversified. Note that when buying stocks, try not to buy stocks in similar fields. For example, buying stocks of two automobile manufacturers, or two financial organizations, would be limiting your diversification. Sometimes stocks move together for reasons that are not outwardly apparent, as you will see in Figure 11.3 in the comparison of Wal-Mart and Johnson & Johnson. It may be worthwhile to look at the stock prices for the last five to 10 years to make sure you don't buy stocks whose prices move in lock-step.

Figure 11.2 shows an example where the two stock prices have *not* moved in concert and would therefore be viable stocks to be purchased for diversity.

Figure 11.3 shows two stocks that would *not* do well as far as diversity is concerned, since they track fairly closely together. The two stocks are Wal-Mart and Johnson & Johnson. Note that it is not outwardly obvious that these two stocks should track together.

Note that in this case the two stocks' prices are similar, which is just coincidental. The thing of note is that the prices of the two stocks move together proportionally.

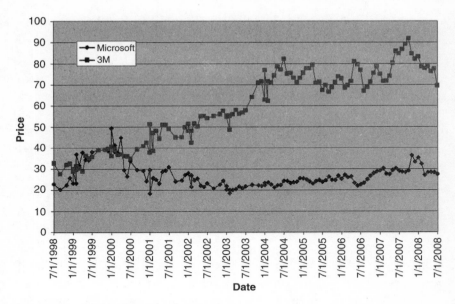

Figure 11.2   3M and Microsoft Stock Prices
SOURCE: MMM and MSFT historical prices, http://finance.yahoo.com.

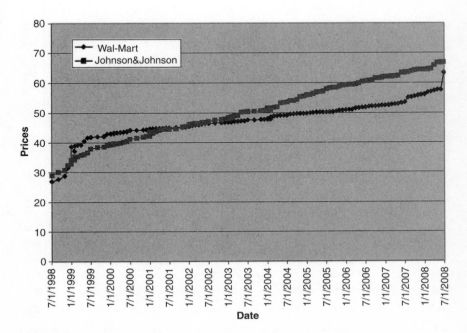

Figure 11.3   Wal-Mart and Johnson & Johnson Stock Prices
SOURCE: WMT and JNJ historical prices, http://finance.yahoo.com.

Which Individual Stocks Should You Buy?

We already mentioned that the prices of stocks are largely determined by mutual fund managers who are buying stocks for the short term, generally for less than one year. Your own investment horizon would generally be longer. You want to be able to buy stocks with long-term potential so that you can hold them long enough to qualify for the capital gains tax; but these stocks aren't always easy to find without massive amounts of detailed research.

Use the Free Expertise of the Staff of the *Wall Street Journal*

What if you could find a group of experts who had no motives to sell you stocks? And what if you could get them to select stocks of great substantial companies that are stable, represent this country's industry, and are likely to continue to grow and prosper for many years? Incidentally, it would be nice if they would do this for free.

Well, the expert-picked stocks are already out there for you to use. The stocks in the Dow are picked by the staff of the *Wall Street Journal* for the reasons just discussed. So, why not just buy a Dow Index fund? We already mentioned the problems of company changes in the index, fad stocks, and stocks no longer viable over the long term. The companies representing the Dow, as is true with all companies, have an earnings life cycle, in which the companies are initially growing and dynamic, then mature and stable, and finally slowly dying as new and more aggressive companies take their place. When a company becomes part of the Dow, it usually stays on the Dow until it is clearly in the dying stage. Figure 11.4 is a visual representation of a company's life cycle.

Buying the Most Recent Additions to the Dow

You would like to buy stocks in the early growing stage of the life cycle. To do this, buy the stocks that were *most recently added* to the Dow. You can look on the Internet to see the most recent additions. Here are the

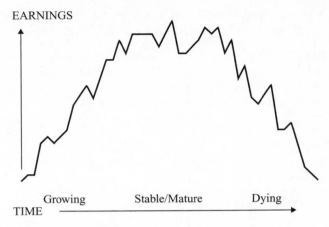

EARNINGS

Growing   Stable/Mature   Dying

TIME

Figure 11.4 Typical Earnings Life Cycle of a Company

most recent at the time of this book's writing.

- 2008: Bank of America, Chevron
- 2004: American International Group, Pfizer, Verizon Communications
- 1999: Home Depot, Microsoft, Intel
- 1997: Wal-Mart, Travelers Group, Hewlett-Packard, Johnson & Johnson
- 1991: Caterpillar, Walt Disney, J. P. Morgan
- 1987: Coca-Cola
- 1985: McDonald's, Philip Morris (Altria)
- 1982: American Express
- 1979: IBM, Merck
- 1976: 3M
- 1959: Alcoa, Owen's-Illinois, Swift & Co

Results of Most Recent Additions to the Dow for 5- and 10-Year Holds

In Tables 11.1 and 11.2, let's look at how these stocks have done against the S&P 500 for 5- and 10-year holds. I am only showing the ones for which I have data that include the effect of dividends and splits and have sufficient data for the 10-year holds. For this example, I assume purchase of the stock one year after they were added to the Dow.

Table 11.1 Gain Percentage After 5-Year Holds

Buy Year	Company	S&P 500 Gain	Company Gain	Company/S&P 500
1977	3M	94%	575%	6.12
1980	IBM	98%	393%	4.01
1983	American Express	103%	614%	5.96
1986	McDonald's	104%	143%	1.38
1986	Altria	104%	1973%	18.97
1988	Coca-Cola	97%	654%	6.74
1992	Caterpillar	152%	389%	2.56
1992	Walt Disney	152%	148%	0.97
1992	J. P. Morgan	152%	226%	1.49

SOURCE: http://finance.yahoo.com, historical prices.

Testing for significant differences between the S&P 500 gains as opposed to the gains on the most recent adds to the Dow for a 5-year hold, using the S&P 500 as the population, we can be 99 percent confident that the superior results of the recent adds to the Dow were *not* due to random cause. Random cause means "just due to luck."

Testing for significant differences between the S&P 500 gains as opposed to the gains on the most recent adds to the Dow for a 10-year hold, using the S&P 500 as the population, we can be 97.5 percent confident that the superior results of the recent adds to the Dow were not due to random cause.

Note that for both the 5-year and 10-year holds, the individual stocks beat the S&P 89 percent of the time, and often by a substantial amount.

Table 11.2 Gain Percentage After 10-Year Holds

Buy Year	Company	S&P 500 Gain	Company Gain	Company/S&P 500
1977	3M	315%	9728%	30.9
1980	IBM	268%	778%	2.9
1983	American Express	302%	1857%	6.15
1986	McDonald's	238%	737%	3.1
1986	Altria	238%	6094%	25.6
1988	Coca-Cola	480%	3224%	6.72
1992	Caterpillar	144%	375%	2.6
1992	Walt Disney	144%	76%	0.53
1992	J. P. Morgan	144%	169%	1.17

SOURCE: http://finance.yahoo.com, historical prices.

Detail on the 10-Year Holds

Now, let's look at the 10-year charts for each of these individual stocks and see if we can glean even more insight on these stocks. Figures 11.5 through 11.13 are plotted logarithmically, so that a constant increase will appear as an upwardly sloped line.

You can see that Walt Disney was the only stock that did not beat the S&P 500 for the 10-year hold period. It was also the only company stock that was not substantially ahead of the S&P 500 after five years, so perhaps this should have served as a warning that this stock was not without problems. However, for the 10 years, it still had a return of 6.5 percent per year, which is not a disaster. Table 11.3 shows the annual yields of the previous nine company stocks as opposed to the S&P 500 for the related 10-year hold period.

The average annual percentage that the company stocks beat the S&P 500 was 16.0 percent. The following comparisons were based on buying the most recent addition to the Dow in the year following its addition. However, we said earlier that we only wanted to buy stocks when the overall market was low priced. That is why we developed the formula based on the price/dividend ratio.

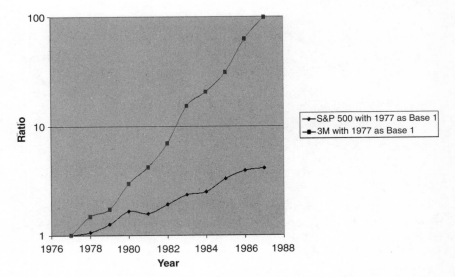

Figure 11.5   S&P 500 Total Return vs. 3M Total Return, with 1977 as Base 1
Source: http://finance.yahoo.com, ^GSPC and MMM historical prices.

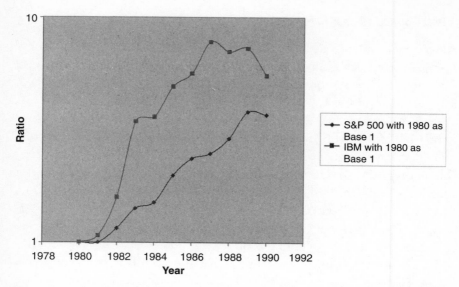

Figure 11.6   S&P 500 Total Return vs. IBM Total Return, with 1980 as Base 1
Source: http://finance.yahoo.com, ^GSPC and IBM historical prices.

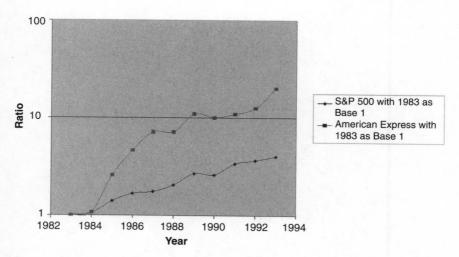

Figure 11.7   S&P Total Return vs. American Express Total Return, with 1983 as Base 1
Source: http://finance.yahoo.com, ^GSPC and AXP historical prices.

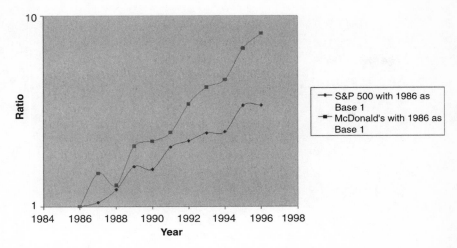

Figure 11.8   S&P 500 Total Return vs. McDonald's Total Return, with 1986 as
Base 1
SOURCE: http://finance.yahoo.com, ^GSPC and MCD historical prices.

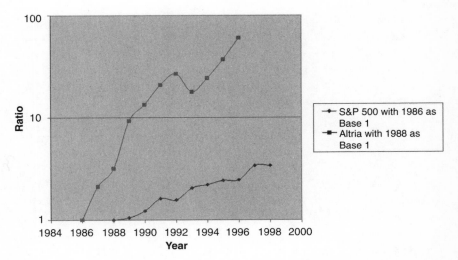

Figure 11.9   S&P Total Return vs. Altria Total Return, with 1986 as Base 1
SOURCE: http://finance.yahoo.com, ^GSPC and MO historical prices.

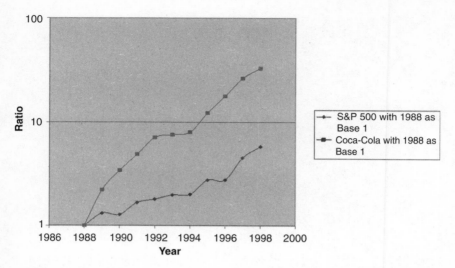

Figure 11.10 S&P 500 Total Return vs. Coca-Cola Total Return, with 1988 as Base 1
SOURCE: http://finance.yahoo.com, ^GSPC and KO historical prices.

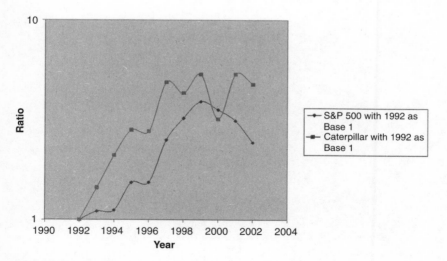

Figure 11.11 S&P 500 Total Return vs. Caterpillar Total Return with 1992 as Base 1
SOURCE: http://finance.yahoo.com, ^GSPC and CAT historical prices.

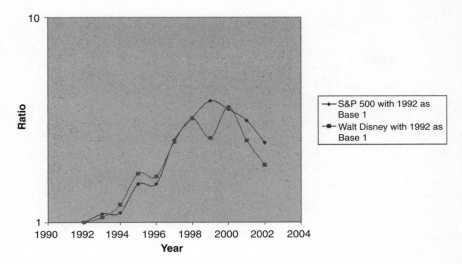

Figure 11.12   S&P 500 Total Return vs. Walt Disney Total Return with 1992 as Base 1
SOURCE: http://finance.yahoo.com, ^GSPC and DIS historical prices.

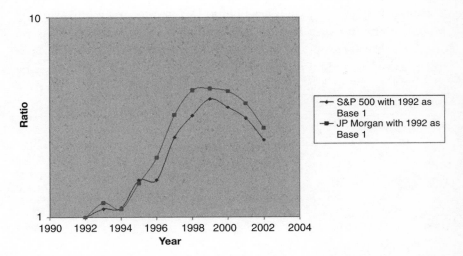

Figure 11.13   S&P 500 Total Return vs. JP Morgan Total Return, with 1992 as Base 1
SOURCE: http://finance.yahoo.com, ^GSPC and JPM historical prices.

Table 11.3   Annual Yields of the Company Stocks vs. the S&P 500 for the Related 10-Year Hold.

Years	S&P 500 Annual Yield	Company	Company Annual Yield
1977–1987	15.20%	3M	58%
1980–1990	14.00%	IBM	18.50%
1983–1993	15.00%	American Express	35%
1986–1986	13.00%	McDonald's	23.30%
1986–1996	13.00%	Altria	50%
1988–1998	19.20%	Coca-Cola	42%
1992–2002	9.30%	Caterpillar	17.00%
1992–2002	9.30%	Walt Disney	6.50%
1992–2002	9.30%	J.P. Morgan	10.90%

SOURCE: http://finance.yahoo.com, historical prices.

Results of Recent Dow Additions as Opposed to the S&P 500 When Purchased Using the Formula Purchase Dates

Let's see how the most recent additions to the Dow do when purchased per the dates shown as formula buy years, using the previous formula low-price trigger, as shown on Figure 11.3, rather than automatically buying them the year after they were added to the Dow. Again, we are limited to looking at the dates and stocks where we have full stock information, including the effect of reinvested dividends and splits. The results in Tables 11.4 and 11.5 are compared to the total S&P 500 data, which also includes the effect of reinvested dividends.

Table 11.4   Recent Dow Stock Gains vs. S&P 500 Using Formula Buy Days

Buy Year	Sell Year	Company	S&P 500 Total Gain	Company Total Gain
1974	1986	Alcoa	528%	3600%
1978	1986	3M	272%	4070%
1979	1986	3M	212%	3471%
1980	1986	IBM	135%	463%
1981	1986	IBM	147%	424%
1982	1986	IBM	104%	254%

SOURCE: http://finance.yahoo.com, historical prices.

Table 11.5   Recent Dow Stock Yields vs. S&P 500 Using Formula Buy Days

Start Year	End Year	S&P 500 Annual Yield	Company	Company Annual Yield
1974	1986	16.50%	Alcoa	36%
1978	1986	17.80%	3M	60%
1979	1986	17.70%	3M	67%
1980	1986	15.30%	IBM	36%
1981	1986	19.80%	IBM	43%
1982	1986	19.40%	IBM	41%

SOURCE: http://finance.yahoo.com, historical prices.

Based on years when the price/dividend ratio was below 17.2, the formula buy dates are 1974, 1978, 1979, 1980, 1981, and 1982. The formula sell date for all these stocks, based on when the price/dividend ratio was over 28, is 1986.

The average weighted annual yield difference between the S&P 500 and these company stocks that were bought and sold per the formula dates was 29.6 percent. So, the recent additions to the Dow bought according to the formula low-price trigger dates beat the S&P 500 by almost 30 percent per year! This is versus the 16 percent difference when the stocks were bought the year after getting in the Dow and then held for 10 years. The formula buy trigger, which is the price/dividend being at or below 17.2, makes the "buy the most recent stock in the Dow" method look even more attractive.

There is no magic about why this works. Recent Dow stocks become overpriced when the market is doing well because of the publicity they receive. These stocks would have already been well known, and adding them to the Dow just gives them even more visibility. When the market tanks, these overpriced stocks get hit extra hard in the drop because they were overpriced. Then, once the stock market again becomes favorable, the recent Dow stocks are the ones the public and the mutual fund managers like and the stocks to which they return. So, it is strictly market timing that makes this work. Incidentally, there is something called *beta* that is a measure of a stock's relative movement as opposed to the total market. If a stock's price swings, or volatility, is greater than the market's, than its beta will be greater than one. The recent Dow additions will generally have high betas during a severe market downturn or upswing.

Although six pieces of data are usually enough to determine if averages are statistically and significantly different, since only three companies are involved in the previous analysis, and the data are overlapping, the data are not truly independent. So, statistical significance tests cannot be run. However, the results look so impressive that we want to test them with the full formula method.

Formula Method on Recent Dow Additions Where We Buy TIPS When the Market Price/Dividend Ratio Is Too High

Now let's try the formula method on the recent Dow additions (Table 11.6) where we are buying TIPS when the market price/dividend ratio is too high. If you recall, in the formula we do the following:

Buy stocks (in this case, the most recent additions to the Dow) whenever the price/dividend ratio of the S&P 500 is at or below 17.2. We will not only be putting new investment money into buying these stocks, but we will also sell all the TIPS we have accumulated and use those funds to buy stocks. When the price/dividend of the S&P 500 again goes above 17.2, we will stop buying stocks with new investment money and start buying TIPS. If the price/dividend of the S&P 500 then goes above 28, we will sell any stocks we have accumulated and use the funds from the sale to buy TIPS.

We will start in 1955 since we have no total individual stock information (including the effect of dividends and splits) before that year. As in the prior model, $100 per year in 2007 dollars is invested as a way of keeping score. The costs of trades are not included because the cost of buying individual stocks per the formula method and the cost of buying an S&P 500 index fund would be similar, so the comparisons are valid with or without these trade costs. These comparisons are shown in Table 11.6. The numbers within the table represent dollars (in 2007 dollar equivalents).

You can see that the TIPS/stock formula buys are currently worth almost three times what the straight S&P 500 investment is worth. And

Table 11.6 Most Recent Dow Stocks Bought and Sold According to the Formula

Accum Alcoa	Accum 3M	Accum IBM	Accum Formula Stock	Accum TIPS	Year (Bold When Buy Stocks)	Accum Formula TIPS&Stks	Accum S&P
			0	13	1955	13	13
			0	27	1956	27	28
			0	42	1957	42	39
			0	58	1958	58	69
			0	75	1959	75	92
			0	93	1960	93	107
			0	112	1961	112	150
			0	132	1962	132	152
			0	153	1963	153	201
			0	174	1964	174	250
			0	198	1965	198	296
			0	227	1966	227	282
			0	257	1967	257	365
			0	294	1968	294	423
			0	338	1969	338	405
			0	386	1970	386	440
			0	429	1971	429	522
			0	478	1972	478	642
			0	554	1973	554	568
663			663	0	**1974**	663	441
677			677	26	1975	703	631
691			691	56	1976	747	809
706			706	90	1977	795	780
721	131		852	0	**1978**	852	862
736	187		922	0	**1979**	922	1056
2207	320	38	2565	0	**1980**	2565	1437
2943	452	83	3479	0	**1981**	3479	1409
5150	745	171	6066	0	**1982**	6066	1759
12509	1624	417	14549	48	1983	14598	2205
13980	2183	487	16650	102	1984	16752	2393
20601	3301	717	24620	161	1985	24781	3205
			0	35022	1986	35022	3857
			0	37680	1987	37680	4114
			0	40533	1988	40533	4855
			0	43693	1989	43693	6453

(Continued)

Table 11.6 (*Continued*)

Accum Alcoa	Accum 3M	Accum IBM	Accum Formula Stock	Accum TIPS	Year (Bold When Buy Stocks)	Accum Formula TIPS&Stks	Accum S&P
			0	47733	1990	47733	6315
			0	50695	1991	50695	8306
			0	53754	1992	53754	9007
			0	56915	1993	56915	9985
			0	60217	1994	60217	10189
			0	63626	1995	63626	14092
			0	67725	1996	67725	14201
			0	70988	1997	70988	23311
			0	74342	1998	74342	30053
			0	78649	1999	78649	36458
			0	83756	2000	83756	33222
			0	87943	2001	87943	29359
			0	92060	2002	92060	22945
			0	96908	2003	96908	29573
			0	102011	2004	102011	32569
			0	107382	2005	107382	34455
			0	113037	2006	113037	39538
			0	118989	2007	118989	41127

SOURCE: http://finance.yahoo.com and www.econ.yale.edu/~shiller/data/ie_data.htm.
NOTE: The numbers within the table, except the year, are dollars in 2007 dollar equivalents.

if the stock market takes a dive and loses over half its value as predicted, that will make the formula method of buying the most recent additions to the Dow even more attractive as opposed to the S&P 500. Let's look at these results on a logarithmic graph, Figure 11.14.

You can see that the two methods tracked each other for the first 19 years, and then the formula method sold all the TIPS and began buying the most recent stock additions to the Dow. All these stocks were sold in 1986, and since then all the purchases have been TIPS.

The formula method, which uses the price/dividend ratio to determine when to buy and sell stocks, is far less risky than buying the S&P 500 on a regular basis. This is because, as shown here, stocks were owned only 12 of the 52 years of the example. This means that we were in the market less than 25 percent of the time, with the other 75 percent of the time owning only TIPS, a very low-risk investment.

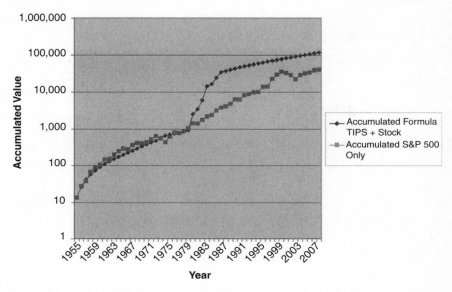

Figure 11.14 Most Recent Dow + TIPS vs. S&P 500

SOURCES: http://finance.yahoo.com and www.econ.yale.edu/~shiller/data/ie_data.htm.

Since only three stocks were included in this example that used the Dow additions in conjunction with the formula, this is too small a sample to be certain that these results will repeat. But, since we were able to do statistical tests on the earlier sample of nine stocks that were just admitted to the Dow (without including the formula timing), this gives us some sense that this investment method is at least worth considering, especially given the outstanding results.

In the example, only three stocks are shown even though there were six buy years. The reason only three stocks are shown is that the complete returns data (including the effects of dividends) on the three other recent additions to the Dow were not available. This may have been due to companies being bought by other companies, mergers, or some limitations in the references I was using for this data. In following the formula in a real-world scenario, six different stocks would have been purchased from the recent additions to the Dow list to give diversity to the portfolio of stocks.

This method of investing in the most recent additions to the Dow in combination with the formula is presented only as an example of how buying individual stocks may be better than an index fund. The number of stocks and incidences referenced here are not enough to be sure this approach is statistically valid.

Referenced Books on Beating the Market

Some of the books listed in the References at the end of this book claim to show how the overall performance of the stock market can be exceeded by following that book's own specific investment strategy. If the improved market performance as shown in these books was truly valid, it could be incorporated into any savings assumptions, and the resultant higher yields would greatly reduce any retirement savings requirements. However, when these books' theories for beating the market are analyzed closely, they seem to have some problems.

First, there are some general problems with some of the analyses in the referenced books, especially analyses related to each author's own theories of beating the market. The authors didn't seem to make statistical errors when they were discussing the stock market in general, but they did when they were trying to prove their own theories.

The reference books chosen were generally limited to those that showed or described the data they used in forming their conclusions. People, even scientists, often slant data that supports their preconceived notions. The test goal in this book was to be able to independently validate the conclusions of the authors of the reference books and to check any statistical methods used, since this is often another source of error. It was necessary to make sure that the authors weren't just mining data (looking at reams of data) until some sort of correlation was found that supported their theories even if it had no real basis in logic. After all, most statistical tests are conducted to a 95 percent confidence level, so if you look at 20 random events, one is likely to test as being statistically significant just due to random cause.

Most of the books referenced were published after the year 2000. This requirement was included because the market drop in 2000 gives an additional significant market event that should be included in any analysis.

Books that emphasized the detail of digging into a company's balance sheets were not referenced. This is because that type of analysis is already being done by countless experts working at the major brokerage firms. They have powerful computers, vast databases, and complex programs with which no individual (or writer) can hope to compete. Everyone doing that type of analysis tends to reach the same general conclusions, and any effect is usually already included in the stock price.

The stock market has been studied by countless people. Any new way of beating the market should be suspect: after all, why haven't other intelligent people already discovered this finding? Perhaps the observations made in reviewing the reference books will give you pause when you find *any* book, including this one, making a point on the market and seemingly to be proving it with data. The reader must apply his or her own logic tests.

A book called *Winning with the Dow's Losers,* by Charles Carlson, tests the theory that the Dow Jones Industrial Average's poorest performers for a given year will do better the following year. This is not a new idea, which Mr. Carlson acknowledges. He just gives a different spin to the concept, which he backs up with many years of data. This back-up data is what he believes makes his book unique and valid. In some of his examples, he uses a 73-year investment time period to "prove" his theory, which, as we previously discussed, may be of statistical interest but has little real-world application. Generally, no one's investment window is 73 years.

Mr. Carlson also compares 5-year and 10-year outputs against the overall Dow and concludes that the *variation* with his plan is less than the variation of the Dow. Five or 10 pieces of annual data are enough to compare averages, but not enough to make a valid statistical comparison of *variation* with any degree of confidence. So his conclusion is not statistically defensible.

In other analyses, Mr. Carlson includes six months of 2003 as an equivalent full year because six months is all the data he had in 2003 before publishing. Without including 2003, many of his conclusions weren't quite as impressive! Using six months of data that is a primary support of a theory, even if the intent is not to mislead, is suspect where everything else is yearly data.

In *Yes, You Can Time the Market*, by Ben Stein and Phil DeMuth, the chapter "The Power of Price," shows an analysis comparing buying stocks when the S&P 500 price is below its 15-year moving average (the book's plan) versus buying the S&P 500 stocks on a consistent-buy-basis, disregarding the price. They chose a time period from 1977 to 2002.

At the beginning eight years of this period the market price *is* below the 15-year S&P 500 moving average price, so the book "allows" the book's plan to *double* the investment (versus the consistent-buy-basis plan) during this favorable time period. At the end of the total 25-year example period, the authors show that the book's plan did 89 percent better than buying the market for the example time period.

The comparison, however, is not valid because they had different investment amounts invested at different time periods. This is comparing apples to oranges. Also, the actual difference between the two methods, as far as comparing the *total* gains, was only 4 percent. Nowhere in the book's analysis did they account for the fact that the book's "plan" was allowed to invest almost $10,000 extra (doubling) at the beginning of the time period, with no consideration for discounting whatever loss occurred from taking the funds from another investment. This is also a problem in several other places in the book.

The time period chosen for this example is convenient for the authors. Had the example stopped one year earlier, the result would have favored the consistent investment plan, not the book's investment method.

Early in the book, the authors of *Yes, You Can Time the Market* seem to demonstrate some misunderstanding of Dollar Cost Averaging. They *negatively state* that, in Dollar Cost Averaging, when the stock market goes up in price you buy fewer shares of stock with the same dollars.

This is *not* a negative. That is the whole *essence* of dollar averaging: that you buy more shares when the price is low and buy fewer shares when the stock price is high. In this way, with the up-and-down variations of the market over time, the average price *paid per share* of stock would be less than the average price of the stock during the same time period. This is because the normal mathematical way to calculate an "average" would be to assume that you bought the same *number of shares* each time you purchased shares, whereas in Dollar Cost Averaging the constant is the *number of dollars* each time you purchase shares.

Since investment plans through payroll deduction are based on number of dollars, not number of shares, many investors practice dollar averaging without even realizing it.

In *The Four Pillars of Investing*, by William Bernstein, generally an excellent book, there is confusing advice in the chapter "Measuring the Beast." After many pages of careful analysis, the author concludes that, in the future, real stock returns will be close to 3.5 percent. He then goes on to say that an aggressive investor should have no more than 80 percent invested in stocks. If the author really believes his own conclusion about future returns on stocks being only 3.5 percent, not much more than risk-free TIPS, investing 80 percent in stocks wouldn't be aggressive, it would be foolhardy!

The portfolios William Bernstein pushes at the end of the book, which seemingly include every domestic and overseas investment instrument currently available, would take a full-time investment advisor to manage. Of course, since he *is* a professional investment advisor, there could be a self-serving view of investment needs here!

Andrew Smithers and Stephen Wright's *Valuing Wall Street* is a book about something called the q ratio, which is the ratio of "Stock Price" divided by "Corporate Net Worth per Share." The book shows that there is an almost 100 percent correlation between the percent change in the q ratio and the percent change in the stock price. So why not just use stock price change directly and get away from the acknowledged problem of the accuracy of the included Corporate Net Worth per Share measurement?

In fact, in *Yes, You Can Time the Market*, the authors show that price alone is somewhat superior to the q ratio when tested on historical results. It should be noted, however, that the Corporate Net Worth per Share value is obtained in a somewhat different manner from book to book.

Winning the Loser's Game, by Charles D. Ellis, presents a somewhat confusing statistic. Without going through all the preliminary data of the example in the chapter "Time," the author concludes that an annualized rate of return is between a profit of 405 percent and a loss of 372 percent. Besides giving a range of outcomes that is so wide as to be meaningless, how can you lose more than 100 percent without selling shares short, which is not part of the book's methodology?

Summary

Index funds are a better investment than mutual funds. The Random Walk and Efficient Market Theories don't seem to be valid when tested against the long-term upward trend of the market. This upward trend is certainly not random.

Buying a mix of individual stocks may be superior to buying index funds, because you are not buying stocks that are past their prime growth. Buying recent additions to the Dow is one way to select stocks, and when they are purchased using the formula that keeps money in TIPS when the market is high priced, the results have been excellent.

Several beating-the-market theories espoused by various books are discussed, but none seem to stand up to independent scrutiny.

Part III

SURVIVING AND SAVING DURING THE COMING DEPRESSION

The priorities for most people during this depression will be to keep their job and home. But people will still want to save for a child's education or for retirement. Part III helps quantify how much someone should be saving annually for a future major expenditure or for retirement, and how much is needed to retire soon. This requires some inflation assumptions and some judgment as to the future of Social Security retirement benefits.

Economic bubbles are extremely dangerous for people trying to save. If you buy any asset whose value is artificially high due to a bubble, it could be many years before you can even get your money back, much less make money on your investment.

Chapter 12, How to Survive the Coming Depression: Keep a job, limit debts, and stay away from the stock market until it tanks.

Chapter 13, Saving Before and During the Depression: You have to be realistic about how much savings it takes to reach a financial goal with available interest rates. Use the charts in this chapter to determine required savings.

Chapter 14, Retirement Savings Charts for People Planning to Retire in 15 to 40 Years: These savings tables include the effect of inflation and assume realistic returns on savings.

Chapter 15, I Want to Retire Soon. How Much Money Will I Need? Anyone retiring soon should be sure of having sufficient funds, especially given the fact that people retiring within the next few years may spend their whole retirement in an economic depression. Use the charts in this chapter to determine how much money is required.

Chapter 12

How to Survive the Coming Depression

F ew people under the age of 75 have much remembrance of the Great Depression of the thirties. Some of us have discussed this era with older relatives or friends, or have read books like Steinbeck's *The Grapes of Wrath* that have given us some glimpse of how hard those times were for so many people. But few of us have any personal experience to help us prepare. So, the coming years are going to be a new and challenging time for most of us.

In this chapter, I try to give some insight on how to best survive the coming years. By necessity the discussion has to be general, because every individual has his own risk factors related to jobs and finances. But few people will go through the coming years without being personally affected and having to adjust to the depression realities.

The Basics, Obvious but Important

In this section, we will discuss some seemingly obvious ways to profit during the next great depression.

Hang on to Your Job

Obviously, having a job during the depression is critical, unless someone is already very comfortably retired or is extremely wealthy. During most recessions and depressions, the majority of people *do* stay employed. Anyone thinking of leaving a job at this time may want to review that decision, given that a depression is starting. This is probably not the time to initiate a war with your boss or to tell him exactly what you think about him or your job! Also, it probably is not a good time to start a business that is relying on growth in the general economy.

As the economy slows and companies downsize, remaining employees will often be asked to do more. Unless the resulting workload becomes absolutely unbearable, cooperate. One of the few good outcomes of economic slowdowns is that companies learn to be more efficient. In good times, the number of people required to do a given task often grows because of an unnoticed expansion of bureaucratic support, which becomes imbedded within the real work requirements.

In the coming depression, as opposed to the 2000 stock market drop, or even the 1929 depression, more of the middle class and upper-middle class are going to be dramatically affected. Some people in these comfortable classes will have their homes foreclosed because they are so extended in their mortgages and other debts. Not only are they at risk of losing their jobs, but also their homes and cars. Many families have payments that rely on two incomes, so even the loss of one of the family jobs will put their whole economic existence at risk.

Make Sure Your Home or Rent Payment Is Affordable

Those who are overburdened with a mortgage payment, a situation that was encouraged by the recent very low mortgage rates that encouraged refinancing or buying with little or no down payment, should take this opportunity to downsize if they are able to sell their existing home, even if it means taking a small loss on the current home. If a family has two incomes, strive to make the mortgage payment, or rent payment, low enough such that one of you could lose their job without jeopardizing the ability to make the payment. You can lose your expensive car or your credit cards can be cancelled. Not good, but not the end of the world, either. Losing these is nothing compared to losing your job or your home.

This doesn't mean that those who have homes that are paid for, or whose mortgage payments are not overwhelming, should sell and downsize. When all the dust settles and the recovery is in full swing, real assets like a home will still have value that will then start to appreciate. And you will be able to live in relative comfort during the depression, while many others are not doing so well. This is nothing that should cause guilt. Most people have had the opportunity to control their expenses versus their income, and you should get the rewards that come from frugality. Those who used their seed corn to fill their stomachs should not be surprised or whine when they have no crops the following year.

Be Attuned to General Risks to Society

Having many people from the middle or upper-middle classes in economic straits is extremely dangerous for the government. This group has experienced power and can mobilize itself to action, and not always in a positive vein. They *will* find someone else to blame for their woes. The victims of their ire will not only be the normal groups that are persecuted, like the minorities and immigrants, but also those who are extremely wealthy or powerful. Of special risk will be CEOs and government leaders who are still drawing obscene salaries during the depression. It is very likely that, for this elite group, the fear of terrorists will be replaced by a fear of internal groups or individuals looking to avenge their own devastating financial situation. During the 1929 depression, communism became attractive to many in the United States, and Hitler and the Nazis came to power during hard economic times in Germany. People will be attracted to any group that gives them a simplistic explanation of the depression and that holds some promise for a quick recovery, even if this solution involves hurting other innocent groups.

Limit Debts and Be Conservative with Investments

Not being overly in debt is critical so that any rise in living costs and interest rates doesn't drive you into bankruptcy. You want enough of a cushion such that a reduction in wages or work hours does not push you over some economic cliff. You want to be able to quietly stand aside from the turmoil that will dominate society until the depression bottoms out and the slow recovery begins. This turmoil will last many years because it will not be easy to mollify all the forces that are coming together to cause this depression. But the turmoil will eventually end!

Having savings in inflation protected government securities (TIPS) is an option, and being out of the stock market until the depression bottoms is critical. At the depression bottom, there will be great opportunities for depression survivors. Relative bargains will be available on homes and other high-dollar items. One of these relative bargains will be stocks, either because no one will want to buy them or because other potential investors will have already lost all their money. Both earlier and later chapters discuss how funds should be saved until you are able to capitalize on these bottom-of-depression opportunities.

We have seen in the earlier chapters that current stock prices are historically very high, and a drop in the stock market is likely to continue for the near future. Even if the stock market were to stay at its current level for several years, the only real benefit in owning stocks would be the current 2 percent dividend. This is lower than the 3 percent we assumed for TIPS.

Note that I have not included burying gold bullion or arming yourself with AK-47s, because I don't think that our country is at risk of a complete meltdown. However, to make sure your money in the bank is safe, limit your bank savings to FDIC insured accounts, with no more than $250,000 per depositor, per bank.

Take Pride in Living on Less and Identify a Support Group

Lower you cost of living. You can lower it a lot more than you think, and you should start doing it now! Take great pride in living on *less* rather than impressing others with *more*. This actually becomes a rewarding task.

Since it is after-tax money you are saving, its effect on your finances is far greater than an equivalent dollar difference in salary.

Help each other and identify backups. This is especially important for family members. Most extended families will have members who lose a job or home, in many cases through no fault of their own. This is the time to forget past family differences and help each other. The help could be emotional, financial, or even having relatives move in with each other to reduce expenses. People without these backups are the ones who become homeless or severely hurt in other ways.

Summary

In this chapter we discussed the basic ways to endure the next great depression. Below is a summary of action steps:

- Hold on to your job if at all possible. Do the little-bit-extra!
- Hold on to you home or downsize if possible.
- Get out of high-interest or adjustable-rate debt.
- Don't have savings in the stock market. Consider TIPS as an alternative.
- Lower your cost of living. You can lower it a lot more than you think, and you should start doing it now!
- Take great pride in living on *less* rather than impressing others with *more*.
- Help each other, and identify backups. This is especially important for family members. Families may have to move in with each other or the elderly may have to be cared for in a relative's home.

Chapter 13

Saving Before and During the Depression

This depression will be very long and hard. The Great Depression really didn't end until the fifties, at least as far as the stock market goes, and it is difficult to determine whether World War II shortened or lengthened that depression. Fifteen or 20 years would be a reasonable estimate for how long this depression will last. So, for many people, a third of their working career may be spent living through this depression. Because of this, we must consider how you can save for the future while you are trying to survive a depression. As we saw in Figure 2.1, most people have not been saving for many years, so this is going to be a dramatic departure from their borrow-and-spend style of living!

Even in a severe depression, people will still have goals such as saving for a child's college education or for their own comfortable retirement. Life will go on during and after the depression, and so will planning for the future, especially for those fortunate enough to still be employed.

However, blindly putting money into a mutual fund in the hope that the savings will skyrocket in value probably never was a very effective plan, and it certainly isn't going to work during the depression. Buy-and-hold as a stock investment plan will become buy-and-weep! Savings before and during the initial stages of this depression will have to be very conservative and out of the stock market.

In this chapter, I show that people have to get realistic about how much savings it takes to reach a financial goal with available interest rates. People also have to make some judgment on Social Security, pensions, and IRAs for the future. *Money never has liked to work very hard. The end of the last century temporarily hid this fact, but only the very wealthy have ever been able to live solely on the earnings from their money.* You must satisfy yourself that real gains of 10 percent per year on your savings are not going to be obtainable. They generally weren't available in the past and certainly are not going to be in the immediate future.

Simple Savings to Get a Known Lump Dollar Sum

Before we review required annual savings, it helps to understand how to calculate these savings requirements. Those who truly hate data can just skim through the following detail, but having an understanding of calculating even simple savings requirements will give some insight on how savings calculations are complicated by the inclusion of inflation considerations. However, understanding this is not required to use the savings tables and formulas in this book.

Let's look at the simplest type of savings calculation, where we already know how much we want to have saved (in a lump sum) in a specific number of years, like wanting $10,000 saved in 10 years. We will assume we are saving the money in TIPS at 3 percent interest, and, for our example, we will initially assume zero inflation. Table 13.1 shows how much you would have to save annually to have various amounts from $10,000 to $1,000,000 after a number of years, at 3 percent interest.

Three percent interest on money, even after inflation, will seem strikingly low to many of you. But think how great this 3 percent per year looks compared to those who bought stock at the beginning of 2008 and by mid-2008 had already lost 16 percent. And think how good that

Table 13.1 Annual Savings Required to Reach Various Goals at 3 Percent Interest
Various Lump Sum Savings Goals

Years	$10,000	$25,000	$50,000	$100,000	$250,000	$500,000	$1,000,000
2	$4,858	$12,144	$24,289	$48,577	$121,443	$242,886	$485,772
4	$2,356	$5,890	$11,780	$23,561	$58,902	$117,804	$235,608
6	$1,523	$3,808	$7,616	$15,233	$38,082	$76,164	$152,328
8	$1,108	$2,769	$5,538	$11,076	$27,690	$55,380	$110,760
10	$859	$2,147	$4,294	$8,587	$21,468	$42,936	$85,872
12	$693	$1,733	$3,467	$6,934	$17,334	$34,668	$69,336
14	$576	$1,439	$2,878	$5,756	$14,391	$28,782	$57,564
16	$488	$1,219	$2,438	$4,877	$12,192	$24,384	$48,768
18	$420	$1,049	$2,098	$4,196	$10,491	$20,982	$41,964
20	$366	$914	$1,828	$3,655	$9,138	$18,276	$36,552
22	$321	$804	$1,607	$3,215	$8,037	$16,074	$32,148
24	$285	$713	$1,425	$2,850	$7,125	$14,250	$28,500
26	$254	$636	$1,272	$2,544	$6,360	$12,720	$25,440
28	$228	$571	$1,142	$2,284	$5,709	$11,418	$22,836
30	$206	$515	$1,030	$2,059	$5,148	$10,296	$20,592
32	$186	$466	$932	$1,865	$4,662	$9,324	$18,648
34	$170	$424	$848	$1,696	$4,239	$8,478	$16,956
36	$155	$386	$773	$1,546	$3,864	$7,728	$15,456
38	$141	$353	$707	$1,414	$3,534	$7,068	$14,136
40	$130	$324	$648	$1,296	$3,240	$6,480	$12,960

3 percent per year will look several years from now, compared to those same stockholders whose stock values will drop an additional 60 percent or more from their mid-2008 value!

The numbers in Table 13.1 are the annual savings required. The numbers across the top of the table are the various lump sum savings goals.

If you want to save other than the specific amounts shown in Table 13.1, just proportion your annual savings accordingly. For example, if you wanted to save $20,000 in 10 years, you would multiply the $859 shown in the table for $10,000 by two to get a required annual savings of $1,718.

As noted, our example assumed zero inflation. However, that's not very realistic. Someone ignoring inflation will probably end up with too little savings at the end of their savings period. TIPS will adjust for any inflation on existing savings, so if the savings are in TIPS, and the yearly amount being saved is *also* adjusted annually for inflation, the eventual saved amount after the given number of years will be in current dollar purchasing power. For example, if you wanted to save $10,000 in 10 years, according to Table 13.1, your initial annual savings would be $859. However, if after one year, the government announces that inflation in the previous year was 5 percent, then your annual savings should be increased 5 percent, to $902. If, in the following year, inflation really takes off and goes up another 10 percent, then the $902 annual savings will have to be increased 10 percent to $992 per year.

So, Table 13.1 *is* valid during inflationary periods if the annual savings are adjusted every year for inflation and the savings are in TIPS.

Let's test if this really works. We want a $10,000 savings goal to have current purchasing power in 10 years. If there is any inflation at all, the actual dollar savings in 10 years will have to be greater than $10,000. Since historical inflation has been 3.5 percent per year, let's see what final savings amount will be required assuming 3.5 percent inflation. To get the actual total dollars we will need in 10 years, we multiply $10,000 times 1.035 and continue doing this nine more times. This is $10,000 $\times$ 1.035^10 = $14,106. Note that if someone *didn't* save in a manner that adjusted for inflation, their $10,000 after 10 years would only have $10,000/$14,106 = 0.71, or 71 percent of their desired real purchasing power.

Let's see if using Table 13.1 and an initial annual savings amount of $859 gets us to our goal of $14,106 in actual saved dollars in 10 years if we increase our annual savings amount every year with inflation. To test this, here is Table 13.2 showing each year's savings with 3.5 percent inflation added and the accumulated savings increasing each year by 3 percent interest plus 3.5 percent inflation. This is what will happen when the savings are in TIPS, at the assumed 3 percent interest, and we index our annual savings up 3.5 percent every year to account for inflation.

The accumulative savings shown can vary somewhat based on the timing of when the interest is assumed to be applied to the savings, which is why the final number doesn't exactly match $14,106. But the example shows that this approach generally allows the saver to meet the goal of having $10,000 worth of *real* purchasing power after 10 years. Although the last savings year will require $1,171 in savings, versus the first year's $859 savings amount, the higher savings requirement in the

Table 13.2 Ten-Year Savings with 3.5 Percent Inflation and 3 Percent Interest

Year	Annual Savings	Accumulated savings
1	$859	$859
2	$889	$1,862
3	$920	$2,963
4	$952	$4,170
5	$986	$5,490
6	$1,020	$6,934
7	$1,056	$8,509
8	$1,093	$10,226
9	$1,131	$12,095
10	$1,171	$14,128

last year should "feel" about the same as the first year's savings because the higher amount is in inflated future dollars. It is assumed that the saver's income will generally increase with inflation.

The savings determination shown here would be valid for things like saving for a college education for your child. You would estimate the cost of the planned-for education in today's dollars and assume that the cost of the education in future years will increase with inflation. Recently, education costs have been rising *faster* than inflation. But since it is impossible to predict exact future cost increases, assuming a rise in college cost matching inflation is probably the best you can do, and it will get you much closer to your goal than if no inflation allowance were made.

The calculations used here for determining monthly savings would also be valid for calculating retirement savings *if* you knew exactly what lump sum, in current dollars, you needed at retirement. However, that is usually *not* known and we have to estimate it. This is covered later in this chapter.

Social Security in the Future

We have noted that, for many readers, one-third of their earning years will be during the depression that has now started. Because of that, besides just surviving the depression, they will have to be looking forward to a time of retirement and planning to have sufficient funds. Before we get into specifics on calculating retirement savings amounts, we need to decide what will be the future of Social Security benefits.

One of the biggest advantages of Social Security retirement benefits is that they are indexed up with inflation once a person retires, just like the TIPS savings we are advocating, as opposed to company pensions and annuities, which are normally "fixed" at the time withdrawal is begun. This indexing of Social Security benefits with inflation can make a huge difference for retirees as they progress through retirement. Social Security retirement benefits often start out with a value less than a company pension, but after years of inflation, Social Security can become the largest contributor to retirement income. Social Security is currently the major income source for many retirees. We therefore have to predict what Social Security retirement benefits will be available in the future, especially given the fact that we are going into a depression where *all* government programs will be at risk.

Most people are aware of the coming funding crisis with Social Security. The dominant issue in the coming years is the forecasted increase in retirees (due to aging baby boomers and people living longer), while the number of people in the support worker base will be declining. When Social Security was first implemented in 1935, the average life expectancy was less than 70. According to the Social Security Administration, life expectancy will be 80 by 2050. In 2008, there were a little over three workers per each retiree receiving Social Security. Projections show that, by 2030, there will only be two workers supporting each retiree if the Social Security retirement plan stays the way it is. This will cause the Social Security Retirement System to eventually run out of funds; unless some changes are made in benefits, the retirement age, or the Social Security taxes of workers.

Technically, the Social Security plan was supposed to have been accumulating funds in an account built from the excess contributions paid in previous years, when the pension payments received from workers was more than the money paid out in Social Security benefits. However, the government spent this money on other things, just leaving IOUs in the Social Security fund. Since the government is already borrowing at an outrageous rate and they haven't got the money to honor their IOUs, these IOUs may not satisfy the need for ready funds to pay retirees in future years.

In 1983, the full retirement age was raised from 65 to 67, to be implemented slowly until 2027. This was the first step in trying to address the issue of Social Security future funding. Delaying the retirement age not only reduces the resultant benefits (because people are on Social Security fewer years before they die), but also keeps people in the workforce longer. This helps address the problem of the proportion of workers to retirees. However, the delay in retirement age must be taken to age 70 to fully address the current funding crisis.

By delaying retirement to age 70, the net effect of both the reduced number of people getting retirement benefits, and the resultant larger workforce, will be to increase the ratio of the number of contributing workers versus the number of retirees receiving Social Security in 2030 to 3.1, close to what it is in 2008! A delay of retirement age to 70 is the minimum delay, given the coming depression. With a higher unemployment number expected during the depression, the number of supporting workers may actually be less than what is assumed here, and retirement age may have to be changed to 72. However, for our calculations we will use age 70, knowing that some adjustment in planned retirement age may have to be made as the realities of the depression unfold.

Since so many people are questioning whether Social Security will even survive, an increase in retirement age will be accepted as a necessary evil. Also, the government has already shown its willingness to adjust retirement age in its earlier delay of retirement to age 67. There will be years of congressional meetings and pulling of hair by Congress and the president, but a further delay in retirement age is what they will eventually implement. There will still be a reduced retirement option at 65 years old, but with *greatly* reduced benefits. This early-retirement option will pacify those still wanting an early out, at least until they see just how very reduced the benefits are!

Given this analysis, we will assume that people will be able to get full Social Security retirement funds (equivalent to the amount someone recently got at age 65), but not until they are 70 years old. For our example, we will assume that these benefits will be $2,400 per month for a couple. In the calculations used later in the chapter, $25,920 per year is used, which is slightly less than $2,200 per month to allow for some taxes on the Social Security benefits.

Other Social Security retirement funding solutions all have unacceptable ramifications. For example, President Bush's proposed private savings plan, that would have put some portion of current Social Security withholdings into a stock market private savings plan, would not only put future Social Security savings at stock market risk, but it would also devastate the current Social Security system. The current retirement system is in reality pay-as-you-go, and current payroll withholdings are used to pay the benefits of those already retired.

If you reduce the withholdings going to current retirees by removing some of the funds for stock purchases, the current system will not have enough money remaining to make payments to current retirees. Some have suggested that the government borrow the needed trillions of dollars to enable the overlap of both plans. Even Congress, which has shown no fiscal restraint in recent years, is not going to fall for that! They don't want any more borrowing! The financial burden the government is going to face, starting in 2009 or 2010, will put *all* new spending off-limits, since the government will be hard put to sustain current programs with the declining tax income that will occur during the depression and all the additional costs of work programs for the large numbers of unemployed.

Increasing taxes on current workers to keep the current retirement age for future retirees would require a doubling of Social Security withholdings. This would cause a worker revolt and an even deeper downturn of the economy, since workers would have less ready funds to spend.

There is also some consideration of changing the formula on how base Social Security benefits are calculated such that retirees get reduced benefits. Given that approximately 10 percent of our current retirees are living below the poverty line, I don't think Congress will go along with any reduced benefit program that will put even *more* of the elderly into dire straits.

Roth IRA

For our analysis, we assume that retirement funds are saved in a Roth IRA and, as already stated, the investment mode is TIPS (Treasury

Inflation Protected Securities). The Roth IRA is a way to control taxes on savings and their related gains. TIPS are one of the many ways that money can be invested *within* a Roth IRA.

When funds are saved in a regular IRA (Individual Retirement Account), the money is saved pretax, and you pay all taxes at a later date when the funds are withdrawn, generally after age 59½. Taxes are then paid not only on the initial deposited funds, but also on any gains those funds generated. In a Roth IRA, the funds are saved *after taxes*, so taxes are paid up front on the funds as they are being saved. There are no additional taxes on those funds, *nor on any of the related gains*, when the funds are withdrawn, again generally after age 59½.

The savings and withdrawal restrictions are less stringent on a Roth IRA than on a traditional IRA. But the biggest advantage for the retiree is that, when savings are in a Roth IRA, you *know* how much will be available at retirement. Net savings will not be at the whim of whatever income tax rate happens to be in effect at fund withdrawal. Nor will retirees have to worry about other income that would affect their tax rate.

Table 13.3 shows the income and contribution limits on a Roth IRA at the time of writing. Any person or couple whose wages exceed the partial contribution wage limits in this table are not eligible for a Roth IRA. Since this changes periodically and with inflation, current government limits should be reviewed at the time of saving.

Since all future retirement savings are assumed to be in a Roth IRA and in TIPS, concerns about taxes and inflation are reduced.

Company Pensions

The next element of retirement savings we must discuss is company pensions. The pension payout amount is normally fixed at the time of retirement and usually stays constant throughout the retirement years. In any period with inflation, the real purchasing power of the company pension is essentially reduced. This is especially an issue when inflation is high, which is likely to occur during this depression. In our calculations, we assume an annual inflation of 3.5 percent, which will cut the real purchasing power of any pension in half in 21 years. However, in times of

Table 13.3   Income and Contribution Limits on a Roth IRA

	Full Contribution Wage Limit	Partial Contribution Wage Limit
Single/head of household	$99,000	$114,000
Married filing jointly	$156,000	$166,000
Contribution limits (per person)	Under Age 50	Age 50 or Older
Year		
2008	$4,000	$5,000
2009+	$4,000 + Inflation	$5,000 + Inflation

SOURCE: IRS Government Publication 590 (2007) Individual Retirement Accounts (IRAs).

high inflation, for example 10 percent per year, the pension purchasing power is reduced by 50 percent in only seven years. That is why we want all elements of our savings, other than the company pension, to be inflation protected. This is why we specified TIPS as a savings mode. In the retirement savings tables that are shown later in the chapter, the diminishing effect of the pension, with 3.5 percent inflation, is already factored into the table's required savings values.

Companies generally quote any pension in the actual dollars the employee will receive at the time of retirement at age 65, assuming employment until then. Of course, companies estimate the pension this way because it makes the pension look more impressive that it takes place many years from now, hence with probable inflated dollars. The effect of inflation on diminishing the pension purchasing power is generally not discussed by the company. For example, let's look at a nominal company pension estimated at $20,000 per year (after taxes) at age 65. The person with the example pension is currently 35 years old, so he or she has another 30 years to work until age 65.

Let's see what $20,000 per year is worth 30 years from now in current dollars, assuming 3.5 percent annual inflation, which is the historical average inflation. To calculate this value, divide $20,000 by $1.035^{30} =$ $7,125. This means that the future pension is worth $7,125 per year in current dollars. This is not a trivial amount, but the pension certainly looks less impressive when expressed in current dollars, which gives a more truly representative value of its purchasing power. Since pensions are normally estimated for age 65, where the tables in this book assume the actual retirement is at age 70, the retirement charts assume an additional 10 percent value over the nominal pension amount because of the five additional years of work. Also, as we noted, since the pension payment amount is fixed, its effective value continues to decline during retirement as inflation does its thing! All of these adjustments are already included in the following charts for estimating retirement savings needs.

Seventy percent to 90 percent of the prior working income is usually estimated for retirement income needs (the estimated amount you will need per year once you retire). So, when estimating your retirement needs, use an assumption of approximately 80 percent of current income, after taxes.

Company-Supported IRAs

Some companies offer IRAs where the company matches the savings amount, or some percentage of the savings amount, of the employee. Obviously, these savings should be counted toward the savings requirements. However, if TIPS, or some other inflation-adjusted investment vehicle, is not an option in the plan, you will be forced to pick some other investment option. At the current stock market prices, you should consider a non-stock-market option, such as money-market or government bonds, until the stock market reaches a more sensible level. You will have to watch inflation levels and know that some portion of your savings is at risk due to its not being indexed in value with inflation.

You can either account for a reduced value of these savings being applied to your goal or recognize that the retirement income on which you are planning may have to be adjusted due to the inflationary effect. In any case, you will have to use a multiplier in the savings to account for the taxes you will have to pay on any gain realized on your investment. If the prior savings and yields are not tax-free, only assume 75 percent of existing savings when using the charts in this book.

Summary

This chapter shows how much savings it takes to reach a financial goal. I also showed why Social Security retirement age is likely to be changed to age 70, and how inflation diminishes the real value of a fixed pension. A Roth IRA has the advantage that earnings on investments will be tax-free, and retirees will be more certain what their savings will actually be at retirement, rather than having to worry about the tax rate at retirement time. Company-supported IRAs are great, except that they often limit investment choices to investments that do not directly adjust for inflation

Chapter 14

Retirement Savings Charts for People Planning to Retire in 15 to 40 Years

I n this chapter are tables to be used for people planning to retire at least 15 years from now. Don't get overwhelmed by the number of tables in this section. People wanting to reference these tables can go directly to the one that applies to them, or they can peruse the whole section to get a better understanding of how these tables were developed. Perusing the whole section and seeing the examples is best. (The next chapter has tables and formulas for those who plan to retire sooner, within a relatively few years. Feel free to jump ahead, if applicable.)

The tables in this chapter are in two groupings. The first group is for those planning to retire at age 70 (Tables 14.1 through 14.6); the second group of tables is for those planning to retire at age 65 (Tables 14.7

through 14.12). In each grouping there is a table for retiring in 40 years, 35 years, 30 years, 25 years, 20 years, and 15 years.

The retirement savings shown in this chapter assume that savings are drained by age 93. Once savings are drained, the only remaining income will be Social Security and a diminished real-value pension. But, by drawing on other assets like home value, retirement lifestyles can be maintained to age 100 and beyond. At the bottom of each table there is also a correction factor for those who want to assume an extended life beyond the age of 93.

Assuming Social Security retirement kicks in at age 70 and actual retirement is also at age 70, Tables 14.1 through 14.6 show annual savings requirements with different options of years-to-retirement, various income needs, different nominal pensions, and varied existing savings amounts. The actual pension is assumed to be 10 percent larger than the shown nominal pension due to a delayed retirement beyond the usual age of 65, and this correction is already included in the table calculations. The nominal pension amount is assumed to be after estimated taxes. Savings are in TIPS. Existing savings and resulting yields are assumed to be tax-free because they are saved in TIPS within a Roth IRA. If the prior savings and yields are not tax-free, only assume 75 percent of existing savings when using the charts.

Immediately following the tables for retirement at age 70 are Tables 14.7 through 14.12 for those who intend to retire at age 65. In these tables, the extra 10 percent on the nominal pension is *not* included, since retirement is at the company-calculated age for the pension.

Note that no stock market benefits are included in any of the retirement savings charts in this book. If someone is fortunate enough to be able to invest in the stock market after it drops over 60 percent, any gains resulting from that activity should be used to reduce required savings only after those gains are truly realized and you are back out of the stock market.

Both the nominal pension and prior savings are assumed to be after taxes. The "prior savings" are what you currently have saved for retirement. The numbers within the tables are what you have to save every year. These annual savings requirements will have to be adjusted every year for inflation. The desired income is the after-tax retirement income you desire in current dollars.

Retiring at Age 70

The following are a series of tables that can be used for people who are planning to retire at the age of 70.

Table 14.1 shows the annual savings for people who are retiring at the age of 70 in 40 years.

Table 14.2 shows the annual savings for people who are retiring at the age of 70 in 35 years.

Table 14.3 shows the annual savings for people who are retiring at the age of 70 in 30 years.

Table 14.4 shows the annual savings for people who are retiring at the age of 70 in 25 years.

Table 14.5 shows the annual savings for people who are retiring at the age of 70 in 20 years.

Table 14.6 shows the annual savings for people who are retiring at the age of 70 in 15 years.

As mentioned earlier, the savings are assumed to be drained by age 93, and the retirement income at that point will be Social Security and the initial pension amount. However, draining other assets, like home value, will probably allow lifestyle continuance to age 100. If the live-to-age-93 assumption is felt to be risky because you plan to live to be 120, then the tabled savings shown must be increased by 92 percent. This will allow the real desired income to "last forever," which is assumed to be age 120 since the income on the larger resulting TIPS investment will be sufficient for a longer period of time. However, this is an expensive option that few will be able to afford. Note that the detailed derivation of the live-forever additional savings is covered in Appendix B.

The savings values in the following tables are, by necessity, approximate. However, they will bring you close to your goal; certainly closer than if you had no guidelines or were using tables based on fantasy future stock market performance, which most published retirement savings formulas do.

To make sure that you can use these charts, I suggest that you work through the following simple examples. For further understanding, refer to Appendix B.

Table 14.1 Annual Savings for Retiring in 40 Years, at Age 70

Desired Income	Nominal Pension	Prior Savings: $0 Annual Savings	$50,000 Annual Savings	$100,000 Annual Savings	$150,000 Annual Savings	$200,000 Annual Savings	$250,000 Annual Savings	$500,000 Annual Savings
$40,000	$0	$3,198	$2,550	$1,902	$1,254	$606	$0	$0
$40,000	$10,000	$2,737	$2,089	$1,441	$793	$145	$0	$0
$40,000	$20,000	$2,276	$1,628	$980	$332	$0	$0	$0
$40,000	$30,000	$1,816	$1,168	$520	$0	$0	$0	$0
$40,000	$40,000	$1,355	$707	$59	$0	$0	$0	$0
$40,000	$50,000	$895	$247	$0	$0	$0	$0	$0
$40,000	$60,000	$434	$0	$0	$0	$0	$0	$0
$50,000	$0	$5,469	$4,821	$4,173	$3,525	$2,877	$2,229	$0
$50,000	$10,000	$5,008	$4,360	$3,712	$3,064	$2,416	$1,768	$0
$50,000	$20,000	$4,547	$3,899	$3,251	$2,603	$1,955	$1,307	$0
$50,000	$30,000	$4,087	$3,439	$2,791	$2,143	$1,495	$847	$0
$50,000	$40,000	$3,626	$2,978	$2,330	$1,682	$1,034	$386	$0
$50,000	$50,000	$3,166	$2,518	$1,870	$1,222	$574	$0	$0
$50,000	$60,000	$2,705	$2,057	$1,409	$761	$113	$0	$0
$60,000	$0	$7,740	$7,092	$6,444	$5,796	$5,148	$4,500	$1,260
$60,000	$10,000	$7,279	$6,631	$5,983	$5,335	$4,687	$4,039	$799
$60,000	$20,000	$6,818	$6,170	$5,522	$4,874	$4,226	$3,578	$338
$60,000	$30,000	$6,358	$5,710	$5,062	$4,414	$3,766	$3,118	$0
$60,000	$40,000	$5,897	$5,249	$4,601	$3,953	$3,305	$2,657	$0
$60,000	$50,000	$5,437	$4,789	$4,141	$3,493	$2,845	$2,197	$0
$60,000	$60,000	$4,976	$4,328	$3,680	$3,032	$2,384	$1,736	$0

Prior Savings:		$0	$50,000	$100,000	$150,000	$200,000	$250,000	$500,000
Desired Income	Nominal Pension	Annual Savings	Annual Savings	Annual Savings	Annual Savings	Annual Savings	Annual Savings	Annual Savings
$70,000	$0	$10,239	$9,526	$8,814	$8,101	$7,419	$6,771	$3,531
$70,000	$10,000	$9,732	$9,020	$8,307	$7,623	$6,958	$6,310	$3,070
$70,000	$20,000	$9,226	$8,513	$7,800	$7,146	$6,498	$5,850	$2,610
$70,000	$30,000	$8,719	$8,016	$7,336	$6,685	$6,037	$5,389	$2,130
$70,000	$40,000	$8,212	$7,520	$6,872	$6,224	$5,576	$4,928	$1,651
$70,000	$50,000	$7,729	$7,060	$6,412	$5,764	$5,116	$4,468	$1,202
$70,000	$60,000	$7,247	$6,599	$5,951	$5,303	$4,655	$4,007	$753
$80,000	$0	$12,738	$11,961	$11,183	$10,406	$9,690	$9,042	$5,802
$80,000	$10,000	$12,186	$11,408	$10,631	$9,911	$9,230	$8,582	$5,342
$80,000	$20,000	$11,633	$10,856	$10,078	$9,417	$8,769	$8,121	$4,881
$80,000	$30,000	$11,080	$10,323	$9,611	$8,956	$8,308	$7,660	$4,420
$80,000	$40,000	$10,527	$9,791	$9,143	$8,495	$7,847	$7,199	$3,959
$80,000	$50,000	$10,022	$9,331	$8,683	$8,035	$7,387	$6,739	$3,499
$80,000	$60,000	$9,518	$8,870	$8,222	$7,574	$6,926	$6,278	$3,038

NOTE: For "living forever," add 92 percent to the values in the table.

Table 14.2 Annual Savings for Retiring in 35 Years, at Age 70

Desired Income	Nominal Pension	Prior Savings: $0 Annual Savings	$50,000 Annual Savings	$100,000 Annual Savings	$150,000 Annual Savings	$200,000 Annual Savings	$250,000 Annual Savings	$500,000 Annual Savings
$40,000	$0	$3,993	$3,181	$2,372	$1,557	$745	$0	$0
$40,000	$10,000	$3,310	$2,498	$1,689	$874	$59	$0	$0
$40,000	$20,000	$2,627	$1,815	$1,006	$191	$0	$0	$0
$40,000	$30,000	$1,944	$1,132	$323	$0	$0	$0	$0
$40,000	$40,000	$1,260	$448	$0	$0	$0	$0	$0
$40,000	$50,000	$577	$0	$0	$0	$0	$0	$0
$40,000	$60,000	$0	$0	$0	$0	$0	$0	$0
$50,000	$0	$6,829	$6,017	$5,208	$4,393	$3,581	$2,777	$0
$50,000	$10,000	$6,146	$5,334	$4,525	$3,710	$2,897	$2,087	$0
$50,000	$20,000	$5,463	$4,651	$3,842	$3,027	$2,212	$1,397	$0
$50,000	$30,000	$4,780	$3,968	$3,159	$2,344	$1,528	$711	$0
$50,000	$40,000	$4,096	$3,284	$2,476	$1,661	$843	$25	$0
$50,000	$50,000	$3,413	$2,601	$1,793	$978	$163	$0	$0
$50,000	$60,000	$2,729	$1,917	$1,110	$295	$0	$0	$0
$60,000	$0	$9,665	$8,853	$8,044	$7,229	$6,417	$5,613	$1,562
$60,000	$10,000	$8,982	$8,170	$7,361	$6,546	$5,734	$4,930	$879
$60,000	$20,000	$8,299	$7,487	$6,678	$5,863	$5,051	$4,247	$196
$60,000	$30,000	$7,616	$6,804	$5,995	$5,180	$4,368	$3,564	$0
$60,000	$40,000	$6,932	$6,120	$5,311	$4,496	$3,684	$2,880	$0
$60,000	$50,000	$6,249	$5,437	$4,628	$3,813	$3,001	$2,197	$0
$60,000	$60,000	$5,566	$4,754	$3,945	$3,130	$2,318	$1,514	$0

Desired Income	Nominal Pension	Prior Savings: $0	$50,000	$100,000	$150,000	$200,000	$250,000	$500,000
		Annual Savings	Annual Savings	Annual Savings	Annual Savings	Annual Savings	Annual Savings	Annual Savings
$70,000	$0	$13,035	$12,142	$11,252	$10,355	$9,462	$8,578	$4,398
$70,000	$10,000	$12,283	$11,390	$10,500	$9,604	$8,711	$7,830	$3,715
$70,000	$20,000	$11,532	$10,639	$9,749	$8,853	$7,959	$7,083	$3,032
$70,000	$30,000	$10,780	$9,887	$8,997	$8,101	$7,240	$6,400	$2,349
$70,000	$40,000	$10,028	$9,135	$8,245	$7,349	$6,520	$5,716	$1,666
$70,000	$50,000	$9,277	$8,384	$7,513	$6,657	$5,837	$5,033	$983
$70,000	$60,000	$8,526	$7,633	$6,781	$5,966	$5,154	$4,350	$300
$80,000	$0	$16,404	$15,430	$14,459	$13,481	$12,507	$11,542	$7,234
$80,000	$10,000	$15,585	$14,610	$13,640	$12,662	$11,687	$10,731	$6,551
$80,000	$20,000	$14,765	$13,791	$12,820	$11,842	$10,868	$9,919	$5,868
$80,000	$30,000	$13,945	$12,971	$12,000	$11,022	$10,112	$9,236	$5,185
$80,000	$40,000	$13,125	$12,150	$11,180	$10,202	$9,356	$8,552	$4,501
$80,000	$50,000	$12,305	$11,331	$10,398	$9,502	$8,673	$7,869	$3,818
$80,000	$60,000	$11,486	$10,511	$9,617	$8,802	$7,990	$7,186	$3,135

NOTE: For "living forever," add 92 percent to the values in the table.

Table 14.3 Annual Savings for Retiring in 30 Years, at Age 70

Prior Savings:		$0	$50,000	$100,000	$150,000	$200,000	$250,000	$500,000
Desired Income	Nominal Pension	Annual Savings	Annual Savings	Annual Savings	Annual Savings	Annual Savings	Annual Savings	Annual Savings
$40,000	$0	$5,081	$4,051	$3,022	$1,991	$961	$0	$0
$40,000	$10,000	$4,049	$3,019	$1,990	$961	$0	$0	$0
$40,000	$20,000	$3,016	$1,986	$957	$0	$0	$0	$0
$40,000	$30,000	$1,984	$954	$0	$0	$0	$0	$0
$40,000	$40,000	$951	$0	$0	$0	$0	$0	$0
$40,000	$50,000	$0	$0	$0	$0	$0	$0	$0
$40,000	$60,000	$0	$0	$0	$0	$0	$0	$0
$50,000	$0	$8,920	$7,787	$6,655	$5,600	$4,570	$3,540	$0
$50,000	$10,000	$7,784	$6,691	$5,611	$4,569	$3,539	$2,509	$0
$50,000	$20,000	$6,648	$5,595	$4,566	$3,537	$2,507	$1,477	$0
$50,000	$30,000	$5,604	$4,499	$3,522	$2,506	$1,476	$446	$0
$50,000	$40,000	$4,560	$3,403	$2,477	$1,474	$444	$0	$0
$50,000	$50,000	$3,516	$2,307	$1,433	$443	$0	$0	$0
$50,000	$60,000	$2,472	$1,211	$388	$0	$0	$0	$0
$60,000	$0	$12,759	$11,523	$10,288	$9,209	$8,179	$7,151	$2,003
$60,000	$10,000	$11,520	$10,363	$9,232	$8,177	$7,147	$6,119	$971
$60,000	$20,000	$10,281	$9,204	$8,175	$7,144	$6,114	$5,086	$0
$60,000	$30,000	$9,225	$8,172	$7,143	$6,112	$5,082	$4,054	$0
$60,000	$40,000	$8,169	$7,139	$6,110	$5,079	$4,049	$3,021	$0
$60,000	$50,000	$7,137	$6,107	$5,078	$4,047	$3,017	$1,989	$0
$60,000	$60,000	$6,104	$5,074	$4,045	$3,014	$1,984	$956	$0

Prior Savings:		$0	$50,000	$100,000	$150,000	$200,000	$250,000	$500,000
Desired Income	Nominal Pension	Annual Savings	Annual Savings	Annual Savings	Annual Savings	Annual Savings	Annual Savings	Annual Savings
$70,000	$0	$17,090	$15,854	$14,619	$13,461	$12,328	$11,197	$5,612
$70,000	$10,000	$15,851	$14,654	$13,471	$12,325	$11,192	$10,061	$4,464
$70,000	$20,000	$14,612	$13,455	$12,323	$11,189	$10,056	$8,925	$3,317
$70,000	$30,000	$13,464	$12,319	$11,188	$10,053	$8,920	$7,790	$2,387
$70,000	$40,000	$12,317	$11,184	$10,052	$8,918	$7,785	$6,654	$1,458
$70,000	$50,000	$11,181	$10,048	$8,916	$7,782	$6,689	$5,609	$529
$70,000	$60,000	$10,045	$8,912	$7,780	$6,646	$5,593	$4,565	$0
$80,000	$0	$21,420	$20,184	$18,950	$17,712	$16,476	$15,243	$9,221
$80,000	$10,000	$20,181	$18,945	$17,711	$16,473	$15,237	$14,004	$8,189
$80,000	$20,000	$18,942	$17,706	$16,472	$15,234	$13,998	$12,765	$7,156
$80,000	$30,000	$17,703	$16,467	$15,233	$13,995	$12,759	$11,526	$6,124
$80,000	$40,000	$16,464	$15,228	$13,994	$12,756	$11,520	$10,287	$5,091
$80,000	$50,000	$15,225	$13,989	$12,755	$11,517	$10,361	$9,230	$4,059
$80,000	$60,000	$13,986	$12,750	$11,516	$10,278	$9,202	$8,174	$3,026

NOTE: For "living forever," add 92 percent to the values in the table.

Table 14.4 Annual Savings for Retiring in 25 Years, at Age 70

Prior Savings:		$0	$50,000	$100,000	$150,000	$200,000	$250,000	$500,000
Desired Income	Nominal Pension	Annual Savings	Annual Savings	Annual Savings	Annual Savings	Annual Savings	Annual Savings	Annual Savings
$40,000	$0	$6,639	$5,290	$3,942	$2,592	$1,243	$0	$0
$40,000	$10,000	$4,995	$3,646	$2,298	$950	$0	$0	$0
$40,000	$20,000	$3,351	$2,002	$654	$0	$0	$0	$0
$40,000	$30,000	$1,707	$358	$0	$0	$0	$0	$0
$40,000	$40,000	$63	$0	$0	$0	$0	$0	$0
$40,000	$50,000	$0	$0	$0	$0	$0	$0	$0
$40,000	$60,000	$0	$0	$0	$0	$0	$0	$0
$50,000	$0	$11,962	$10,478	$8,995	$7,510	$6,026	$4,542	$0
$50,000	$10,000	$10,153	$8,669	$7,186	$5,703	$4,219	$2,736	$0
$50,000	$20,000	$8,345	$6,861	$5,378	$3,895	$2,412	$930	$0
$50,000	$30,000	$6,536	$5,052	$3,570	$2,087	$606	$0	$0
$50,000	$40,000	$4,728	$3,244	$1,761	$278	$0	$0	$0
$50,000	$50,000	$2,920	$1,436	$0	$0	$0	$0	$0
$50,000	$60,000	$1,111	$0	$0	$0	$0	$0	$0
$60,000	$0	$17,284	$15,665	$14,048	$12,428	$10,809	$9,327	$2,585
$60,000	$10,000	$15,311	$13,692	$12,075	$10,581	$9,097	$7,683	$785
$60,000	$20,000	$13,338	$11,720	$10,102	$8,735	$7,386	$6,039	$0
$60,000	$30,000	$11,416	$9,932	$8,450	$7,091	$5,742	$4,395	$0
$60,000	$40,000	$9,494	$8,145	$6,797	$5,447	$4,098	$2,751	$0
$60,000	$50,000	$7,850	$6,501	$5,153	$3,803	$2,454	$1,105	$0
$60,000	$60,000	$6,206	$4,857	$3,509	$2,159	$810	$0	$0

Prior Savings:		$0	$50,000	$100,000	$150,000	$200,000	$250,000	$500,000
Desired Income	Nominal Pension	Annual Savings	Annual Savings	Annual Savings	Annual Savings	Annual Savings	Annual Savings	Annual Savings
$70,000	$0	$22,943	$21,324	$19,706	$18,086	$16,467	$14,918	$7,502
$70,000	$10,000	$20,970	$19,351	$17,733	$16,177	$14,625	$13,110	$5,484
$70,000	$20,000	$18,997	$17,378	$15,761	$14,267	$12,783	$11,302	$3,466
$70,000	$30,000	$17,050	$15,498	$13,948	$12,459	$10,975	$9,493	$1,986
$70,000	$40,000	$15,102	$13,618	$12,135	$10,650	$9,166	$7,685	$506
$70,000	$50,000	$13,294	$11,810	$10,327	$8,842	$7,358	$5,875	$0
$70,000	$60,000	$11,485	$10,001	$8,519	$7,034	$5,550	$4,066	$0
$80,000	$0	$28,601	$26,982	$25,365	$23,745	$22,126	$20,510	$12,419
$80,000	$10,000	$26,628	$25,010	$23,392	$21,772	$20,153	$18,537	$10,574
$80,000	$20,000	$24,656	$23,037	$21,419	$19,799	$18,180	$16,564	$8,728
$80,000	$30,000	$22,683	$21,064	$19,446	$17,826	$16,208	$14,591	$7,084
$80,000	$40,000	$20,710	$19,091	$17,474	$15,854	$14,235	$12,618	$5,440
$80,000	$50,000	$18,737	$17,118	$15,501	$13,881	$12,262	$10,756	$3,796
$80,000	$60,000	$16,764	$15,146	$13,528	$11,908	$10,289	$8,894	$2,152

NOTE: For "living forever," add 92 percent to the values in the table.

Table 14.5 Annual Savings for Retiring in 20 Years, at Age 70

Prior Savings:		$0	$50,000	$100,000	$150,000	$200,000	$250,000	$500,000
Desired Income	Nominal Pension	Annual Savings	Annual Savings	Annual Savings	Annual Savings	Annual Savings	Annual Savings	Annual Savings
$40,000	$0	$9,020	$7,192	$5,365	$3,536	$1,708	$0	$0
$40,000	$10,000	$6,431	$4,603	$2,776	$949	$0	$0	$0
$40,000	$20,000	$3,841	$2,013	$186	$0	$0	$0	$0
$40,000	$30,000	$1,252	$0	$0	$0	$0	$0	$0
$40,000	$40,000	$0	$0	$0	$0	$0	$0	$0
$40,000	$50,000	$0	$0	$0	$0	$0	$0	$0
$40,000	$60,000	$0	$0	$0	$0	$0	$0	$0
$50,000	$0	$16,609	$14,598	$12,589	$10,577	$8,566	$6,555	$0
$50,000	$10,000	$13,761	$11,750	$9,740	$7,729	$5,719	$3,709	$0
$50,000	$20,000	$10,912	$8,902	$6,892	$4,882	$2,872	$863	$0
$50,000	$30,000	$8,064	$6,053	$4,043	$2,035	$26	$0	$0
$50,000	$40,000	$5,215	$3,205	$1,195	$0	$0	$0	$0
$50,000	$50,000	$2,367	$356	$0	$0	$0	$0	$0
$50,000	$60,000	$0	$0	$0	$0	$0	$0	$0
$60,000	$0	$24,198	$22,005	$19,812	$17,618	$15,424	$13,233	$3,556
$60,000	$10,000	$21,091	$18,897	$16,705	$14,510	$12,383	$10,374	$697
$60,000	$20,000	$17,984	$15,790	$13,598	$11,403	$9,341	$7,515	$0
$60,000	$30,000	$14,876	$12,718	$10,708	$8,696	$6,752	$4,926	$0
$60,000	$40,000	$11,769	$9,646	$7,819	$5,990	$4,162	$2,336	$0
$60,000	$50,000	$9,032	$7,057	$5,230	$3,401	$1,573	$0	$0
$60,000	$60,000	$6,296	$4,468	$2,641	$812	$0	$0	$0

Prior Savings:		$0	$50,000	$100,000	$150,000	$200,000	$250,000	$500,000
Desired Income	Nominal Pension	Annual Savings	Annual Savings	Annual Savings	Annual Savings	Annual Savings	Annual Savings	Annual Savings
$70,000	$0	$31,885	$29,691	$27,499	$25,304	$23,111	$20,919	$10,598
$70,000	$10,000	$28,786	$26,592	$24,400	$22,205	$20,045	$17,945	$7,077
$70,000	$20,000	$25,687	$23,493	$21,301	$19,106	$16,979	$14,970	$3,556
$70,000	$30,000	$22,572	$20,396	$18,295	$16,191	$14,122	$12,113	$35
$70,000	$40,000	$19,456	$17,298	$15,288	$13,276	$11,265	$9,257	$0
$70,000	$50,000	$16,234	$14,150	$12,140	$10,128	$8,117	$6,107	$0
$70,000	$60,000	$13,013	$11,002	$8,992	$6,980	$4,969	$2,957	$0
$80,000	$0	$39,572	$37,378	$35,186	$32,991	$30,797	$28,606	$17,640
$80,000	$10,000	$36,481	$34,287	$32,095	$29,900	$27,707	$25,515	$14,550
$80,000	$20,000	$33,390	$31,197	$29,004	$26,810	$24,616	$22,425	$11,459
$80,000	$30,000	$30,267	$28,073	$25,881	$23,686	$21,492	$19,301	$8,735
$80,000	$40,000	$27,143	$24,950	$22,757	$20,562	$18,369	$16,178	$6,010
$80,000	$50,000	$23,436	$21,243	$19,050	$16,856	$14,662	$12,574	$3,002
$80,000	$60,000	$19,730	$17,536	$15,344	$13,149	$10,955	$8,970	$0

NOTE: For "living forever," add 92 percent to the values in the table.

Table 14.6 Annual Savings for Retiring in 15 Years, at Age 70

Desired Income	Nominal Pension	Prior Savings: $0 Annual Savings	$50,000 Annual Savings	$100,000 Annual Savings	$150,000 Annual Savings	$200,000 Annual Savings	$250,000 Annual Savings	$500,000 Annual Savings
$40,000	$0	$13,655	$10,466	$7,264	$5,072	$2,414	$0	$0
$40,000	$10,000	$9,009	$6,085	$3,162	$238	$0	$0	$0
$40,000	$20,000	$4,363	$1,705	$0	$0	$0	$0	$0
$40,000	$30,000	$0	$0	$0	$0	$0	$0	$0
$40,000	$40,000	$0	$0	$0	$0	$0	$0	$0
$40,000	$50,000	$0	$0	$0	$0	$0	$0	$0
$40,000	$60,000	$0	$0	$0	$0	$0	$0	$0
$50,000	$0	$24,774	$21,585	$18,383	$15,698	$12,775	$9,851	$0
$50,000	$10,000	$19,846	$16,790	$13,727	$10,923	$7,999	$5,075	$0
$50,000	$20,000	$14,919	$11,995	$9,071	$6,147	$3,223	$300	$0
$50,000	$30,000	$9,991	$7,200	$4,409	$1,618	$0	$0	$0
$50,000	$40,000	$5,063	$2,405	$0	$0	$0	$0	$0
$50,000	$50,000	$135	$0	$0	$0	$0	$0	$0
$50,000	$60,000	$0	$0	$0	$0	$0	$0	$0
$60,000	$0	$35,894	$32,704	$29,502	$26,325	$23,135	$19,943	$4,995
$60,000	$10,000	$30,684	$27,494	$24,293	$21,115	$17,925	$14,773	$0
$60,000	$20,000	$25,474	$22,284	$19,083	$15,905	$12,716	$9,603	$0
$60,000	$30,000	$20,264	$17,075	$13,984	$11,072	$8,148	$5,262	$0
$60,000	$40,000	$15,054	$11,865	$8,886	$6,238	$3,580	$920	$0
$60,000	$50,000	$10,292	$7,368	$4,545	$1,721	$0	$0	$0
$60,000	$60,000	$5,529	$2,871	$203	$0	$0	$0	$0

Prior Savings:		$0	$50,000	$100,000	$150,000	$200,000	$250,000	$500,000
Desired Income	Nominal Pension	Annual Savings	Annual Savings	Annual Savings	Annual Savings	Annual Savings	Annual Savings	Annual Savings
$70,000	$0	$47,013	$43,823	$40,622	$37,444	$34,254	$31,062	$15,614
$70,000	$10,000	$41,803	$38,613	$35,412	$32,234	$29,045	$25,872	$10,304
$70,000	$20,000	$36,593	$33,404	$30,202	$27,024	$23,835	$20,683	$4,995
$70,000	$30,000	$31,383	$28,194	$25,048	$22,003	$18,946	$15,907	$0
$70,000	$40,000	$26,174	$22,984	$19,894	$16,981	$14,057	$11,131	$0
$70,000	$50,000	$21,187	$18,131	$15,118	$11,959	$9,168	$6,356	$0
$70,000	$60,000	$16,201	$13,277	$10,343	$6,938	$4,280	$1,580	$0
$80,000	$0	$58,132	$54,942	$51,741	$48,563	$45,374	$42,182	$26,232
$80,000	$10,000	$52,922	$49,733	$46,531	$43,353	$40,164	$36,972	$21,023
$80,000	$20,000	$47,712	$44,523	$41,321	$38,144	$34,954	$31,762	$15,813
$80,000	$30,000	$42,503	$39,313	$36,111	$32,934	$29,744	$26,552	$10,987
$80,000	$40,000	$37,293	$34,103	$30,902	$27,724	$24,534	$21,342	$6,161
$80,000	$50,000	$32,083	$28,893	$25,692	$22,514	$19,325	$16,133	$1,335
$80,000	$60,000	$26,873	$23,684	$20,482	$17,304	$14,115	$10,923	$0

NOTE: For "living forever," add 92 percent to the values in the table.

Example 1

A couple is 40-years-old and plan to retire at age 70. So they have 30 additional years to work. Their current combined income is $75,000 after taxes. Using 80 percent as the factor to determine their retirement income needs, their required after-tax retirement income will be 0.8 × $75,000 = $60,000 in current dollars.

The combined company pensions that the couple will receive at age 65 are $40,000 per year, after taxes. To adjust the company-quoted pension for expected taxes, when in doubt reduce the company-quoted pension by 20 percent. The tables assume that the nominal pension shown is *after* any tax adjustment. The couple currently has no savings for the purpose of retirement.

Using Table 14.3, which is for people retiring in 30 years, we find $60,000 in the first column, which is desired income. In the next column we find $40,000, which is the couple's combined nominal pension (as estimated by the company at age 65, but after taxes). Since the couple has no retirement savings, we look in the next column to find the $8,169 after-tax annual savings requirement. Below is a replication of the lines from this chart that we used to find these values.

Prior Savings:		$0	$50,000	$100,000	$150,000	$200,000	$250,000	$500,000
Desired Income	Nominal Pension	Annual Savings	Annual Savings	Annual Savings	Annual Savings	Annual Savings	Annual Savings	Annual Savings
$60,000	$40,000	$8,169	$7,139	$6,110	$5,079	$4,049	$3,021	$0

This $8,169 after-tax annual savings will have to be indexed up every year for inflation. For example, if inflation is 5 percent after the first year of saving, the second year's saving will have to be 1.05 × $8,169 = $8,577. If the following year has 6 percent inflation, then the amount saved will again have to be increased: 1.06 × $8,577 = $9,092. It is expected that wage increases will largely compensate for these increases.

Example 2

A single person is 51-years-old and plans to retire at age 70. This person has $50,000 saved for retirement. The person's income is $60,000 after taxes, so using 80 percent as the factor to determine retirement income, the after-tax retirement income required will be 0.8 × $60,000 = $48,000 in current dollars.

The person expects a company pension that is forecasted to be $19,000 (after taxes), at age 65.

Since the tables don't have numbers that exactly match the above values, we will use the closest numbers. It is possible to extrapolate into closer numbers, but, with the degree of unknowns in the future economy, this effort is generally not worthwhile. We will use 20 years as the years left to work, $50,000 as the desired income, and a nominal pension of $20,000. The individual already has prior savings of $50,000 set aside for retirement.

Below is the data used from Table 14.5.

Prior Savings:		$0	$50,000	$100,000	$150,000	$200,000	$250,000	$500,000
Desired Income	Nominal Pension	Annual Savings	Annual Savings	Annual Savings	Annual Savings	Annual Savings	Annual Savings	Annual Savings
$50,000	$20,000	$10,912	$8,902	$6,892	$4,882	$2,872	$863	$0

From this excerpt, we get an annual after-tax savings requirement of $8,902. The annual savings will then be adjusted every year for inflation.

These tables are applicable to both couples and singles. The single person will generally have less Social Security income than the couple, and more of their annual savings will be above the Roth IRA savings limits and therefore subject to later taxes. However, the single person will generally have a larger pension because it won't have the survivor provision taken by most couples. Also, with a couple there is a higher likelihood that at least one of them will live to be over 93 years of age. Thus, there is a general wash of plusses and minuses when determining retirement savings for singles and couples, so we use the same tables for both. However, the current income, and therefore the projected required retirement income, is often lower for a single person than it would be for a couple with two incomes, so even though the same table is used, the resultant required annual savings will generally be lower for the single person.

Many of you reading this book will be shocked at the size of the annual required savings amounts. Few of the currently retired people have sufficient funds, which is why the bankruptcy rate among the elderly is the highest of any age group and why 10 percent of retirees are living below the poverty line.

Retirement, as we currently define it, is a true luxury. Not too many years ago, the elderly were taken into their children's homes, and their living costs were generally only food and limited medicines. Now a retiree expects independent living, perhaps first in their own home in the sunny South where they move after retirement, then in an assisted-living facility, and finally in a nursing home at incredible costs. In the future, few retirees will be able to afford this scenario, even though many people will have these goals. However, following the savings requirement shown in this book will give someone a realistic shot at living a good retirement with adequate funds. Someone retiring after saving at the rates shown in this book's tables is unlikely to get into the dire straits of many of those currently retired and of many of those planning to retire during or after this depression, without adequate planning.

Retiring Early, at Age 65

Even though Social Security benefits will likely not come into play until age 70, there will be those who want to save for retiring before then. Here are savings Tables 14.7 through 14.12 for retiring at 65. Even though there will likely be a reduced Social Security benefit option for age 65, the calculations in these tables assume that the retiree waits until age 70 to collect Social Security benefits, therefore getting a nonreduced Social Security benefit.

Table 14.7 shows the annual savings for people who are retiring at the age of 65 in 40 years.

Table 14.8 shows the annual savings for people who are retiring at the age of 65 in 35 years.

Table 14.9 shows the annual savings for people who are retiring at the age of 65 in 30 years.

Table 14.10 shows the annual savings for people who are retiring at the age of 65 in 25 years.

Table 14.11 shows the annual savings for people who are retiring at the age of 65 in 20 years.

Table 14.12 shows the annual savings for people who are retiring at the age of 65 in 15 years.

Table 14.7 Annual Savings for Retiring in 40 Years, at Age 65

Prior Savings:		$0	$50,000	$100,000	$150,000	$200,000	$250,000	$500,000
Desired Income	Nominal Pension	Annual Savings	Annual Savings	Annual Savings	Annual Savings	Annual Savings	Annual Savings	Annual Savings
$40,000	$0	$5,150	$4,502	$3,854	$3,206	$2,558	$1,910	$0
$40,000	$10,000	$4,721	$4,073	$3,425	$2,777	$2,129	$1,481	$0
$40,000	$20,000	$4,292	$3,644	$2,996	$2,348	$1,700	$1,052	$0
$40,000	$30,000	$3,863	$3,215	$2,567	$1,919	$1,271	$623	$0
$40,000	$40,000	$3,434	$2,786	$2,138	$1,490	$842	$194	$0
$40,000	$50,000	$3,506	$2,858	$2,210	$1,562	$914	$266	$0
$40,000	$60,000	$2,577	$1,929	$1,281	$633	$0	$0	$0
$50,000	$0	$7,684	$7,036	$6,388	$5,740	$5,092	$4,444	$1,204
$50,000	$10,000	$7,255	$6,607	$5,959	$5,311	$4,663	$4,015	$775
$50,000	$20,000	$6,826	$6,178	$5,530	$4,882	$4,234	$3,586	$346
$50,000	$30,000	$6,397	$5,749	$5,101	$4,453	$3,805	$3,157	$0
$50,000	$40,000	$5,969	$5,321	$4,673	$4,025	$3,377	$2,729	$0
$50,000	$50,000	$5,540	$4,892	$4,244	$3,596	$2,948	$2,300	$0
$50,000	$60,000	$5,111	$4,463	$3,815	$3,167	$2,519	$1,871	$0
$60,000	$0	$10,262	$9,614	$8,966	$8,318	$7,670	$7,022	$3,782
$60,000	$10,000	$9,789	$9,141	$8,493	$7,845	$7,197	$6,549	$3,309
$60,000	$20,000	$9,360	$8,712	$8,064	$7,416	$6,768	$6,120	$2,880
$60,000	$30,000	$8,931	$8,283	$7,635	$6,987	$6,339	$5,691	$2,451
$60,000	$40,000	$8,503	$7,855	$7,207	$6,559	$5,911	$5,263	$2,023
$60,000	$50,000	$8,074	$7,426	$6,778	$6,130	$5,482	$4,834	$1,594
$60,000	$60,000	$7,645	$6,997	$6,349	$5,701	$5,053	$4,405	$1,165

(Continued)

Table 14.7 *(Continued)*

Prior Savings:		$0	$50,000	$100,000	$150,000	$200,000	$250,000	$500,000
Desired Income	Nominal Pension	Annual Savings	Annual Savings	Annual Savings	Annual Savings	Annual Savings	Annual Savings	Annual Savings
$70,000	$0	$13,302	$12,654	$12,006	$11,358	$10,710	$10,062	$6,822
$70,000	$10,000	$12,788	$12,140	$11,492	$10,844	$10,196	$9,548	$6,308
$70,000	$20,000	$12,273	$11,625	$10,977	$10,329	$9,681	$9,033	$5,793
$70,000	$30,000	$11,758	$11,110	$10,462	$9,814	$9,166	$8,518	$5,278
$70,000	$40,000	$11,244	$10,596	$9,948	$9,300	$8,652	$8,004	$4,764
$70,000	$50,000	$10,730	$10,082	$9,434	$8,786	$8,138	$7,490	$4,250
$70,000	$60,000	$10,215	$9,567	$8,919	$8,271	$7,623	$6,975	$3,735
$80,000	$0	$16,343	$15,627	$14,911	$14,195	$13,479	$12,763	$9,185
$80,000	$10,000	$15,828	$15,112	$14,396	$13,680	$12,964	$12,248	$8,670
$80,000	$20,000	$15,314	$14,598	$13,882	$13,166	$12,450	$11,734	$8,156
$80,000	$30,000	$14,799	$14,083	$13,367	$12,651	$11,935	$11,219	$7,641
$80,000	$40,000	$14,284	$13,568	$12,852	$12,136	$11,420	$10,704	$7,126
$80,000	$50,000	$13,770	$13,054	$12,338	$11,622	$10,906	$10,190	$6,612
$80,000	$60,000	$13,256	$12,540	$11,824	$11,108	$10,392	$9,676	$6,098

NOTE: For "living forever," add 55 percent to the values in the table.

Table 14.8 Annual Savings for Retiring in 35 Years, at Age 65

Desired Income	Nominal Pension	Prior Savings: $0 Annual Savings	$50,000 Annual Savings	$100,000 Annual Savings	$150,000 Annual Savings	$200,000 Annual Savings	$250,000 Annual Savings	$500,000 Annual Savings
$40,000	$0	$6,433	$5,621	$4,809	$3,997	$3,185	$2,373	$0
$40,000	$10,000	$5,797	$4,985	$4,173	$3,361	$2,549	$1,737	$0
$40,000	$20,000	$5,161	$4,349	$3,537	$2,725	$1,913	$1,101	$0
$40,000	$30,000	$4,524	$3,712	$2,900	$2,088	$1,276	$464	$0
$40,000	$40,000	$3,888	$3,076	$2,264	$1,452	$640	$0	$0
$40,000	$50,000	$3,252	$2,440	$1,628	$816	$4	$0	$0
$40,000	$60,000	$2,616	$1,804	$992	$180	$0	$0	$0
$50,000	$0	$9,599	$8,784	$7,969	$7,154	$6,339	$5,524	$1,434
$50,000	$10,000	$8,963	$8,148	$7,333	$6,518	$5,703	$4,888	$798
$50,000	$20,000	$8,326	$7,511	$6,696	$5,881	$5,066	$4,251	$161
$50,000	$30,000	$7,690	$6,875	$6,060	$5,245	$4,430	$3,615	$0
$50,000	$40,000	$7,054	$6,239	$5,424	$4,609	$3,794	$2,979	$0
$50,000	$50,000	$6,418	$5,603	$4,788	$3,973	$3,158	$2,343	$0
$50,000	$60,000	$5,781	$4,966	$4,151	$3,336	$2,521	$1,706	$0
$60,000	$0	$13,317	$12,505	$11,693	$10,881	$10,069	$9,257	$5,197
$60,000	$10,000	$12,554	$11,742	$10,930	$10,118	$9,306	$8,494	$4,434
$60,000	$20,000	$11,790	$10,978	$10,166	$9,354	$8,542	$7,730	$3,670
$60,000	$30,000	$11,027	$10,215	$9,403	$8,591	$7,779	$6,967	$2,907
$60,000	$40,000	$10,263	$9,451	$8,639	$7,827	$7,015	$6,203	$2,143
$60,000	$50,000	$9,583	$8,771	$7,959	$7,147	$6,335	$5,523	$1,463
$60,000	$60,000	$8,947	$8,135	$7,323	$6,511	$5,699	$4,887	$827

(*Continued*)

217

Table 14.8 *(Continued)*

Desired Income	Nominal Pension	Prior Savings: $0 Annual Savings	$50,000 Annual Savings	$100,000 Annual Savings	$150,000 Annual Savings	$200,000 Annual Savings	$250,000 Annual Savings	$500,000 Annual Savings
$70,000	$0	$17,116	$16,223	$15,330	$14,437	$13,544	$12,651	$8,186
$70,000	$10,000	$16,353	$15,460	$14,567	$13,674	$12,781	$11,888	$7,423
$70,000	$20,000	$15,589	$14,696	$13,803	$12,910	$12,017	$11,124	$6,659
$70,000	$30,000	$14,826	$13,933	$13,040	$12,147	$11,254	$10,361	$5,896
$70,000	$40,000	$14,062	$13,169	$12,276	$11,383	$10,490	$9,597	$5,132
$70,000	$50,000	$13,298	$12,405	$11,512	$10,619	$9,726	$8,833	$4,368
$70,000	$60,000	$12,535	$11,642	$10,749	$9,856	$8,963	$8,070	$3,605
$80,000	$0	$20,896	$19,922	$18,948	$17,974	$17,000	$16,026	$11,156
$80,000	$10,000	$20,132	$19,158	$18,184	$17,210	$16,236	$15,262	$10,392
$80,000	$20,000	$19,368	$18,394	$17,420	$16,446	$15,472	$14,498	$9,628
$80,000	$30,000	$18,605	$17,631	$16,657	$15,683	$14,709	$13,735	$8,865
$80,000	$40,000	$17,841	$16,867	$15,893	$14,919	$13,945	$12,971	$8,101
$80,000	$50,000	$17,078	$16,104	$15,130	$14,156	$13,182	$12,208	$7,338
$80,000	$60,000	$16,314	$15,340	$14,366	$13,392	$12,418	$11,444	$6,574

NOTE: For "living forever," add 55 percent to the values in the table.

218

Table 14.9 Annual Savings for Retiring in 30 Years, at Age 65

Desired Income	Nominal Pension	Prior Savings: $0 Annual Savings	$50,000 Annual Savings	$100,000 Annual Savings	$150,000 Annual Savings	$200,000 Annual Savings	$250,000 Annual Savings	$500,000 Annual Savings
$40,000	$0	$8,182	$7,152	$6,122	$5,092	$4,062	$3,032	$0
$40,000	$10,000	$7,221	$6,191	$5,161	$4,131	$3,101	$2,071	$0
$40,000	$20,000	$6,260	$5,230	$4,200	$3,170	$2,140	$1,110	$0
$40,000	$30,000	$5,299	$4,269	$3,239	$2,209	$1,179	$149	$0
$40,000	$40,000	$4,338	$3,308	$2,278	$1,248	$218	$0	$0
$40,000	$50,000	$3,377	$2,347	$1,317	$287	$0	$0	$0
$40,000	$60,000	$2,416	$1,386	$356	$0	$0	$0	$0
$50,000	$0	$12,649	$11,549	$10,449	$9,349	$8,249	$7,149	$1,649
$50,000	$10,000	$11,496	$10,396	$9,296	$8,196	$7,096	$5,996	$496
$50,000	$20,000	$10,343	$9,243	$8,143	$7,043	$5,943	$4,843	$0
$50,000	$30,000	$9,325	$8,225	$7,125	$6,025	$4,925	$3,825	$0
$50,000	$40,000	$8,364	$7,264	$6,164	$5,064	$3,964	$2,864	$0
$50,000	$50,000	$7,403	$6,303	$5,203	$4,103	$3,003	$1,903	$0
$50,000	$60,000	$6,442	$5,342	$4,242	$3,142	$2,042	$942	$0
$60,000	$0	$17,480	$16,330	$15,180	$14,030	$12,880	$11,730	$5,980
$60,000	$10,000	$16,327	$15,177	$14,027	$12,877	$11,727	$10,577	$4,827
$60,000	$20,000	$15,174	$14,024	$12,874	$11,724	$10,574	$9,424	$3,674
$60,000	$30,000	$14,021	$12,871	$11,721	$10,571	$9,421	$8,271	$2,521
$60,000	$40,000	$12,868	$11,718	$10,568	$9,418	$8,268	$7,118	$1,368
$60,000	$50,000	$11,714	$10,564	$9,414	$8,264	$7,114	$5,964	$214
$60,000	$60,000	$10,561	$9,411	$8,261	$7,111	$5,961	$4,811	$0

Table 14.9 (*Continued*)

Desired Income	Nominal Pension	Prior Savings: $0 Annual Savings	$50,000 Annual Savings	$100,000 Annual Savings	$150,000 Annual Savings	$200,000 Annual Savings	$250,000 Annual Savings	$500,000 Annual Savings
$70,000	$0	$22,311	$21,111	$19,911	$18,711	$17,511	$16,311	$9,311
$70,000	$10,000	$21,158	$19,958	$18,758	$17,558	$16,358	$15,158	$8,158
$70,000	$20,000	$20,005	$18,805	$17,605	$16,405	$15,205	$14,005	$7,005
$70,000	$30,000	$18,852	$17,652	$16,452	$15,252	$14,052	$12,852	$5,852
$70,000	$40,000	$17,699	$16,499	$15,299	$14,099	$12,899	$11,699	$4,699
$70,000	$50,000	$16,545	$15,345	$14,145	$12,945	$11,745	$10,545	$3,545
$70,000	$60,000	$15,392	$14,192	$12,992	$11,792	$10,592	$9,392	$2,392
$80,000	$0	$27,143	$25,907	$24,671	$23,435	$22,199	$20,963	$14,783
$80,000	$10,000	$25,989	$24,753	$23,517	$22,281	$21,045	$19,809	$13,629
$80,000	$20,000	$24,836	$23,600	$22,364	$21,128	$19,892	$18,656	$12,476
$80,000	$30,000	$23,683	$22,447	$21,211	$19,975	$18,739	$17,503	$11,323
$80,000	$40,000	$22,530	$21,294	$20,058	$18,822	$17,586	$16,350	$10,170
$80,000	$50,000	$21,377	$20,141	$18,905	$17,669	$16,433	$15,197	$9,017
$80,000	$60,000	$20,223	$18,987	$17,751	$16,515	$15,279	$14,043	$7,863

NOTE: For "living forever," add 55 percent to the values in the table.

220

Table 14.10 Annual Savings for Retiring in 25 Years, at Age 65

Prior Savings:		$0	$50,000	$100,000	$150,000	$200,000	$250,000	$500,000
Desired Income	Nominal Pension	Annual Savings	Annual Savings	Annual Savings	Annual Savings	Annual Savings	Annual Savings	Annual Savings
$40,000	$0	$10,827	$9,478	$8,129	$6,780	$5,431	$4,082	$0
$40,000	$10,000	$9,198	$7,849	$6,500	$5,151	$3,802	$2,453	$0
$40,000	$20,000	$7,707	$6,358	$5,009	$3,660	$2,311	$962	$0
$40,000	$30,000	$6,216	$4,867	$3,518	$2,169	$820	$0	$0
$40,000	$40,000	$4,725	$3,376	$2,027	$678	$0	$0	$0
$40,000	$50,000	$3,233	$1,884	$535	$0	$0	$0	$0
$40,000	$60,000	$1,742	$393	$0	$0	$0	$0	$0
$50,000	$0	$17,139	$15,655	$14,171	$12,687	$11,203	$9,719	$2,299
$50,000	$10,000	$15,349	$13,865	$12,381	$10,897	$9,413	$7,929	$509
$50,000	$20,000	$13,560	$12,076	$10,592	$9,108	$7,624	$6,140	$0
$50,000	$30,000	$11,770	$10,286	$8,802	$7,318	$5,834	$4,350	$0
$50,000	$40,000	$9,984	$8,500	$7,016	$5,532	$4,048	$2,564	$0
$50,000	$50,000	$8,493	$7,009	$5,525	$4,041	$2,557	$1,073	$0
$50,000	$60,000	$7,002	$5,518	$4,034	$2,550	$1,066	$0	$0
$60,000	$0	$23,450	$21,831	$20,212	$18,593	$16,974	$15,355	$7,260
$60,000	$10,000	$21,661	$20,042	$18,423	$16,804	$15,185	$13,566	$5,471
$60,000	$20,000	$19,872	$18,253	$16,634	$15,015	$13,396	$11,777	$3,682
$60,000	$30,000	$18,082	$16,463	$14,844	$13,225	$11,606	$9,987	$1,892
$60,000	$40,000	$16,293	$14,674	$13,055	$11,436	$9,817	$8,198	$103
$60,000	$50,000	$14,504	$12,885	$11,266	$9,647	$8,028	$6,409	$0
$60,000	$60,000	$12,714	$11,095	$9,476	$7,857	$6,238	$4,619	$0

(Continued)

Table 14.10 (*Continued*)

Desired Income	Nominal Pension	$0 Annual Savings	$50,000 Annual Savings	$100,000 Annual Savings	$150,000 Annual Savings	$200,000 Annual Savings	$250,000 Annual Savings	$500,000 Annual Savings
$70,000	$0	$29,762	$28,143	$26,524	$24,905	$23,286	$21,667	$13,572
$70,000	$10,000	$27,973	$26,354	$24,735	$23,116	$21,497	$19,878	$11,783
$70,000	$20,000	$26,183	$24,564	$22,945	$21,326	$19,707	$18,088	$9,993
$70,000	$30,000	$24,394	$22,775	$21,156	$19,537	$17,918	$16,299	$8,204
$70,000	$40,000	$22,605	$20,986	$19,367	$17,748	$16,129	$14,510	$6,415
$70,000	$50,000	$20,815	$19,196	$17,577	$15,958	$14,339	$12,720	$4,625
$70,000	$60,000	$19,026	$17,407	$15,788	$14,169	$12,550	$10,931	$2,836
$80,000	$0	$36,074	$34,455	$32,836	$31,217	$29,598	$27,979	$19,884
$80,000	$10,000	$34,284	$32,665	$31,046	$29,427	$27,808	$26,189	$18,094
$80,000	$20,000	$32,495	$30,876	$29,257	$27,638	$26,019	$24,400	$16,305
$80,000	$30,000	$30,706	$29,087	$27,468	$25,849	$24,230	$22,611	$14,516
$80,000	$40,000	$28,916	$27,297	$25,678	$24,059	$22,440	$20,821	$12,726
$80,000	$50,000	$27,127	$25,508	$23,889	$22,270	$20,651	$19,032	$10,937
$80,000	$60,000	$25,338	$23,719	$22,100	$20,481	$18,862	$17,243	$9,148

NOTE: For "living forever," add 55 percent to the values in the table.

222

Table 14.11 Annual Savings for Retiring in 20 Years, at Age 65

Desired Income	Nominal Pension	Prior Savings: $0 Annual Savings	$50,000 Annual Savings	$100,000 Annual Savings	$150,000 Annual Savings	$200,000 Annual Savings	$250,000 Annual Savings	$500,000 Annual Savings
$40,000	$0	$15,428	$13,600	$11,772	$9,944	$8,116	$6,288	$3,894
$40,000	$10,000	$12,541	$10,713	$8,885	$7,057	$5,229	$3,401	$1,007
$40,000	$20,000	$9,711	$7,883	$6,055	$4,227	$2,399	$571	$0
$40,000	$30,000	$7,305	$5,477	$3,649	$1,821	$0	$0	$0
$40,000	$40,000	$4,898	$3,070	$1,242	$0	$0	$0	$0
$40,000	$50,000	$2,492	$664	$0	$0	$0	$0	$0
$40,000	$60,000	$86	$0	$0	$0	$0	$0	$0
$50,000	$0	$24,004	$21,993	$19,982	$17,971	$15,960	$13,949	
$50,000	$10,000	$21,117	$19,106	$17,095	$15,084	$13,073	$11,062	
$50,000	$20,000	$18,229	$16,218	$14,207	$12,196	$10,185	$8,174	
$50,000	$30,000	$15,342	$13,331	$11,320	$9,309	$7,298	$5,287	
$50,000	$40,000	$12,454	$10,443	$8,432	$6,421	$4,410	$2,399	
$50,000	$50,000	$9,639	$7,628	$5,617	$3,606	$1,595	$0	
$50,000	$60,000	$7,233	$5,222	$3,211	$1,200	$0	$0	
$60,000	$0	$32,580	$30,386	$28,192	$25,998	$23,804	$21,610	$10,640
$60,000	$10,000	$29,693	$27,499	$25,305	$23,111	$20,917	$18,723	$7,753
$60,000	$20,000	$26,805	$24,611	$22,417	$20,223	$18,029	$15,835	$4,865
$60,000	$30,000	$23,918	$21,724	$19,530	$17,336	$15,142	$12,948	$1,978
$60,000	$40,000	$21,030	$18,836	$16,642	$14,448	$12,254	$10,060	$0
$60,000	$50,000	$18,143	$15,949	$13,755	$11,561	$9,367	$7,173	$0
$60,000	$60,000	$15,255	$13,061	$10,867	$8,673	$6,479	$4,285	$0

(Continued)

Table 14.11 (*Continued*)

Desired Income	Nominal Pension	$0 Annual Savings	$50,000 Annual Savings	$100,000 Annual Savings	$150,000 Annual Savings	$200,000 Annual Savings	$250,000 Annual Savings	$500,000 Annual Savings
$70,000	$0	$41,156	$38,962	$36,768	$34,574	$32,380	$30,186	$19,216
$70,000	$10,000	$38,269	$36,075	$33,881	$31,687	$29,493	$27,299	$16,329
$70,000	$20,000	$35,381	$33,187	$30,993	$28,799	$26,605	$24,411	$13,441
$70,000	$30,000	$32,494	$30,300	$28,106	$25,912	$23,718	$21,524	$10,554
$70,000	$40,000	$29,606	$27,412	$25,218	$23,024	$20,830	$18,636	$7,666
$70,000	$50,000	$26,718	$24,524	$22,330	$20,136	$17,942	$15,748	$4,778
$70,000	$60,000	$23,831	$21,637	$19,443	$17,249	$15,055	$12,861	$1,891
$80,000	$0	$49,732	$47,538	$45,344	$43,150	$40,956	$38,762	$27,792
$80,000	$10,000	$46,845	$44,651	$42,457	$40,263	$38,069	$35,875	$24,905
$80,000	$20,000	$43,957	$41,763	$39,569	$37,375	$35,181	$32,987	$22,017
$80,000	$30,000	$41,069	$38,875	$36,681	$34,487	$32,293	$30,099	$19,129
$80,000	$40,000	$38,182	$35,988	$33,794	$31,600	$29,406	$27,212	$16,242
$80,000	$50,000	$35,294	$33,100	$30,906	$28,712	$26,518	$24,324	$13,354
$80,000	$60,000	$32,407	$30,213	$28,019	$25,825	$23,631	$21,437	$10,467

NOTE: For "living forever," add 55 percent to the values in the table.

Table 14.12 Annual Savings for Retiring in 15 Years, at Age 65

Prior Savings:		$0	$50,000	$100,000	$150,000	$200,000	$250,000	$500,000
Desired Income	Nominal Pension	Annual Savings	Annual Savings	Annual Savings	Annual Savings	Annual Savings	Annual Savings	Annual Savings
$40,000	$0	$23,210	$20,020	$16,830	$13,640	$10,450	$7,260	$3,715
$40,000	$10,000	$18,249	$15,059	$11,869	$8,679	$5,489	$2,299	$0
$40,000	$20,000	$13,288	$10,098	$6,908	$3,718	$528	$0	$0
$40,000	$30,000	$8,606	$5,416	$2,226	$0	$0	$0	$0
$40,000	$40,000	$4,472	$1,282	$0	$0	$0	$0	$0
$40,000	$50,000	$338	$0	$0	$0	$0	$0	$0
$40,000	$60,000	$0	$0	$0	$0	$0	$0	$0
$50,000	$0	$35,615	$32,425	$29,235	$26,045	$22,855	$19,665	$3,715
$50,000	$10,000	$30,655	$27,465	$24,275	$21,085	$17,895	$14,705	$0
$50,000	$20,000	$25,694	$22,504	$19,314	$16,124	$12,934	$9,744	$0
$50,000	$30,000	$20,733	$17,543	$14,353	$11,163	$7,973	$4,783	$0
$50,000	$40,000	$15,772	$12,582	$9,392	$6,202	$3,012	$0	$0
$50,000	$50,000	$10,811	$7,621	$4,431	$1,241	$0	$0	$0
$50,000	$60,000	$6,542	$3,352	$162	$0	$0	$0	$0
$60,000	$0	$48,021	$44,831	$41,641	$38,451	$35,261	$32,071	$16,121
$60,000	$10,000	$43,060	$39,870	$36,680	$33,490	$30,300	$27,110	$11,160
$60,000	$20,000	$38,099	$34,909	$31,719	$28,529	$25,339	$22,149	$6,199
$60,000	$30,000	$33,138	$29,948	$26,758	$23,568	$20,378	$17,188	$1,238
$60,000	$40,000	$28,177	$24,987	$21,797	$18,607	$15,417	$12,227	$0
$60,000	$50,000	$23,217	$20,027	$16,837	$13,647	$10,457	$7,267	$0
$60,000	$60,000	$18,256	$15,066	$11,876	$8,686	$5,496	$2,306	$0

(Continued)

Table 14.12 *(Continued)*

Desired Income	Nominal Pension	Prior Savings: $0 Annual Savings	$50,000 Annual Savings	$100,000 Annual Savings	$150,000 Annual Savings	$200,000 Annual Savings	$250,000 Annual Savings	$500,000 Annual Savings
$70,000	$0	$60,426	$57,236	$54,046	$50,856	$47,666	$44,476	$28,526
$70,000	$10,000	$55,465	$52,275	$49,085	$45,895	$42,705	$39,515	$23,565
$70,000	$20,000	$50,504	$47,314	$44,124	$40,934	$37,744	$34,554	$18,604
$70,000	$30,000	$45,543	$42,353	$39,163	$35,973	$32,783	$29,593	$13,643
$70,000	$40,000	$40,583	$37,393	$34,203	$31,013	$27,823	$24,633	$8,683
$70,000	$50,000	$35,622	$32,432	$29,242	$26,052	$22,862	$19,672	$3,722
$70,000	$60,000	$30,661	$27,471	$24,281	$21,091	$17,901	$14,711	$0
$80,000	$0	$72,831	$69,641	$66,451	$63,261	$60,071	$56,881	$40,931
$80,000	$10,000	$67,870	$64,680	$61,490	$58,300	$55,110	$51,920	$35,970
$80,000	$20,000	$62,909	$59,719	$56,529	$53,339	$50,149	$46,959	$31,009
$80,000	$30,000	$57,949	$54,759	$51,569	$48,379	$45,189	$41,999	$26,049
$80,000	$40,000	$52,988	$49,798	$46,608	$43,418	$40,228	$37,038	$21,088
$80,000	$50,000	$48,027	$44,837	$41,647	$38,457	$35,267	$32,077	$16,127
$80,000	$60,000	$43,066	$39,876	$36,686	$33,496	$30,306	$27,116	$11,166

NOTE: For "living forever," add 55 percent to the values in the table.

Both the savings amounts and the withdrawal amounts after retirement are to be indexed annually for inflation.

As in the retire-at-age-70 tables, the savings as calculated assume that funds will run out at age 93, with the exception of Social Security and the fixed pension. If someone is uncomfortable with this assumption, by adding 55 percent to the savings values in the tables the retiree can keep a constant lifestyle "forever," which is assumed to be to age 120 in the example. The reason this adjustment is less than the 92 percent additional needed in the retire-at-age-70 tables is that the calculations to retire at age 65 already have an adjustment in the savings for living five years longer in retirement, so the 55 percent additional amount is being added onto a far larger savings base.

Let's do the same two examples we did earlier under the retire-at-age-70 assumption, but now assuming a retirement age of 65. We will then compare the amount of savings required in both cases.

Example 3

A couple is 40-years-old and plan to retire at age 65. (Example 3 is similar to Example 1, but assumes retirement at the age of 65.) So, they have 25 additional years to work. Their current combined income is $75,000 after taxes. Using 80 percent as the factor to determine their retirement income needs, their required after-tax retirement income will be 0.8 × $75,000 = $60,000 in current dollars.

The combined nominal company pensions that their companies have projected the couple would receive at age 65 is $40,000 per year (after taxes in future dollars). They currently have no savings for the purpose of retirement. The following is from Table 14.10.

Prior Savings:		$0	$50,000	$100,000	$150,000	$200,000	$250,000	$500,000
Desired Income	Nominal Pension	Annual Savings	Annual Savings	Annual Savings	Annual Savings	Annual Savings	Annual Savings	Annual Savings
$60,000	$40,000	$16,293	$14,674	$13,055	$11,436	$9,817	$8,198	$103

This $16,293 after-tax annual savings will have to be indexed up every year for inflation. Note that this annual savings requirement is approximately twice the $8,169 annual savings required to retire at age

70. Few will be able to afford to save the annual amounts needed to retire "early" at age 65.

Example 4

A single person is 51-years-old and plans to retire at age 65. (Example 4 is similar to Example 2, but assumes retirement at the age of 65.) This person has $50,000 saved for retirement. The person's income is $60,000 after taxes, so using 80 percent as the factor to determine retirement income needs, the retirement income required will be 0.8 × $60,000 = $48,000 in current dollars.

The person expects a company pension that is forecasted to be $19,000 after taxes, at age 65.

Since the tables don't have numbers that exactly match the above values, we will use the closest numbers. It is possible to extrapolate to closer numbers, but, with the degree of variation in the future economy, this effort is probably not worthwhile. We will use 15 years as the years left to work, $50,000 as the desired income, and a nominal pension of $20,000 after taxes. The individual already has prior savings of $50,000 set aside for retirement. The following is from Table 14.12.

Prior Savings:		$0	$50,000	$100,000	$150,000	$200,000	$250,000	$500,000
Desired Income	Nominal Pension	Annual Savings	Annual Savings	Annual Savings	Annual Savings	Annual Savings	Annual Savings	Annual Savings
$50,000	$20,000	$25,694	$22,504	$19,314	$16,124	$12,934	$9,744	$0

From this table we get an annual after-tax savings requirement of $22,504. The annual savings will then be adjusted every year for inflation. Note that the $22,504 annual savings requirement is 153 percent higher than the $8,902 annual savings required for retiring at age 70. Truly, retiring before age 70 will be an expensive luxury!

Summary

This chapter contains tables to be used for people planning to retire at least 15 years from now. Readers wanting to refer to these tables can go directly to the one that applies to them, or they can peruse the whole section to get a better understanding on how these tables were developed.

The tables in this chapter are in two groupings. The first group is for those planning to retire at age 70 (Tables 14.1 through 14.6); the second group of tables is for those planning to retire at age 65 (Tables 14.7 through 14.12). In each grouping there is a table for retiring in 40 years, 35 years, 30 years, 25 years, 20 years, and 15 years.

Both the nominal pension and prior savings are assumed to be after taxes. The "prior savings" are what you currently have saved for retirement. The numbers within the tables are what you have to save every year. These annual savings requirements will have to be adjusted every year for inflation. The desired income is the after-tax retirement income you desire in current dollars.

Chapter 15

I Want to Retire Soon. How Much Money Will I Need?

This chapter is for someone planning to retire within a few years. However, this should be a chapter of interest even for those who won't be retiring for many years, because it highlights just how much money is required. These numbers are generally quite sobering.

In the early part of this chapter are tables that can be used to estimate both retirement income and required savings. To get more exact numbers, there are formulas near the end of the chapter into which exact values can be input. It generally is worthwhile to use both. The tables will get you close, and the formulas will allow you to input your exact values. By doing the table first, you can have some confidence that you did the formula correctly by comparing the two answers.

The earlier chapter did not include the formula option because, with all the variables that exist in a calculation for retirement far in the future, the accuracy just was not needed. However, with the retirement date being near, items like how much Social Security you will receive, or the size of your pension, will be known with more accuracy, and it then becomes advantageous to enter these values into the formulas to get more accurate output.

Verify That You Have Sufficient Funds If You Plan to Retire Soon!

People retiring soon should be sure that they have sufficient funds, especially given that people retiring within the next few years may spend their whole retirement in a depression, and we are not talking about the mental kind (that is, unless you ignore the guidelines in this book)! Some former retirees who came to the realization that they had insufficient funds have been able to go back to work, albeit in jobs that paid little, such as waitresses, cashiers, or even greeters at Wal-Mart. In a depression, such jobs will not be available. Also, those looking at retirement in the next few years are likely to have been influenced by the perceived high stock market gains of the nineties and may have unrealistic expectations of what their savings can earn. This chapter will be extremely valuable for putting savings requirements into the proper prospective and bringing people back to reality.

No one planning on retiring soon should have any needed funds in the stock market. None! In the best of times this would be good advice for anyone nearing retirement; with the coming depression, this is an absolute necessity.

Most people reading this chapter will be shocked at how much savings it takes to retire and to be self-sufficient for the rest of your life. It is important that you react to this shock in an intelligent way. If you are planning to retire in just a few years, it is probably too late to increase your savings rate, at least not enough to make a big difference. If you have insufficient funds saved, you have only two options: delay retirement or reduce your cost of living during retirement. The tables and formulas in this chapter show you different options of retiring at age 60, 65, or 70. As the retirement age is delayed, everything becomes easier. You won't have as many years to live during retirement, any pension you receive will be larger, you have additional time to save, and your Social Security benefit will be larger.

The other option is to reduce retirement living costs. Here are just a few examples of the type of savings you can incorporate into your retirement lifestyle, usually with little change in your life's values. If you are a couple owning two automobiles, one a fairly new SUV and the other a small car that gets good gas mileage, sell the SUV and get along with the other automobile. After all, you are retired with a freer schedule that no longer includes going to a workplace, so that you can adapt to one less automobile. The savings on gas, depreciation, insurance, and taxes could easily be over $5,000 per year. As you will see later, reducing costs by $5,300 per year is equivalent to having an additional $100,000 saved in TIPS! If you live in San Francisco and have $400,000 equity on your $800,000 home, consider selling your home and moving to some place like Ohio. You can pay cash for an even nicer home, have no house payment, and save more than half on taxes and insurance. This savings could be in excess of $25,000 per year. Again, this is the equivalent of having an additional half-a-million dollars savings in TIPS! Switch from going out to eat at a restaurant every week to eating out once a month and pocket maybe $1,500 per year. You'll probably eat healthier, besides saving a lot of money. Give up the Starbucks lattes every day and save $1,200 per year. And do you really need all those cable channels and two cell phones with unlimited calling around the world? We have all gotten accustomed to extras that are often very costly and that we can easily do without. The only way you will identify all these items is to itemize all your expenditures and see which ones you really need. Reducing retirement costs is so much easier than trying to accumulate additional savings, especially if you are close to retirement.

I mentioned that it is important that you react to the shock of the size of required savings in an intelligent way. I have an acquaintance who responded in a way that I would *not* judge as being very intelligent. This person signed on for the services of a financial manager a few years ago, explaining to the financial manager that he "needed" 8 percent real annual gain on his money every year (after the financial manager's fees and after inflation), and the financial manager readily agreed to these goals. What did the financial manager have to lose if the goals weren't reached? He was still getting *his* fees.

The value of this acquaintance's investments has *not* kept up with the 8 percent goal, but the financial manager has assured my friend that the market will turn around. The financial manager stated that since no one can predict the economy in the short run, therefore no one can predict the stock market in the short run. The secret of successful investing, according to the financial manager's sage advice, is to "ride out the lows." Of course, the financial manager still takes *his* 2 percent fees, even during the lows, and, since the financial manager takes no responsibility for the short run, my acquaintance friend will only know that he has a real financial problem in the long run!

It doesn't work to first determine your financial "need" then assume that you can find some investment that will satisfy that "need". This is what my acquaintance was doing when he told the financial manager that he "needed" 8 percent real annual gain on his savings. He had backed into that number using his existing savings and assumed retirement costs. If investing was really that easy, he could have saved even less, then looked for investments that made 12 percent, or even 15 percent! How about 20 percent?

Tables Showing Retirement Income and Related Retirement Savings, for Those Retiring Within a Few Years

The following savings tables are for determining what retirement income you can expect at different savings and pension amounts; and, alternatively, what savings are required to support a given retirement income. It is assumed that the after-tax retirement income is desired to be constant (as to purchasing power), so retirement income will index up every year with inflation. Otherwise, you would become poorer in the later retirement years.

As was true on the previous chapter's tables, no stock market benefits are included in the tables in this chapter. If someone is fortunate enough to be able to invest in the stock market (with extra funds) after it drops 70 percent, any gains resulting from that activity should be recognized only after those gains are truly realized and you are back out of the stock market.

In the following tables, Social Security is assumed to be somewhat less than what was assumed in the last chapter's charts. This is because the earlier chapter's charts assumed Social Security benefits starting at age 70 because retirement took place many years in the future. Although the benefits were assumed to be on the same base as current Social Security, simply delayed, the additional years of work would have qualified more people to a somewhat higher Social Security benefit. However, using the formulas that are later in this chapter will allow readers to input their exact Social Security benefits.

Retire at Age 65, Live to Age 93

Not only are many people getting ready to retire in a few years with little savings, but many nearing retirement do not know how much they should have saved if they live until age 93 with a comfortable lifestyle without running out of money. As mentioned in earlier chapters, after age 93 the value of other assets, like the home, can often be drained to extend the same lifestyle to age 100 or so.

Table 15.1 shows how much yearly retirement income you can use without running out of money before age 93. This table assumes retirement at age 65, with Social Security at $20,000 per year after taxes. Table output options are given for various savings amounts and pension amounts. Retirement income is assumed to be adjusted up every year with inflation, as is Social Security. Savings are assumed to be in TIPS and to be tax-free or after taxes. Pension is fixed and after taxes. The numbers within the table are annual after-tax retirement income dollars the retiree can use for living expenses.

For example, using Table 15.1, if a couple have existing savings of $200,000 in TIPS or equivalent after taxes, and are expecting a pension of $30,000 per year after taxes, they can live on an after-tax retirement income of $50,926 per year, which is then indexed up annually with inflation.

Or if they know how much they need for retirement income during retirement and want to make sure they have enough money saved, they can use Table 15.2. This table assumes retirement at age 65, Social Security at $20,000 per year after taxes, and various saved amounts and pension amounts. Retirement income is assumed to go up every year

Table 15.1   Retirement Income, Assuming Retirement Soon at Age 65 and Living to 93

Pension:	$0	$10,000	$20,000	$30,000	$40,000	$50,000	$60,000
Savings							
$0	$20,000	$26,800	$33,600	$40,400	$47,200	$54,000	$60,800
$50,000	$22,632	$29,432	$36,232	$43,032	$49,832	$56,632	$63,432
$100,000	$25,263	$32,063	$38,863	$45,663	$52,463	$59,263	$66,063
$150,000	$27,895	$34,695	$41,495	$48,295	$55,095	$61,895	$68,695
$200,000	$30,526	$37,326	$44,126	$50,926	$57,726	$64,526	$71,326
$250,000	$33,158	$39,958	$46,758	$53,558	$60,358	$67,158	$73,958
$300,000	$35,789	$42,589	$49,389	$56,189	$62,989	$69,789	$76,589
$350,000	$38,421	$45,221	$52,021	$58,821	$65,621	$72,421	$79,221
$400,000	$41,053	$47,853	$54,653	$61,453	$68,253	$75,053	$81,853
$450,000	$43,684	$50,484	$57,284	$64,084	$70,884	$77,684	$84,484
$500,000	$46,316	$53,116	$59,916	$66,716	$73,516	$80,316	$87,116
$550,000	$48,947	$55,747	$62,547	$69,347	$76,147	$82,947	$89,747
$600,000	$51,579	$58,379	$65,179	$71,979	$78,779	$85,579	$92,379
$650,000	$54,211	$61,011	$67,811	$74,611	$81,411	$88,211	$95,011
$700,000	$56,842	$63,642	$70,442	$77,242	$84,042	$90,842	$97,642
$750,000	$59,474	$66,274	$73,074	$79,874	$86,674	$93,474	$100,274

with inflation, as is Social Security. Savings are assumed to be in TIPS and to be tax-free or after taxes. Pension is fixed and after taxes. Funds are to run out at age 93. The numbers within the table are the savings required at retirement.

For example, using Table 15.2, if people knew they wanted $60,000 to live on during retirement, and they had a pension of $20,000 per year after taxes, Table 16.2 shows that they need to have $501,600 saved in TIPS or equivalent. The $60,000 per year after-tax retirement income is assumed to index every year with inflation and won't run out until age 93.

Retire at Age 65, Live to Age 120

There will be those retiring soon who will be uncomfortable with the assumption of running out of money at age 93, even with the provision of using other assets to enable the retirement lifestyle to continue to age 100. For those people who want to be sure they have required funds if they live over 100 years, the following tables assume funds do

Table 15.2 Required Savings, Assuming Retirement Soon at Age 65 and Living to 93

Pension:	$0	$10,000	$20,000	$30,000	$40,000	$50,000	$60,000
Income							
$20,000	$0	$0	$0	$0	$0	$0	$0
$25,000	$95,000	$0	$0	$0	$0	$0	$0
$30,000	$190,000	$60,800	$0	$0	$0	$0	$0
$35,000	$285,000	$155,800	$26,600	$0	$0	$0	$0
$40,000	$380,000	$250,800	$121,600	$0	$0	$0	$0
$45,000	$475,000	$345,800	$216,600	$87,400	$0	$0	$0
$50,000	$570,000	$440,800	$311,600	$182,400	$53,200	$0	$0
$55,000	$665,000	$535,800	$406,600	$277,400	$148,200	$19,000	$0
$60,000	$760,000	$630,800	$501,600	$372,400	$243,200	$114,000	$0
$65,000	$855,000	$725,800	$596,600	$467,400	$338,200	$209,000	$79,800
$70,000	$950,000	$820,800	$691,600	$562,400	$433,200	$304,000	$174,800
$75,000	$1,045,000	$915,800	$786,600	$657,400	$528,200	$399,000	$269,800
$80,000	$1,140,000	$1,010,800	$881,600	$752,400	$623,200	$494,000	$364,800
$85,000	$1,235,000	$1,105,800	$976,600	$847,400	$718,200	$589,000	$459,800
$90,000	$1,330,000	$1,200,800	$1,071,600	$942,400	$813,200	$684,000	$554,800
$95,000	$1,425,000	$1,295,800	$1,166,600	$1,037,400	$908,200	$779,000	$649,800
$100,000	$1,520,000	$1,390,800	$1,261,600	$1,132,400	$1,003,200	$874,000	$744,800
$105,000	$1,615,000	$1,485,800	$1,356,600	$1,227,400	$1,098,200	$969,000	$839,800
$110,000	$1,710,000	$1,580,800	$1,451,600	$1,322,400	$1,193,200	$1,064,000	$934,800
$115,000	$1,805,000	$1,675,800	$1,546,600	$1,417,400	$1,288,200	$1,159,000	$1,029,800
$120,000	$1,900,000	$1,770,800	$1,641,600	$1,512,400	$1,383,200	$1,254,000	$1,124,800
$125,000	$1,995,000	$1,865,800	$1,736,600	$1,607,400	$1,478,200	$1,349,000	$1,219,800

Table 15.3   Retirement Income, Assuming Retirement Soon at Age 65 and Living to 120

Pension:	$0	$10,000	$20,000	$30,000	$40,000	$50,000	$60,000
Savings							
$0	$20,000	$24,600	$29,200	$33,800	$38,400	$43,000	$47,600
$50,000	$21,786	$26,386	$30,986	$35,586	$40,186	$44,786	$49,386
$100,000	$23,571	$28,171	$32,771	$37,371	$41,971	$46,571	$51,171
$150,000	$25,357	$29,957	$34,557	$39,157	$43,757	$48,357	$52,957
$200,000	$27,143	$31,743	$36,343	$40,943	$45,543	$50,143	$54,743
$250,000	$28,929	$33,529	$38,129	$42,729	$47,329	$51,929	$56,529
$300,000	$30,714	$35,314	$39,914	$44,514	$49,114	$53,714	$58,314
$350,000	$32,500	$37,100	$41,700	$46,300	$50,900	$55,500	$60,100
$400,000	$34,286	$38,886	$43,486	$48,086	$52,686	$57,286	$61,886
$450,000	$36,071	$40,671	$45,271	$49,871	$54,471	$59,071	$63,671
$500,000	$37,857	$42,457	$47,057	$51,657	$56,257	$60,857	$65,457
$550,000	$39,643	$44,243	$48,843	$53,443	$58,043	$62,643	$67,243
$600,000	$41,429	$46,029	$50,629	$55,229	$59,829	$64,429	$69,029
$650,000	$43,214	$47,814	$52,414	$57,014	$61,614	$66,214	$70,814
$700,000	$45,000	$49,600	$54,200	$58,800	$63,400	$68,000	$72,600
$750,000	$46,786	$51,386	$55,986	$60,586	$65,186	$69,786	$74,386

not run out until age 120, and even then can be extended by draining other assets.

Table 15.3 is a chart showing how much after-tax yearly retirement income you can use without running out of money before age 120. This table assumes retirement at age 65, Social Security at $20,000 per year after taxes, and various saved amounts and pension amounts. Retirement income is assumed to go up every year with inflation, as is Social Security. Savings are assumed to be in TIPS and to be tax-free or after taxes. Pension is fixed and after taxes.

For example, using Table 15.3, if people have savings of $200,000 in TIPS or equivalent after taxes, and a pension of $30,000 per year after taxes, they can live on $40,943 per year, which is then indexed up annually with inflation. Note that this is substantially less than the $50,926 retirement income of the live-to-age-93 option.

Or if they know how much they need for living during retirement but just want to make sure they have enough money saved, they can use Table 15.4. This table assumes retirement at age 65, Social Security at $20,000 per year after taxes, and various saved amounts and pension amounts. Retirement income is assumed to be after taxes and to go up every year with inflation, as does Social Security. Savings are assumed to be in TIPS and to be tax-free or after taxes. Pension is fixed and after taxes. Funds are to run out at age 120.

Using Table 15.4, if people knew they wanted $60,000 after taxes to live on during retirement, and they had a pension of $20,000 per year after taxes, Table 15.4 shows that they need to have $862,400 saved in TIPS or equivalent. The $60,000 per year after-tax retirement income is assumed to index every year with inflation and won't run out until age 120. Note that this savings amount is substantially more than the $501,600 savings required in the live-to-age-93 option.

Retire at Age 60, Live to 93

There will be those who want to retire early, at age 60. Here are similar tables for those wishing to retire within a few years, at age 60. It is assumed that $20,000 per year Social Security will be started at age 65 (even though this may be a year earlier than full Social Security) as will the pension. The pension assumed within the tables is reduced 15 percent due to retiring early, but in the table headings, the pension amount is shown as the nominal pension at age 65. The pension headings are left that way because companies quote pensions with the assumption of retirement at age 65 and employment until that time. The pension amount shown, however, is assumed to be after estimated taxes.

So, for the first five years of retirement, only the existing savings will be used to cover retirement income needs. No other income is assumed.

The reason some of the top cells are blank in Table 15.5 is that there aren't enough initial savings to cover the first five years at a constant retirement income.

For example, using Table 15.5, if people have savings of $250,000 in TIPS or equivalent after taxes and a pension of $30,000 per year after taxes, they can live on an after-tax retirement income of $39,978 per year, which is then indexed up annually with inflation.

Or if they know how much they need for retirement income during retirement but just want to make sure they have enough money saved,

Table 15.4 Required Savings, Assuming Retirement Soon at Age 65 and Living to 120

Pension:	$0	$10,000	$20,000	$30,000	$40,000	$50,000	$60,000
Income							
$20,000	$0	$0	$0	$0	$0	$0	$0
$25,000	$140,000	$11,200	$0	$0	$0	$0	$0
$30,000	$280,000	$151,200	$22,400	$0	$0	$0	$0
$35,000	$420,000	$291,200	$162,400	$33,600	$0	$0	$0
$40,000	$560,000	$431,200	$302,400	$173,600	$44,800	$0	$0
$45,000	$700,000	$571,200	$442,400	$313,600	$184,800	$56,000	$0
$50,000	$840,000	$711,200	$582,400	$453,600	$324,800	$196,000	$67,200
$55,000	$980,000	$851,200	$722,400	$593,600	$464,800	$336,000	$207,200
$60,000	$1,120,000	$991,200	$862,400	$733,600	$604,800	$476,000	$347,200
$65,000	$1,260,000	$1,131,200	$1,002,400	$873,600	$744,800	$616,000	$487,200
$70,000	$1,400,000	$1,271,200	$1,142,400	$1,013,600	$884,800	$756,000	$627,200
$75,000	$1,540,000	$1,411,200	$1,282,400	$1,153,600	$1,024,800	$896,000	$767,200
$80,000	$1,680,000	$1,551,200	$1,422,400	$1,293,600	$1,164,800	$1,036,000	$907,200
$85,000	$1,820,000	$1,691,200	$1,562,400	$1,433,600	$1,304,800	$1,176,000	$1,047,200
$90,000	$1,960,000	$1,831,200	$1,702,400	$1,573,600	$1,444,800	$1,316,000	$1,187,200
$95,000	$2,100,000	$1,971,200	$1,842,400	$1,713,600	$1,584,800	$1,456,000	$1,327,200
$100,000	$2,240,000	$2,111,200	$1,982,400	$1,853,600	$1,724,800	$1,596,000	$1,467,200
$105,000	$2,380,000	$2,251,200	$2,122,400	$1,993,600	$1,864,800	$1,736,000	$1,607,200
$110,000	$2,520,000	$2,391,200	$2,262,400	$2,133,600	$2,004,800	$1,876,000	$1,747,200
$115,000	$2,660,000	$2,531,200	$2,402,400	$2,273,600	$2,144,800	$2,016,000	$1,887,200
$120,000	$2,800,000	$2,671,200	$2,542,400	$2,413,600	$2,284,800	$2,156,000	$2,027,200
$125,000	$2,940,000	$2,811,200	$2,682,400	$2,553,600	$2,424,800	$2,296,000	$2,167,200

Table 15.5   Retirement Income, Assuming Retirement Soon at Age 60 and Living 93

Pension:	$0	$10,000	$20,000	$30,000	$40,000	$50,000	$60,000
Savings							
$0							
$50,000							
$100,000	$20,000						
$150,000	$22,083	$26,659					
$200,000	$24,167	$28,743	$33,318	$37,894			
$250,000	$26,250	$30,826	$35,402	$39,978	$44,553	$49,129	
$300,000	$28,333	$32,909	$37,485	$42,061	$46,637	$51,213	$55,788
$350,000	$30,417	$34,993	$39,568	$44,144	$48,720	$53,296	$57,872
$400,000	$32,500	$37,076	$41,652	$46,228	$50,803	$55,379	$59,955
$450,000	$34,583	$39,159	$43,735	$48,311	$52,887	$57,463	$62,038
$500,000	$36,667	$41,243	$45,818	$50,394	$54,970	$59,546	$64,122
$550,000	$38,750	$43,326	$47,902	$52,478	$57,053	$61,629	$66,205
$600,000	$40,833	$45,409	$49,985	$54,561	$59,137	$63,713	$68,288
$650,000	$42,917	$47,493	$52,068	$56,644	$61,220	$65,796	$70,372
$700,000	$45,000	$49,576	$54,152	$58,728	$63,303	$67,879	$72,455
$750,000	$47,083	$51,659	$56,235	$60,811	$65,387	$69,963	$74,538

they can use Table 15.6. This table assumes retirement at age 60, Social Security at $20,000 per year after taxes, and various savings amounts and pension amounts. Retirement income is assumed to be after taxes and indexed up every year with inflation, as is Social Security. Savings are assumed to be in TIPS and to be tax-free or after taxes. Pension is fixed and after taxes. Funds are to run out at age 93.

For example, using Table 15.6, if people know they want $60,000 after taxes to live on during retirement, and they have a pension of $20,000 per year after taxes, Table 15.6 shows that they need to have $840,360 saved in TIPS or equivalent. The $60,000 per year retirement income is assumed to index every year with inflation and won't run out until age 93.

Retire at Age 60, Live to 120

There will be those retiring soon, at age 60, who will be uncomfortable with the assumption of running out of money at age 93, even with

Table 15.6 Required Savings, Assuming Retirement Soon at Age 60 and Living to 93

Pension:	$0	$10,000	$20,000	$30,000	$40,000	$50,000	$60,000
Income							
$20,000	$100,000	$100,000	$100,000	$100,000	$100,000	$100,000	$100,000
$25,000	$220,000	$125,000	$125,000	$125,000	$125,000	$125,000	$125,000
$30,000	$340,000	$230,180	$150,000	$150,000	$150,000	$150,000	$150,000
$35,000	$460,000	$350,180	$240,360	$175,000	$175,000	$175,000	$175,000
$40,000	$580,000	$470,180	$360,360	$250,540	$200,000	$200,000	$200,000
$45,000	$700,000	$590,180	$480,360	$370,540	$260,720	$225,000	$225,000
$50,000	$820,000	$710,180	$600,360	$490,540	$380,720	$270,900	$250,000
$55,000	$940,000	$830,180	$720,360	$610,540	$500,720	$390,900	$281,080
$60,000	$1,060,000	$950,180	$840,360	$730,540	$620,720	$510,900	$401,080
$65,000	$1,180,000	$1,070,180	$960,360	$850,540	$740,720	$630,900	$521,080
$70,000	$1,300,000	$1,190,180	$1,080,360	$970,540	$860,720	$750,900	$641,080
$75,000	$1,420,000	$1,310,180	$1,200,360	$1,090,540	$980,720	$870,900	$761,080
$80,000	$1,540,000	$1,430,180	$1,320,360	$1,210,540	$1,100,720	$990,900	$881,080
$85,000	$1,660,000	$1,550,180	$1,440,360	$1,330,540	$1,220,720	$1,110,900	$1,001,080
$90,000	$1,780,000	$1,670,180	$1,560,360	$1,450,540	$1,340,720	$1,230,900	$1,121,080
$95,000	$1,900,000	$1,790,180	$1,680,360	$1,570,540	$1,460,720	$1,350,900	$1,241,080
$100,000	$2,020,000	$1,910,180	$1,800,360	$1,690,540	$1,580,720	$1,470,900	$1,361,080
$105,000	$2,140,000	$2,030,180	$1,920,360	$1,810,540	$1,700,720	$1,590,900	$1,481,080
$110,000	$2,260,000	$2,150,180	$2,040,360	$1,930,540	$1,820,720	$1,710,900	$1,601,080
$115,000	$2,380,000	$2,270,180	$2,160,360	$2,050,540	$1,940,720	$1,830,900	$1,721,080
$120,000	$2,500,000	$2,390,180	$2,280,360	$2,170,540	$2,060,720	$1,950,900	$1,841,080
$125,000	$2,620,000	$2,510,180	$2,400,360	$2,290,540	$2,180,720	$2,070,900	$1,961,080

Table 15.7 Retirement Income, Assuming Retirement Soon at Age 60 and Living to 120

Pension:	$0	$10,000	$20,000	$30,000	$40,000	$50,000	$60,000
Savings							
$0							
$50,000							
$100,000	$20,000						
$150,000	$21,515	$24,833	$28,150				
$200,000	$23,030	$26,348	$29,665	$32,983	$36,301	$39,618	
$250,000	$24,545	$27,863	$31,181	$34,498	$37,816	$41,133	$44,451
$300,000	$26,061	$29,378	$32,696	$36,013	$39,331	$42,648	$45,966
$350,000	$27,576	$30,893	$34,211	$37,528	$40,846	$44,164	$47,481
$400,000	$29,091	$32,408	$35,726	$39,044	$42,361	$45,679	$48,996
$450,000	$30,606	$33,924	$37,241	$40,559	$43,876	$47,194	$50,512
$500,000	$32,121	$35,439	$38,756	$42,074	$45,392	$48,709	$52,027
$550,000	$33,636	$36,954	$40,272	$43,589	$46,907	$50,224	$53,542
$600,000	$35,152	$38,469	$41,787	$45,104	$48,422	$51,739	$55,057
$650,000	$36,667	$39,984	$43,302	$46,619	$49,937	$53,255	$56,572
$700,000	$38,182	$41,499	$44,817	$48,135	$51,452	$54,770	$58,087
$750,000	$39,697	$43,015	$46,332	$49,650	$52,967	$56,285	$59,602

the provision of using other assets to enable the retirement lifestyle to continue to age 100. For those people who want to be sure they have required funds if they live over 100, Table 15.7 and Table 15.8 assume funds do not run out until age 120, and even then can be extended by draining other assets.

Table 15.7 shows how much yearly retirement you can use without running out of money before age 120. This table assumes retirement at age 60, Social Security at $20,000 per year after taxes, and various savings amounts and pension amounts. Retirement income is assumed to be after taxes and to go up every year with inflation, as is Social Security. Savings are assumed to be in TIPS or in some other format to be tax-free or after taxes. Pension is fixed and after taxes.

For example, using Table 15.7, if people have savings of $200,000 in TIPS and after taxes, and a pension of $30,000 per year after taxes, they can live on an after-tax retirement income of $32,983 per year, which is then indexed up annually with inflation. Note that this is substantially less than the $40,943 retire-at-age-65 option.

Or if they know how much they need for retirement income during retirement but just want to make sure they have enough money saved, they can use Table 15.8. This table assumes retirement at age 60, Social Security at $20,000 per year after taxes, and various savings amounts and pension amounts. Retirement income is assumed to be after taxes and to go up every year with inflation, as is Social Security. Savings are assumed to be in TIPS and to be tax-free or after taxes. Pension is fixed and after taxes. Funds are to run out at age 120.

Using Table 15.8, if people know they want $60,000 after taxes to live on during retirement, and they have a pension of $20,000 per year after taxes, Table 15.8 shows that they need to have $1,201,040 saved in TIPS or equivalent. The $60,000 per year retirement income is assumed to index every year with inflation and won't run out until age 120. Note that this savings amount is substantially more than the $862,400 savings required in the retire-at-age-65 option.

Retire at Age 70, Live to 93

As we mentioned in earlier chapters, after age 93 the value of other assets, like the home, can be drained to extend the same lifestyle to age 100 or so. Table 15.9 shows how much yearly retirement income you can use without running out of money before age 93. This table assumes retirement at age 70 and Social Security at $26,400 per year after taxes, which is 32 percent higher due to the delayed retirement. There are various options for initial savings and pension amounts. Retirement income is assumed to be after taxes and to go up every year with inflation, as is Social Security. Savings are assumed to be in TIPS and to be tax-free or after taxes. Pension is fixed and after taxes, but assumed to be 10 percent higher than the nominal shown in the tables because of the later retirement.

Using Table 15.9, if people have savings of $200,000 in TIPS or equivalent after taxes, and a pension of $30,000 per year after taxes, they can live on a retirement income of $62,915 per year, which is then indexed up annually with inflation. Note that the $62,915 is much higher than the $50,797 they would have had to live on if they retired at 65.

Table 15.8 Required Savings, Assuming Retirement Soon at Age 60 and Living to 120

Pension:	$0	$10,000	$20,000	$30,000	$40,000	$50,000	$60,000
Income							
$20,000	$100,000	$100,000	$100,000	$100,000	$100,000	$100,000	$100,000
$25,000	$265,000	$155,520	$125,000	$125,000	$125,000	$125,000	$125,000
$30,000	$430,000	$320,520	$211,040	$150,000	$150,000	$150,000	$150,000
$35,000	$595,000	$485,520	$376,040	$266,560	$157,080	$175,000	$175,000
$40,000	$760,000	$650,520	$541,040	$431,560	$322,080	$212,600	$200,000
$45,000	$925,000	$815,520	$706,040	$596,560	$487,080	$377,600	$268,120
$50,000	$1,090,000	$980,520	$871,040	$761,560	$652,080	$542,600	$433,120
$55,000	$1,255,000	$1,145,520	$1,036,040	$926,560	$817,080	$707,600	$598,120
$60,000	$1,420,000	$1,310,520	$1,201,040	$1,091,560	$982,080	$872,600	$763,120
$65,000	$1,585,000	$1,475,520	$1,366,040	$1,256,560	$1,147,080	$1,037,600	$928,120
$70,000	$1,750,000	$1,640,520	$1,531,040	$1,421,560	$1,312,080	$1,202,600	$1,093,120
$75,000	$1,915,000	$1,805,520	$1,696,040	$1,586,560	$1,477,080	$1,367,600	$1,258,120
$80,000	$2,080,000	$1,970,520	$1,861,040	$1,751,560	$1,642,080	$1,532,600	$1,423,120
$85,000	$2,245,000	$2,135,520	$2,026,040	$1,916,560	$1,807,080	$1,697,600	$1,588,120
$90,000	$2,410,000	$2,300,520	$2,191,040	$2,081,560	$1,972,080	$1,862,600	$1,753,120
$95,000	$2,575,000	$2,465,520	$2,356,040	$2,246,560	$2,137,080	$2,027,600	$1,918,120
$100,000	$2,740,000	$2,630,520	$2,521,040	$2,411,560	$2,302,080	$2,192,600	$2,083,120
$105,000	$2,905,000	$2,795,520	$2,686,040	$2,576,560	$2,467,080	$2,357,600	$2,248,120
$110,000	$3,070,000	$2,960,520	$2,851,040	$2,741,560	$2,632,080	$2,522,600	$2,413,120
$115,000	$3,235,000	$3,125,520	$3,016,040	$2,906,560	$2,797,080	$2,687,600	$2,578,120
$120,000	$3,400,000	$3,290,520	$3,181,040	$3,071,560	$2,962,080	$2,852,600	$2,743,120
$125,000	$3,565,000	$3,455,520	$3,346,040	$3,236,560	$3,127,080	$3,017,600	$2,908,120

Table 15.9   Retirement Income, Assuming Retirement Soon at Age 70 and Living 93

Pension:	$0	$10,000	$20,000	$30,000	$40,000	$50,000	$60,000
Savings							
$0	$26,400	$34,650	$42,900	$51,150	$59,400	$67,650	$75,900
$50,000	$29,341	$37,591	$45,841	$54,091	$62,341	$70,591	$78,841
$100,000	$32,282	$40,532	$48,782	$57,032	$65,282	$73,532	$81,782
$150,000	$35,224	$43,474	$51,724	$59,974	$68,224	$76,474	$84,724
$200,000	$38,165	$46,415	$54,665	$62,915	$71,165	$79,415	$87,665
$250,000	$41,106	$49,356	$57,606	$65,856	$74,106	$82,356	$90,606
$300,000	$44,047	$52,297	$60,547	$68,797	$77,047	$85,297	$93,547
$350,000	$46,988	$55,238	$63,488	$71,738	$79,988	$88,238	$96,488
$400,000	$49,929	$58,179	$66,429	$74,679	$82,929	$91,179	$99,429
$450,000	$52,871	$61,121	$69,371	$77,621	$85,871	$94,121	$102,371
$500,000	$55,812	$64,062	$72,312	$80,562	$88,812	$97,062	$105,312
$550,000	$58,753	$67,003	$75,253	$83,503	$91,753	$100,003	$108,253
$600,000	$61,694	$69,944	$78,194	$86,444	$94,694	$102,944	$111,194
$650,000	$64,635	$72,885	$81,135	$89,385	$97,635	$105,885	$114,135
$700,000	$67,576	$75,826	$84,076	$92,326	$100,576	$108,826	$117,076
$750,000	$70,518	$78,768	$87,018	$95,268	$103,518	$111,768	$120,018

If people know how much they need for living during retirement but just want to make sure they have enough money saved, they can use Table 15.10. This table assumes retirement at age 70, Social Security at $26,400 per year after taxes, and has various saved amount and pension amount options. Retirement income is assumed to be after taxes and to go up every year with inflation, as is Social Security. Savings are assumed to be in TIPS and tax-free or after taxes. Pension is fixed but is assumed to be 10 percent higher than the nominal shown because of a delayed retirement. Pension is after taxes. Funds are to run out at age 93.

For example, using Table 15.10, if people know they want $60,000 after taxes to live on during retirement, and they have a pension of $20,000 per year after taxes, Table 15.10 shows that they need to have $290,700 saved in TIPS or equivalent. The $60,000 per year retirement income is assumed to index every year with inflation and won't run out until age 93. Note that the $290,700 required savings is substantially less than the $501,600 savings required when retirement was at age 65.

Table 15.10 Required Savings, Assuming Retirement Soon at Age 70 and Living to 93

Pension:	$0	$10,000	$20,000	$30,000	$40,000	$50,000	$60,000
Income							
$20,000	$0	$0	$0	$0	$0	$0	$0
$25,000	$0	$0	$0	$0	$0	$0	$0
$30,000	$61,200	$0	$0	$0	$0	$0	$0
$35,000	$146,200	$5,950	$0	$0	$0	$0	$0
$40,000	$231,200	$90,950	$0	$0	$0	$0	$0
$45,000	$316,200	$175,950	$35,700	$0	$0	$0	$0
$50,000	$401,200	$260,950	$120,700	$0	$0	$0	$0
$55,000	$486,200	$345,950	$205,700	$65,450	$0	$0	$0
$60,000	$571,200	$430,950	$290,700	$150,450	$10,200	$0	$0
$65,000	$656,200	$515,950	$375,700	$235,450	$95,200	$0	$0
$70,000	$741,200	$600,950	$460,700	$320,450	$180,200	$39,950	$0
$75,000	$826,200	$685,950	$545,700	$405,450	$265,200	$124,950	$0
$80,000	$911,200	$770,950	$630,700	$490,450	$350,200	$209,950	$69,700
$85,000	$996,200	$855,950	$715,700	$575,450	$435,200	$294,950	$154,700
$90,000	$1,081,200	$940,950	$800,700	$660,450	$520,200	$379,950	$239,700
$95,000	$1,166,200	$1,025,950	$885,700	$745,450	$605,200	$464,950	$324,700
$100,000	$1,251,200	$1,110,950	$970,700	$830,450	$690,200	$549,950	$409,700
$105,000	$1,336,200	$1,195,950	$1,055,700	$915,450	$775,200	$634,950	$494,700
$110,000	$1,421,200	$1,280,950	$1,140,700	$1,000,450	$860,200	$719,950	$579,700
$115,000	$1,506,200	$1,365,950	$1,225,700	$1,085,450	$945,200	$804,950	$664,700
$120,000	$1,591,200	$1,450,950	$1,310,700	$1,170,450	$1,030,200	$889,950	$749,700
$125,000	$1,676,200	$1,535,950	$1,395,700	$1,255,450	$1,115,200	$974,950	$834,700

Retire at Age 70, Live to 120

There will be those retiring soon who will be uncomfortable with the assumption of running out of money at age 93, even with the provision of using other assets to enable the retirement lifestyle to continue to age 100. For people who want to be sure they have the required funds if they live over 100 years, the following tables assume funds that do not run out until age 120, and even then can be extended by draining other assets.

Table 15.11 shows how much yearly retirement you can use without running out of money before age 120. This table assumes retirement at age 70, Social Security at $26,400 per year after taxes, and has various savings amounts and pension amount options. Retirement income is assumed to be after taxes and to go up every year with inflation, as is Social Security. Savings are assumed to be in TIPS and to be tax-free or after taxes. Pension is fixed and after taxes, but is 10 percent higher than the nominal shown because of the delayed retirement.

Table 15.11   Retirement Income, Assuming Retirement Soon at Age 70 and Living 120

Pension:	$0	$10,000	$20,000	$30,000	$40,000	$50,000	$60,000
Savings							
$0	$26,400	$31,790	$37,180	$42,570	$47,960	$53,350	$58,740
$50,000	$28,252	$33,642	$39,032	$44,422	$49,812	$55,202	$60,592
$100,000	$30,104	$35,494	$40,884	$46,274	$51,664	$57,054	$62,444
$150,000	$31,956	$37,346	$42,736	$48,126	$53,516	$58,906	$64,296
$200,000	$33,807	$39,197	$44,587	$49,977	$55,367	$60,757	$66,147
$250,000	$35,659	$41,049	$46,439	$51,829	$57,219	$62,609	$67,999
$300,000	$37,511	$42,901	$48,291	$53,681	$59,071	$64,461	$69,851
$350,000	$39,363	$44,753	$50,143	$55,533	$60,923	$66,313	$71,703
$400,000	$41,215	$46,605	$51,995	$57,385	$62,775	$68,165	$73,555
$450,000	$43,067	$48,457	$53,847	$59,237	$64,627	$70,017	$75,407
$500,000	$44,919	$50,309	$55,699	$61,089	$66,479	$71,869	$77,259
$550,000	$46,770	$52,160	$57,550	$62,940	$68,330	$73,720	$79,110
$600,000	$48,622	$54,012	$59,402	$64,792	$70,182	$75,572	$80,962
$650,000	$50,474	$55,864	$61,254	$66,644	$72,034	$77,424	$82,814
$700,000	$52,326	$57,716	$63,106	$68,496	$73,886	$79,276	$84,666
$750,000	$54,178	$59,568	$64,958	$70,348	$75,738	$81,128	$86,518

For example, using Table 15.11, if people have savings of $200,000 in TIPS after taxes, and a pension of $30,000 per year after taxes, they can live on $49,977 per year, which is then indexed up annually with inflation. Note that this is substantially more than the $40,943 in the retire-at-age-65 option.

If they know how much they need for living during retirement but just want to make sure they have enough money saved, they can use Table 15.12. This table assumes retirement at age 70, Social Security at $26,400 per year after taxes, and has various savings amount and pension amount options. Retirement income is assumed to be after taxes and to go up every year with inflation, as is Social Security. Savings are assumed to be in TIPS and to be tax-free or after taxes. Pension is fixed and after taxes, but is calculated within the table at 10 percent more than the nominal shown due to the delayed retirement. Funds are to run out at age 120.

Using Table 15.12, if people know they want $60,000 after taxes to live on during retirement, and they have a pension of $20,000 per year after taxes, Table 15.12 shows that they need to have $616,140 saved in TIPS or equivalent. The $60,000 per year retirement income is assumed to index every year with inflation and won't run out until age 120. Note that this savings amount is substantially less than the $862,400 savings required in the retire-at-age-65 option.

Just to show how expensive retiring early and "living forever" are, using the prior tables, here is a comparison of the savings requirement for someone wanting $60,000 retirement income with a nominal pension of $20,000.

- Retire age 60, live to 120, savings required = $1,201,040
- Retire age 70, live to 93, savings required = $290,700

Formulas Showing Retirement Income and Retirement Savings for Those Retiring Within a Few Years

Readers who are comfortable using formulas can plug their own specific values into the formulas to calculate more exact values for either retirement income or the TIPS savings that are required. Using the formulas

Table 15.12 Required Savings, Assuming Retirement Soon at Age 70 and Living to 120

Pension:	$0	$10,000	$20,000	$30,000	$40,000	$50,000	$60,000
Income							
$20,000	$0	$0	$0	$0	$0	$0	$0
$25,000	$0	$0	$0	$0	$0	$0	$0
$30,000	$97,200	$0	$0	$0	$0	$0	$0
$35,000	$232,200	$86,670	$0	$0	$0	$0	$0
$40,000	$367,200	$221,670	$76,140	$0	$0	$0	$0
$45,000	$502,200	$356,670	$211,140	$65,610	$0	$0	$0
$50,000	$637,200	$491,670	$346,140	$200,610	$55,080	$0	$0
$55,000	$772,200	$626,670	$481,140	$335,610	$190,080	$44,550	$0
$60,000	$907,200	$761,670	$616,140	$470,610	$325,080	$179,550	$34,020
$65,000	$1,042,200	$896,670	$751,140	$605,610	$460,080	$314,550	$169,020
$70,000	$1,177,200	$1,031,670	$886,140	$740,610	$595,080	$449,550	$304,020
$75,000	$1,312,200	$1,166,670	$1,021,140	$875,610	$730,080	$584,550	$439,020
$80,000	$1,447,200	$1,301,670	$1,156,140	$1,010,610	$865,080	$719,550	$574,020
$85,000	$1,582,200	$1,436,670	$1,291,140	$1,145,610	$1,000,080	$854,550	$709,020
$90,000	$1,717,200	$1,571,670	$1,426,140	$1,280,610	$1,135,080	$989,550	$844,020
$95,000	$1,852,200	$1,706,670	$1,561,140	$1,415,610	$1,270,080	$1,124,550	$979,020
$100,000	$1,987,200	$1,841,670	$1,696,140	$1,550,610	$1,405,080	$1,259,550	$1,114,020
$105,000	$2,122,200	$1,976,670	$1,831,140	$1,685,610	$1,540,080	$1,394,550	$1,249,020
$110,000	$2,257,200	$2,111,670	$1,966,140	$1,820,610	$1,675,080	$1,529,550	$1,384,020
$115,000	$2,392,200	$2,246,670	$2,101,140	$1,955,610	$1,810,080	$1,664,550	$1,519,020
$120,000	$2,527,200	$2,381,670	$2,236,140	$2,090,610	$1,945,080	$1,799,550	$1,654,020
$125,000	$2,662,200	$2,516,670	$2,371,140	$2,225,610	$2,080,080	$1,934,550	$1,789,020

allows someone to input numbers other than the ones shown on the prior tables. Those of you who get headaches from math details may want to skip the rest of this chapter.

In the formulas, we will use RI to represent the after-tax "retirement income," SS for the "Social Security benefit," TS for the required "TIPS savings," and PN for the "pension benefit."

Determine Retirement Income If You Retire at Age 65 and Live to Age 93

In order to determine your retirement income if you retire at the age of 65 and live to age 93, you must use the following formula:

$$RI = TS/19 + SS + 0.68 \times PN$$

Let's try this formula and check the results against Table 15.1. Assume someone has TIPS savings of $450,000 and a pension of $40,000 after taxes. For this example, as we assumed in Table 15.1, we will use Social Security being $20,000 per year after taxes.

$$RI = TS/19 + SS + 0.68 \times PN$$
$$RI = \$450,000/19 + \$20,000 + 0.68 \times \$40,000$$
$$RI = \$23,684 + \$20,000 + \$27,200$$
$$RI = \$70,884$$

Let's now go to Table 15.1 and look up the table value with a savings of $450,000 and a pension of $40,000. We see it is $70,884, the same as what we calculated. The advantage of using the formula, however, is that, if necessary, you can input values other than those shown in the table.

The above equation shows that for every dollar of retirement income (RI) you need 19 dollars of TIPS savings (TS). The luxury of having an extra automobile that costs $5,250 per year in gas, depreciation, insurance, taxes, and so on requires an extra $100,000 in TIPS savings! Obviously, reducing living expenses is much easier than trying to save additional funds!

For those who are inquisitive, the details on the derivations of the "19" divisor and "0.68" multiplier in the previous formula are covered in Appendix B.

Now let's look at the other formulas. Again, in all the formulas, we will use RI to represent the after-tax retirement income, SS for the Social Security benefit, TS for the required TIPS savings, and PN for the pension benefit.

Determine Required TIPS Savings If You Retire at Age 65 and Live to Age 93

In order to determine your required TIPS savings if you retire at the age of 65 and live to age 93, you must use the following formula:

$$TS = 19 \times (RI - SS - 0.68 \times PN)$$

Let's try this formula and then compare the results with the value in Table 15.2. Assume an after-tax retirement income (RI) of $75,000 and a pension (PN) of $30,000 after taxes. We will use $20,000 for the after-tax Social Security (SS) benefit, as we did in the tables.

$$TS = 19 \times (RI - SS - 0.68 \times PN)$$
$$TS = 19 \times (\$75{,}000 - \$20{,}000 - 0.68 \times \$30{,}000)$$
$$TS = 19 \times (\$75{,}000 - \$20{,}000 - \$20{,}400)$$
$$TS = 19 \times \$34{,}600$$
$$TS = \$657{,}400$$

Checking this against the equivalent value in Table 15.2, we can see that they agree. You will also recognize the multipliers 19 and 0.68 in this formula as being identical to those in the prior formula for retirement income.

Again, in the formulas, we will use RI to represent the after-tax retirement income, SS for the Social Security benefit, TS for the required TIPS savings, and PN for the pension benefit.

Determine Retirement Income If You Retire at Age 65 and Live to Age 120

In order to determine the retirement income if you retire at the age of 65 and live to age 120, you must use the following formula:

$$RI = TS/28 + SS + 0.46 \times PN$$

Let's try this formula and check the results against Table 15.3. Assume someone has TIPS savings of $450,000 and a pension of $40,000 after taxes. As we assumed in Table 15.3, we will use Social Security being $20,000 per year after taxes.

$$RI = TS/28 + SS + 0.46 \times PN$$
$$RI = \$450,000/28 + \$20,000 + 0.46 \times \$40,000$$
$$RI = \$16,071 + \$20,000 + \$18,400$$
$$RI = \$54,471$$

Let's now go to Table 15.3 and look up the table value with a savings of $450,000 and a pension of $40,000. We see it is $54,471, the same as what we calculated.

The TS/28 and 0.46 × PN were determined in exactly the same manner as we did for the earlier formulas for retirement at age 93, except that in this case we required the savings to go negative in 55 years, which gets us from age 65 to age 120.

Determine Required TIPS Savings If You Retire at Age 65 and Live to Age 120

In order to determine your required TIPS savings if you retire at the age of 65 and live to age 120, you must use the following formula:

$$TS = 28 \times (RI - SS - 0.46 \times PN)$$

Let's try this formula and then compare the results with Table 15.4. Assume an after-tax retirement income (RI) of $75,000 and a pension (PN) of $30,000 after taxes. We will use $20,000 for the after-tax Social Security (SS) benefit, as we did in the tables.

$$TS = 28 \times (RI - SS - 0.46 \times PN)$$
$$TS = 28 \times (\$75,000 - \$20,000 - 0.46 \times \$30,000)$$
$$TS = 28 \times (\$75,000 - \$20,000 - \$13,800)$$
$$TS = 28 \times \$41,200$$
$$TS = \$1,153,600$$

This matches the value in Table 15.4.

Determine Retirement Income If You Retire at Age 60 and Live to Age 93

This formula used to determine your retirement income if you retire at the age of 60 and live to the age of 93 becomes a little more complex because the first five years of retirement do not include either Social Security benefits or a pension. Also, it is assumed that the pension is reduced 15 percent because the employee leaves the company five years before the company pension begins, giving fewer employment years credited toward the pension.

We account for the above issues by adding five times the annual retirement income onto the required savings, since these savings will be the only income for the first five years. This additional amount is included within the formula. We also must verify that savings are a minimum of five times the retirement income. Here is the formula:

$$RI = 0.0417TS + 0.4576PN + 0.7917SS$$

(TS must be greater than 5RI, or there will not be sufficient funds for the first five years.)

Let's try this and compare the answer with Table 15.5. Assume someone has TIPS savings of $450,000 and a pension of $40,000 after taxes. As we assumed in Table 15.5, we will use Social Security being $20,000 per year after taxes.

$$RI = 0.0417TS + 0.4576PN + 0.7917SS$$
$$RI = (0.0417 \times \$450,000) + (0.4576 \times \$40,000) + (0.7917 \times \$20,000)$$
$$RI = \$18,765 + \$18,304 + \$15,834$$
$$RI = \$52,903$$

(Since the TS of $450,000 is greater than 5 times the RI of $52,903, we have enough funds for the first five years.)

Let's check this result against Table 15.5. The table value is $52,887, equivalent except for a small amount of rounding error.

Determine Required TIPS Savings If You Retire at Age 60 and Live to Age 93

The first five years of retirement do not include either Social Security benefits or a pension. Also, it is assumed that the pension is reduced 15 percent because the employee leaves the company five years before the company pension begins, giving fewer years toward the pension.

We account for the above issues within the formula by adding five times the annual retirement income onto the required savings, since these savings will be the only income for the first five years. We also must verify savings are a minimum of five times the retirement income. Here is the formula:

$$TS = 24RI - 10.98PN - 19SS$$

(TS must be greater than 5RI, or there will not be sufficient funds for the first five years.)

Let's try this and compare the answer with Table 15.6. Assume an after-tax retirement income (RI) of $65,000 and a pension (PN) of $10,000 after taxes. We will use $20,000 for the after-tax Social Security (SS) benefit, as we did in the tables.

$$TS = 24RI - 10.98PN - 19SS$$
$$TS = (24 \times \$65,000) - (10.98 \times \$10,000) - (19 \times \$20,000)$$
$$TS = \$1,560,000 - \$109,800 - \$380,000$$
$$TS = \$1,070,200$$

This agrees with Table 15.6, other than the rounding error.

(Since the TS of $1,070,200 is greater than 5 times the RI of $65,000, we have enough funds for the first five years.)

Determine Retirement Income If You Retire at Age 60 and Live to Age 120

The first five years of retirement do not include either Social Security benefits or a pension. Also, it is assumed that the pension is reduced 15 percent because the employee leaves the company five years before the company pension begins, giving fewer years toward the pension.

We account for the above issues within the formula by adding five times the annual retirement income onto the required savings, since these savings will be the only income for the first five years. We also must verify that savings are a minimum of five times the retirement income. Here is the formula:

$$RI = 0.0303TS + 0.3318PN + 0.8485SS$$

(TS must be greater than 5RI, or there will not be sufficient funds for the first five years.)

Let's try this and compare the answer with Table 15.7. Assume someone has TIPS savings of $400,000 and a pension of $40,000 after taxes. As we assumed in Table 16.7, we will use Social Security being $20,000 per year after taxes.

$RI = 0.0303TS + 0.3318PN + 0.8485SS$

$RI = (0.0303 \times \$400,000) + (0.3318 \times \$40,000) + (0.8485 \times \$20,000)$

$RI = \$12,120 + \$13,272 + \$16,970$

$RI = \$42,362$

Looking at Table 15.7, the results agree. (Since the TS of $400,000 is greater than five times the RI of $42,362, we have enough funds for the first five years.)

Determine Required TIPS Savings If You Retire at Age 60 and Live to Age 120

The first five years of retirement do not include either Social Security benefits or a pension. Also, it is assumed that the pension is reduced 15 percent because the employee leaves the company five years before the company pension begins, giving fewer years toward the pension.

We account for the above issues within the formula by adding five times the annual retirement income onto the required savings, since these savings will be the only income for the first five years. We also must verify that savings are a minimum of five times the retirement income. Here is the formula:

$$TS = 33RI - 10.95PN - 28SS$$

(TS must be greater than 5RI, or there will not be sufficient funds for the first five years.)

Let's try this and compare the answer with Table 15.8. Assume an after-tax retirement income (RI) of $85,000 and a pension (PN) of $10,000 after taxes. We will use $20,000 for the after-tax Social Security (SS) benefit, as in the tables.

$$TS = 33RI - 10.95PN - 28SS$$
$$TS = (33 \times \$85,000) - (10.95 \times \$10,000) - (28 \times \$20,000)$$
$$TS = \$2,805,000 - \$109,500 - \$560,000$$
$$TS = \$2,135,500$$

Looking at Table 15.8, the results agree other than the rounding error. (Since the TS of $2,135,500 is greater than 5 times the RI of $85,000, we have enough funds for the first 5 years.)

Determine Retirement Income If You Retire at Age 70 and Live to Age 93

In order to determine your retirement income if you retire at the age of 70 and live to age 93, you must use the following formula:

$$RI = (TS/17) + SS + (0.825 \times PN)$$

Let's try this formula and check the results against Table 15.9. Assume someone has TIPS savings of $450,000 and a nominal pension of $40,000 after taxes. In the formula, the pension is increased 10 percent over the nominal due to the five years extended employment. As we assumed in Table 16.9, we will use Social Security being $26,400 per year after taxes.

$$RI = (TS/17) + SS + (0.825 \times PN)$$
$$RI = \$450,000/17 + \$26,400 + 0.825 \times \$40,000$$
$$RI = \$26,471 + \$26,400 + \$33,000$$
$$RI = \$85,871$$

Let's now go to Table 15.9 and look up the table value with a savings of $450,000 and a pension of $40,000. We see it is $85,871, the same as what we calculated.

Determine Required TIPS Savings If You Retire at Age 70 and Live to Age 93

In order to determine your required TIPS savings if you retire at the age of 70 and live to age 93, you must use the following formula:

$$TS = 17 \times (RI - SS - 0.825PN)$$

Let's try this formula and then compare the results with Table 15.10. Assume an after-tax retirement income (RI) of $75,000 and a nominal pension (PN) of $30,000 after taxes (assumed to be 10 percent bigger in the formula due to five years of additional employment). We will use $26,400 for the after-tax Social Security (SS) benefit, as we did in the tables.

$$TS = 17 \times (RI - SS - 0.825 \times PN)$$
$$TS = 17 \times (\$75,000 - \$26,400 - 0.825 \times \$30,000)$$
$$TS = 17 \times (\$75,000 - 26,400 - \$24,750)$$
$$TS = 17 \times \$23,850$$
$$TS = \$405,450$$

Checking this against the equivalent value in Table 15.10, we can see that they agree.

Determine Retirement Income If You Retire at Age 70 and Live to Age 120

In order to determine your retirement income if you retire at the age of 70 and live to age 120, you must use the following formula:

$$RI = TS/27 + SS + 0.539 \times PN$$

Let's try this formula and check the results against Table 15.11. Assume that someone has TIPS savings of $450,000 and a pension of nominal $40,000 after taxes (increased 10 percent in the formula because of the additional five years of employment). As we assumed in Table 15.11, we will use Social Security being $26,400 per year after taxes.

$$RI = TS/27 + SS + 0.539 \times PN$$
$$RI = \$450,000/27 + \$26,400 + 0.539 \times \$40,000$$
$$RI = \$16,667 + \$26,400 + \$21,560$$
$$RI = \$64,627$$

Let's now go to Table 15.11 and look up the table value with a savings of $450,000 and a pension of $40,000. We see it is $64,627, the same as what we calculated.

Determine Required TIPS Savings If You Retire at Age 70 and Live to Age 120

In order to determine your required TIPS savings if you retire at the age of 70 and live to age 120, you must use the following formula:

$$TS = 27 \times (RI - SS - 0.539PN)$$

Let's try this formula and then compare the results with Table 15.12. Assume an after-tax retirement income (RI) of $75,000 and a nominal pension (PN) of $30,000 after taxes (which is increased 10 percent within the formula to account for the additional five years of employment). We will use $26,400 for the after-tax Social Security (SS) benefit, as we did in the tables.

$$TS = 27 \times (RI - SS - 0.539 \times PN)$$
$$TS = 27 \times (\$75,000 - \$26,400 - 0.539 \times \$30,000)$$

$$TS = 27 \times (\$75,000 - \$26,400 - \$16,170)$$
$$TS = 27 \times \$32,430$$
$$TS = \$875,610$$

This matches the value in Table 15.12.

Summary

This chapter is intended for people planning to retire within a few years. In the early part of this chapter are tables that were used to estimate both retirement income and required savings. To get more exact numbers, there are formulas near the end of the chapter into which exact values can be input. It generally is worthwhile to use both. The tables will get you close, and the formulas will allow you to input your exact values. By doing the table first, you can have some confidence that you did the formula correctly by comparing the two answers.

APPENDIX A

Details on Using the Formula on 5-, 10-, and 20-Year Investing

We will buy stocks anytime the price/dividend ratio on the S&P 500 is at or below 17.2. We will not only be putting new investment money into buying these stocks, but we will also sell all the TIPS (Treasury Inflation Protected Securities) we have accumulated and use those funds to buy stocks. When the price/dividend again goes above 17.2, we will stop buying stocks with new investment money and start buying TIPS. If the price/dividend goes above 28, we will sell all the stocks we have accumulated and use the funds from the sale to buy TIPS. In this Appendix, I will show you how to use the formula based on 5-, 10-, and 20-year investing, assuming a 3 percent TIPS base interest.

5-Year Investing, with a Constant Amount Invested Each Year

In Table A.1 we look at the results of the savings formula versus the S&P 500 in five-year investment scenarios, where we are investing $100

Table A.1   Formula Buy versus Straight S&P 500 Buy, 5-Year Investment, $100 Per Year (2007 $) 3 Percent TIPS

End Year	Formula Gain	Formula Mix Results	S&P 500 Results	S&P 500 Gain
1911	0.0229	**26.49**	25.90	
1912	0.0256	**25.68**	25.04	
1913	0.0527	**23.69**	22.51	
1914	0.0296	**23.30**	22.63	
1915	0.0309	**30.44**	29.53	
1916	0.0431	**32.18**	30.85	
1917	0.0104	**24.50**	24.25	
1918	0.0103	**31.05**	30.74	
1919	0.0103	**37.11**	36.73	
1920		34.26	34.26	
1921		43.51	43.51	
1922		53.60	53.60	
1923		53.65	53.65	
1924		63.66	63.66	
1925	0.1263	**76.44**	67.87	
1926	0.1388	**71.65**	62.92	
1927	0.2862	**92.69**	72.06	
1928	0.3160	**108.82**	82.69	
1929	0.5583	**95.58**	61.34	
1930	0.5589	**64.44**	41.34	
1931	0.4029	**34.47**	24.57	
1932	0.0933	**27.53**	25.18	
1933	0.0359	**41.85**	40.40	
1934	0.0587	**43.54**	41.13	
1935		45.36	**57.39**	0.2653
1936		41.33	**61.72**	0.4932
1937	0.1184	**37.14**	33.21	
1938	0.3053	**52.69**	40.36	
1939	0.3652	**49.24**	36.07	
1940	0.3023	**42.54**	32.67	
1941	0.1857	**37.01**	31.21	
1942	0.1902	**43.80**	36.80	
1943		46.11	46.11	
1944	0.1602	**62.45**	53.82	
1945	0.1353	**76.17**	67.09	
1946	0.4705	**80.42**	54.69	
1947	0.4967	**79.36**	53.03	
1948	0.4118	**75.53**	53.50	

Table A.1 *(Continued)*

End Year	Formula Gain	Formula Mix Results	S&P 500 Results	S&P 500 Gain
1949	0.0827	**66.04**	61.00	
1950	0.0127	**78.35**	77.37	
1951		89.30	89.30	
1952		93.74	93.74	
1953		80.21	80.21	
1954		101.15	101.15	
1955		112.40	112.40	
1956		101.59	**102.36**	0.0076
1957	0.1451	**92.04**	80.38	
1958		79.33	**93.06**	0.1731
1959		75.79	**91.57**	0.2082
1960		76.66	**86.10**	0.1230
1961		77.55	**99.62**	0.2845
1962		78.84	**80.19**	0.0171
1963		80.16	**90.96**	0.1348
1964		81.06	**97.43**	0.2019
1965		82.52	**97.88**	0.1861
1966	0.0065	**84.89**	84.34	
1967		87.16	**94.25**	0.0814
1968		90.70	**97.04**	0.0699
1969	0.0961	**95.30**	86.95	
1970	0.0994	**99.86**	90.83	
1971	0.0322	**103.17**	99.95	
1972		106.60	**115.87**	0.0869
1973	0.1344	**114.98**	101.36	
1974	0.5605	**127.69**	81.82	
1975	0.6302	**189.31**	116.13	
1976	0.6361	**239.50**	146.38	
1977	0.7149	**247.93**	144.58	
1978	0.6310	**258.99**	158.79	
1979	0.6745	**295.04**	176.19	
1980	0.4682	**325.81**	221.91	
1981	0.2266	**261.37**	213.09	
1982		249.76	249.76	
1983	0.1691	**334.33**	285.96	
1984	0.3549	**389.12**	287.19	
1985	0.4535	**516.17**	355.13	
1986	0.4534	**537.40**	369.75	

(Continued)

Table A.1 *(Continued)*

End Year	Formula Gain	Formula Mix Results	S&P 500 Results	S&P 500 Gain
1987	0.5409	**530.22**	344.11	
1988	0.2996	**467.65**	359.83	
1989		396.31	**406.74**	0.0263
1990		337.32	**359.63**	0.0661
1991		346.21	**424.83**	0.2271
1992		357.38	**411.14**	0.1504
1993		368.46	**410.12**	0.1130
1994		379.85	**397.17**	0.0456
1995		392.29	**485.98**	0.2388
1996		405.11	**453.43**	0.1193
1997		413.03	**648.46**	0.5700
1998		420.68	**707.03**	0.6807
1999		431.97	**683.33**	0.5819
2000		445.82	**532.42**	0.1943
2001	0.1383	**455.61**	400.24	
2002	0.4324	**462.93**	323.19	
2003	0.1062	**472.94**	427.53	
2004		495.45	**513.78**	0.0370
2005		506.13	**539.21**	0.0654
2006		512.23	**581.62**	0.1355
2007		525.77	**541.95**	0.0308

Best results are in bold.
SOURCE: Stock Data, www.econ.yale.edu/~shiller/data/ie_data.htm.

every year for five years. As a means of keeping score, we assume the investment is in year 2007 equivalent dollars.

So, if we look at investing a constant real-dollar amount every year when our time period is five years, the formula-based investment equaled or beat the straight S&P 500 investment 67 percent of the time. In addition, the formula method averaged 10.1 percent greater returns for the five-year period. On this basis, the market timing when following the formula is superior to just blindly investing in the S&P 500 when the investment period is five years. In addition, since the formula investment method was out of the stock market half the time, this is a far lower-risk method than being in the market continuously.

Note that nothing about this method involves any trick of beating the market. The only reason the formula method beats the straight S&P

500 investment is because it stays out of the market when the market is historically high priced, instead investing in TIPS. This method works strictly because of market timing.

The fact that the five-year investment period is so good is of special interest because many people start out with the intent of saving for a longer period, but, because of some unforeseen reason, they have to withdraw their savings early. The formula method reduces the risk that they will lose substantial amounts of money if they have to cut their investment window short.

Now let's look at a similar comparison, in Table A.2, when the investment window is 10 years.

10-Year Investing, with a Constant Amount Invested Each Year

In Table A.2, we look at the results of the savings formula versus the S&P 500 in 10-year investment scenarios, where we are investing $100 every year for 10 years. As a means of keeping score, we assume the investment is in year 2007 equivalent dollars.

If we look at investing when the time period is 10 years, the formula-based investment beat the straight S&P 500 investment 66 percent of the time. In addition, the formula method averaged 11.7 percent greater returns per 10-year period. On this basis, the market timing according to the formula is superior to just blindly investing in the S&P 500 when the investment period is 10 years. In addition, since the formula investment method was out of the stock market over half the time, this is a far lower-risk method than being in the market continuously.

Now let's look at a 20-year investment window and see if the formula method is still superior.

20-Year Investing, with a Constant Amount Invested Each Year

In Table A.3, we look at the results of the savings formula versus the S&P 500 in 20-year investment scenarios, where we are investing $100 every year for 20 years. As a means of keeping score, we assume the investment is in year 2007 equivalent dollars.

Table A.2 Formula Buy Compared to Straight S&P 500 Buy, 10-Year Investment, $100 Per Year (2007 $) 3 Percent TIPS

End Year	Formula Gain	Formula Mix Results	S&P 500 Results	S&P 500 Gain
1916	0.0322	**68.97**	66.82	
1917	0.0333	**49.86**	48.26	
1918	0.0312	**62.62**	60.72	
1919	0.0201	**75.68**	74.19	
1920	0.0190	**64.72**	63.51	
1921	0.0183	**77.00**	75.61	
1922	0.0046	**96.96**	96.51	
1923	0.0047	**98.72**	98.26	
1924	0.0048	**120.39**	119.82	
1925	0.0568	**159.45**	150.88	
1926	0.0521	**176.44**	167.71	
1927	0.0981	**230.76**	210.14	
1928	0.0941	**303.76**	277.63	
1929	0.2491	**285.78**	228.79	
1930	0.6107	**233.74**	145.12	
1931	0.5785	**114.08**	72.27	
1932	0.5315	**94.84**	61.93	
1933	0.5036	**127.57**	84.85	
1934	0.5634	**119.51**	76.44	
1935		101.55	**104.06**	0.0247
1936		96.99	**126.86**	0.3080
1937	0.1028	**88.71**	80.44	
1938	0.1381	**120.15**	105.58	
1939	0.1202	**115.45**	103.06	
1940	0.1239	**100.87**	89.75	
1941	0.1362	**81.78**	71.97	
1942	0.1524	**89.68**	77.82	
1943	0.1590	**108.50**	93.62	
1944	0.2604	**132.70**	105.29	
1945	0.2210	**168.39**	137.91	
1946	0.5256	**190.89**	125.12	
1947	0.6002	**200.44**	125.26	
1948	0.4097	**182.27**	129.29	
1949	0.3768	**204.07**	148.22	
1950	0.3485	**244.31**	181.18	
1951	0.3176	**268.39**	203.69	
1952	0.2838	**280.81**	218.73	
1953	0.2458	**247.99**	199.05	

Table A.2   *(Continued)*

End Year	Formula Gain	Formula Mix Results	S&P 500 Results	S&P 500 Gain
1954	0.0524	**290.70**	276.23	
1955	0.0085	**340.03**	337.17	
1956		323.71	**326.42**	0.0084
1957	0.1643	**300.60**	258.18	
1958		268.30	**313.84**	0.1697
1959		239.75	**296.48**	0.2366
1960		221.11	**259.85**	0.1752
1961		205.26	**287.36**	0.4000
1962		192.83	**230.50**	0.1953
1963		178.29	**239.68**	0.3443
1964		174.15	**249.51**	0.4328
1965		177.19	**257.85**	0.4553
1966		183.22	**215.58**	0.1766
1967		188.76	**237.80**	0.2598
1968		197.04	**244.39**	0.2403
1969		208.24	**211.07**	0.0136
1970	0.0614	**218.84**	206.17	
1971		225.33	**226.24**	0.0041
1972		232.46	**251.34**	0.0812
1973	0.2028	**250.81**	208.53	
1974	0.7519	**278.43**	158.93	
1975	0.7482	**388.96**	222.49	
1976	0.7566	**480.03**	273.27	
1977	0.7922	**464.78**	259.34	
1978	0.6965	**482.14**	284.20	
1979	0.6197	**549.88**	339.50	
1980	0.5585	**694.64**	445.71	
1981	0.4790	**635.23**	429.51	
1982	0.3944	**738.48**	529.59	
1983	0.4245	**910.80**	639.40	
1984	0.5308	**977.54**	638.59	
1985	0.4616	**1162.14**	795.10	
1986	0.3201	**1184.16**	897.05	
1987	0.2243	**1076.51**	879.29	
1988	0.1478	**1082.24**	942.85	
1989		1094.78	**1132.29**	0.0343
1990	0.1139	**1135.76**	1019.59	
1991		1118.79	**1180.28**	0.0550
1992		1108.76	**1130.02**	0.0192

(Continued)

Table A.2   (*Continued*)

End Year	Formula Gain	Formula Mix Results	S&P 500 Results	S&P 500 Gain
1993		1020.86	**1119.75**	0.0969
1994		922.59	**1014.35**	0.0995
1995		839.14	**1260.78**	0.5025
1996		864.86	**1156.63**	0.3374
1997		882.24	**1682.98**	0.9076
1998		899.24	**1912.41**	1.1267
1999		925.36	**2077.88**	1.2455
2000		959.47	**1659.79**	0.7299
2001		978.93	**1324.92**	0.3534
2002	0.0456	**995.87**	952.48	
2003		1018.63	**1113.22**	0.0929
2004		1065.22	**1072.22**	0.0066
2005	0.0552	**1088.29**	1031.35	
2006	0.0263	**1106.89**	1078.55	
2007	0.0635	**1131.85**	1064.22	

The best results are in bold.
SOURCE: Stock Data, www.econ.yale.edu/~shiller/data/ie_data.htm.

Table A.3   Formula Buy Compared to Straight S&P 500 Buy, 20–Year Investment, $100 Per Year (2007 $) 3 Percent TIPS

End Year	Formula Gain	Formula Results	S&P 500 Results	S&P 500 Gain
1926	0.0421	**349.37**	335.24	
1927	0.0650	**458.08**	430.13	
1928	0.0604	**634.00**	597.86	
1929	0.1979	**631.46**	527.16	
1930	0.5382	**585.14**	380.41	
1931	0.5220	**320.16**	210.36	
1932	0.4917	**281.49**	188.70	
1933	0.4819	**410.13**	276.76	
1934	0.5719	**405.41**	257.92	
1935	0.1286	**411.39**	364.51	
1936		413.57	**464.03**	0.1220
1937	0.4500	**408.05**	281.41	
1938	0.4602	**505.91**	346.47	

Table A.3   *(Continued)*

End Year	Formula Gain	Formula Results	S&P 500 Results	S&P 500 Gain
1939	0.4508	**460.79**	317.62	
1940	0.4364	**362.98**	252.70	
1941	0.4169	**281.32**	198.56	
1942	0.3969	**309.19**	221.34	
1943	0.3757	**350.55**	254.82	
1944	0.3854	**391.96**	282.93	
1945	0.2462	**451.50**	362.29	
1946	0.6055	**504.46**	314.21	
1947	0.5715	**503.46**	320.37	
1948	0.5305	**510.49**	333.55	
1949	0.5006	**579.98**	386.51	
1950	0.4947	**720.79**	482.23	
1951	0.4942	**811.91**	543.39	
1952	0.4947	**865.21**	578.85	
1953	0.4900	**805.88**	540.87	
1954	0.4976	**1147.14**	765.97	
1955	0.4690	**1405.95**	957.06	
1956	0.4048	**1380.92**	982.99	
1957	0.6521	**1351.76**	818.20	
1958	0.1067	**1222.13**	1104.34	
1959	0.0267	**1189.16**	1158.28	
1960	0.0556	**1133.23**	1073.52	
1961		1044.39	**1224.69**	0.1726
1962		966.60	**1006.30**	0.0411
1963		901.05	**1115.25**	0.2377
1964		752.82	**1178.81**	0.5659
1965		716.74	**1226.30**	0.7109
1966		699.18	**1004.33**	0.4364
1967		668.53	**1102.02**	0.6484
1968		637.34	**1056.81**	0.6582
1969		618.48	**838.38**	0.3556
1970		612.44	**775.10**	0.2656
1971		599.86	**793.18**	0.3223
1972		591.32	**844.38**	0.4280
1973		604.99	**637.29**	0.0534
1974	0.5021	**662.20**	440.84	
1975	0.5558	**899.65**	578.24	
1976	0.6027	**1094.76**	683.09	

(Continued)

Table A.3 *(Continued)*

End Year	Formula Gain	Formula Results	S&P 500 Results	S&P 500 Gain
1977	0.7049	**1019.28**	597.87	
1978	0.7064	**1054.78**	618.14	
1979	0.6930	**1207.26**	713.09	
1980	0.6882	**1537.75**	910.91	
1981	0.6530	**1411.92**	854.14	
1982	0.6351	**1653.79**	1011.44	
1983	0.6431	**1994.26**	1213.71	
1984	0.6408	**2085.79**	1271.19	
1985	0.6146	**2656.23**	1645.17	
1986	0.5760	**2989.29**	1896.81	
1987	0.5671	**3063.52**	1954.90	
1988	0.4063	**3139.66**	2232.58	
1989	0.1342	**3224.39**	2842.84	
1990	0.2589	**3350.96**	2661.79	
1991	0.0080	**3378.62**	3351.82	
1992		3397.74	**3500.75**	0.0303
1993		3420.04	**3690.67**	0.0791
1994		3444.02	**3462.31**	0.0053
1995		3273.21	**4444.11**	0.3577
1996		3125.54	**4190.29**	0.3407
1997		2885.14	**6305.13**	1.1854
1998		2860.18	**7377.47**	1.5794
1999		2872.86	**8110.42**	1.8231
2000		2929.49	**6755.49**	1.3060
2001		2898.16	**5308.91**	0.8318
2002		2874.19	**3711.79**	0.2914
2003		2738.56	**4304.94**	0.5720
2004		2731.83	**4264.03**	0.5609
2005		2728.90	**4056.73**	0.4866
2006		2719.48	**4186.59**	0.5395
2007		2718.87	**3917.33**	0.4408

The best results are in bold.

SOURCE: Stock Data, www.econ.yale.edu/~shiller/data/ie_data.htm.

If we look at investing when the time period is 20 years, the formula-based investment beat the straight S&P 500 investment 63 percent of the time. In addition, the formula method averaged 17.0 percent greater returns per 20-year period. On this basis, the market timing according to the formula is superior to just blindly investing in the S&P 500 when the investment period is 20 years. In addition, since the formula investment method was out of the stock market almost half the time, this is a far lower-risk method than being in the market continuously.

APPENDIX B

Derivation of the Savings Tables and Formulas

Those who have a natural aversion to data analysis and computation may want to skip this section. This appendix is for readers who want to understand the details of how the savings tables and formulas were derived. In this appendix, we will show how the living-forever savings adjustment discussed in Chapter 14 was derived, test the retirement tables presented in Chapter 14 with inflated funds, and see how the divisors and multipliers in the retirement formulas in Chapter 15 were derived.

Derivation of the Living-Forever Savings Adjustment

At the bottom of the savings tables shown in Chapter 14, there is a correction factor to be used for people who want to be very conservative and have enough funds at retirement to live forever or in this case to age 120. We will now show in detail how that correction factor was derived, revisiting two of the examples used in Chapter 15.

273

Example 1 from Chapter 14 Modified to a Live-Forever Assumption

A 40-year-old couple plan to retire at age 70. So they have 30 additional years to work. Their current combined income is $75,000 after taxes. Using 80 percent as the factor to determine their retirement income needs, their required retirement income will be 0.8 × $75,000 = $60,000 in current dollars.

The combined nominal company pensions that their companies have projected the couple will receive at age 65 is $40,000 per year (after tax and in future dollars). They currently have no savings for the purpose of retirement. They want to save enough so that when they retire they can keep their desired lifestyle until age 120.

In the calculations shown in Table B.1, for the live-to-120 option, we had to add 92 percent to the savings that were already calculated in Chapter 14 for the live-to-age-93 assumption. The savings requirement that was calculated for the live-to-age-93 assumption was $8,169, whereas the first-year savings shown in Table B.1 is $15,684, which is 92 percent higher than the $8,169. Some of the additional savings are needed because a portion of the savings are outside the Roth IRA limits, so the amount saved has extra added for expected taxes. This is where the total 92 percent extra savings number came from. We also track desired income and Social Security so we can then use the inflated numbers in Table B.2.

As previously noted, extra had to be saved since some of the accumulated savings is taxable because the savings amount exceeded the Roth maximum savings limits. That is why there is a lower tax-adjusted amount of $1,866,244, which is the amount that will be used for the retirement initial savings. We now have to see if these accumulated savings of $1,866,244 last for the 50 years required from retirement at age 70 to the goal of age 120.

Looking at Table B.2, you can see that with the $1,866,244 initial savings, the accumulated savings in the second column doesn't become negative until the 50th year (age 70 through age 120), so we were successful.

We will now show how the correction factor was derived for Example 3 from Chapter 14, which had an assumed age of 65 for retirement.

Table B.1 Testing the 92 Percent Savings Additional Amount on the Chapter 14, Example 1 Savings

Savings Year	Inflated Annual Actual Savings	Accumulated Savings Including Interest and Inflation	Desired Income Including Inflation	Social Security Including Inflation
1	$15,684	$15,684	$60,000	$25,920
2	$16,233	$32,936	$62,100	$26,827
3	$16,801	$51,878	$64,274	$27,766
4	$17,389	$72,640	$66,523	$28,738
5	$17,998	$95,359	$68,851	$29,744
6	$18,628	$120,185	$71,261	$30,785
7	$19,280	$147,277	$73,755	$31,862
8	$19,954	$176,804	$76,337	$32,977
9	$20,653	$208,949	$79,009	$34,132
10	$21,376	$243,906	$81,774	$35,326
11	$22,124	$281,884	$84,636	$36,563
12	$22,898	$323,105	$87,598	$37,842
13	$23,700	$367,806	$90,664	$39,167
14	$24,529	$416,243	$93,837	$40,538
15	$25,388	$468,686	$97,122	$41,957
16	$26,276	$525,427	$100,521	$43,425
17	$27,196	$586,775	$104,039	$44,945
18	$28,148	$653,064	$107,681	$46,518
19	$29,133	$724,646	$111,449	$48,146
20	$30,153	$801,900	$115,350	$49,831
21	$31,208	$885,231	$119,387	$51,575
22	$32,300	$975,072	$123,566	$53,380
23	$33,431	$1,071,882	$127,891	$55,249
24	$34,601	$1,176,155	$132,367	$57,182
25	$35,812	$1,288,417	$137,000	$59,184
26	$37,065	$1,409,229	$141,795	$61,255
27	$38,362	$1,539,191	$146,758	$63,399
28	$39,705	$1,678,944	$151,894	$65,618
29	$41,095	$1,829,170	$157,210	$67,915
30	$42,533	$1,990,599	$162,713	$70,292
	Tax Adjusted =	$1,866,244		

Table B.2 Testing the 92 Percent Additional Savings on the Retirement Funds in Chapter 14, Example 1

Retire Year	Accumulated Savings Plus Inflation and Interest	Inflated Outgoing Funds (Desired Income)	Inflated Social Security
1	$1,866,244	$168,408	$72,752
2	$1,932,536	$174,302	$75,298
3	$1,999,572	$180,402	$77,934
4	$2,067,276	$186,717	$80,662
5	$2,135,560	$193,252	$83,485
6	$2,204,330	$200,015	$86,407
7	$2,273,478	$207,016	$89,431
8	$2,342,886	$214,262	$92,561
9	$2,412,422	$221,761	$95,801
10	$2,481,942	$229,522	$99,154
11	$2,551,286	$237,556	$102,624
12	$2,620,277	$245,870	$106,216
13	$2,688,723	$254,475	$109,933
14	$2,756,413	$263,382	$113,781
15	$2,823,115	$272,600	$117,763
16	$2,888,576	$282,142	$121,885
17	$2,952,520	$292,016	$126,151
18	$3,014,647	$302,237	$130,566
19	$3,074,630	$312,815	$135,136
20	$3,132,113	$323,764	$139,866
21	$3,186,709	$335,096	$144,761
22	$3,237,999	$346,824	$149,828
23	$3,285,528	$358,963	$155,072
24	$3,328,804	$371,526	$160,499
25	$3,367,292	$384,530	$166,117
26	$3,400,416	$397,988	$171,931
27	$3,427,552	$411,918	$177,949
28	$3,448,026	$426,335	$184,177
29	$3,461,109	$441,257	$190,623
30	$3,466,016	$456,701	$197,295
31	$3,461,899	$472,685	$204,200
32	$3,447,846	$489,229	$211,347
33	$3,422,871	$506,352	$218,744
34	$3,385,915	$524,075	$226,400
35	$3,335,836	$542,417	$234,324
36	$3,271,406	$561,402	$242,526
37	$3,191,304	$581,051	$251,014

Table B.2 *(Continued)*

Retire Year	Accumulated Savings Plus Inflation and Interest	Inflated Outgoing Funds (Desired Income)	Inflated Social Security
38	$3,094,110	$601,388	$259,800
39	$2,978,295	$622,436	$268,893
40	$2,842,220	$644,222	$278,304
41	$2,684,122	$666,770	$288,044
42	$2,502,107	$690,106	$298,126
43	$2,294,145	$714,260	$308,560
44	$2,058,054	$739,259	$319,360
45	$1,791,495	$765,133	$330,538
46	$1,491,958	$791,913	$342,106
47	$1,156,751	$819,630	$354,080
48	$782,990	$848,317	$366,473
49	$367,580	$878,008	$379,300
50	−$92,792	$908,738	$392,575

Example 3 from Chapter 14 Modified to a Live-Forever Assumption

A 40-year-old couple plan to retire at age 65. So they have 25 additional years to work. Their current combined income is $75,000 after taxes. Using 80 percent as the factor to determine their retirement income needs, their required retirement income will be $0.8 \times \$75,000 = \$60,000$ in current dollars.

The combined nominal company pensions that their companies have projected the couple would receive at age 65 is $40,000 per year after taxes (in future dollars). They currently have no savings for the purpose of retirement. They want to save enough that when they retire at age 65 they can keep their desired lifestyle until age 120.

In the calculations shown in Table B.3, we had to add 55 percent to the $16,293 savings that were calculated in Chapter 14 for a live-to-age-93 assumption: 1.55 times $16,293 = $25,254, the first year savings we show in the annual savings column in Table B.3. The last line in the third column, $1,897,516, is the tax-adjusted accumulated savings value. This number represents the savings available after expected taxes that occur because the savings amount exceeded the Roth IRA maximums.

Table B.3 Testing the 55 Percent Additional Savings on the Chapter 14, Example 3 Savings

Savings Year	Inflated Annual Actual Savings	Accumulated Savings Including Interest and Inflation	Desired Income Including Inflation	Social Security Including Inflation
1	$25,254	$26,896	$60,000	$25,920
2	$26,138	$54,782	$62,100	$26,827
3	$27,053	$85,396	$64,274	$27,766
4	$28,000	$118,946	$66,523	$28,738
5	$28,980	$155,657	$68,851	$29,744
6	$29,994	$195,769	$71,261	$30,785
7	$31,044	$239,538	$73,755	$31,862
8	$32,130	$287,238	$76,337	$32,977
9	$33,255	$339,163	$79,009	$34,132
10	$34,419	$395,628	$81,774	$35,326
11	$35,623	$456,967	$84,636	$36,563
12	$36,870	$523,540	$87,598	$37,842
13	$38,161	$595,731	$90,664	$39,167
14	$39,496	$673,950	$93,837	$40,538
15	$40,879	$758,636	$97,122	$41,957
16	$42,310	$850,256	$100,521	$43,425
17	$43,790	$949,314	$104,039	$44,945
18	$45,323	$1,056,342	$107,681	$46,518
19	$46,909	$1,171,913	$111,449	$48,146
20	$48,551	$1,296,639	$115,350	$49,831
21	$50,250	$1,431,171	$119,387	$51,575
22	$52,009	$1,576,206	$123,566	$53,380
23	$53,830	$1,732,489	$127,891	$55,249
24	$55,714	$1,900,814	$132,367	$57,182
25	$57,664	$2,082,031	$137,000	$59,184
	Tax Adjusted =	$1,897,516		

We are tracking desired income and Social Security so we can use the inflated numbers in Table B.4.

We now have to test if the $1,897,516 tax–adjusted savings in Table B.3 will last for the 55 years required from retirement at age 65 to the goal of age 120. Looking at Table B.4, you can see that with the 55 percent additional savings, the second column, which is the accumulated savings, doesn't become negative until the 55th year, so we were successful.

Table B.4 Testing the 55 Percent Additional Savings on the Retirement Funds in Chapter 14, Example 3

Retire Year	Accumulated Savings Plus Inflation and Interest	Inflated Outgoing Funds (Desired Income)	Inflated Social Security
1	$1,897,516	$141,795	$61,255
2	$1,912,443	$146,758	$63,399
3	$1,923,055	$151,894	$65,618
4	$1,928,886	$157,210	$67,915
5	$1,929,435	$162,713	$70,292
6	$1,924,159	$168,408	$72,752
7	$1,989,956	$174,302	$75,298
8	$2,056,465	$180,402	$77,934
9	$2,123,606	$186,717	$80,662
10	$2,191,292	$193,252	$83,485
11	$2,259,424	$200,015	$86,407
12	$2,327,893	$207,016	$89,431
13	$2,396,578	$214,262	$92,561
14	$2,465,345	$221,761	$95,801
15	$2,534,045	$229,522	$99,154
16	$2,602,515	$237,556	$102,624
17	$2,670,576	$245,870	$106,216
18	$2,738,032	$254,475	$109,933
19	$2,804,667	$263,382	$113,781
20	$2,870,245	$272,600	$117,763
21	$2,934,510	$282,142	$121,885
22	$2,997,180	$292,016	$126,151
23	$3,057,950	$302,237	$130,566
24	$3,116,487	$312,815	$135,136
25	$3,172,431	$323,764	$139,866
26	$3,225,387	$335,096	$144,761
27	$3,274,932	$346,824	$149,828
28	$3,320,601	$358,963	$155,072
29	$3,361,897	$371,526	$160,499
30	$3,398,276	$384,530	$166,117
31	$3,429,154	$397,988	$171,931
32	$3,453,898	$411,918	$177,949
33	$3,471,824	$426,335	$184,177
34	$3,482,194	$441,257	$190,623
35	$3,484,211	$456,701	$197,295
36	$3,477,018	$472,685	$204,200

(Continued)

Table B.4　*(Continued)*

Retire Year	Accumulated Savings Plus Inflation and Interest	Inflated Outgoing Funds (Desired Income)	Inflated Social Security
37	$3,459,687	$489,229	$211,347
38	$3,431,222	$506,352	$218,744
39	$3,390,549	$524,075	$226,400
40	$3,336,511	$542,417	$234,324
41	$3,267,865	$561,402	$242,526
42	$3,183,273	$581,051	$251,014
43	$3,081,296	$601,388	$259,800
44	$2,960,389	$622,436	$268,893
45	$2,818,890	$644,222	$278,304
46	$2,655,015	$666,770	$288,044
47	$2,466,849	$690,106	$298,126
48	$2,252,335	$714,260	$308,560
49	$2,009,266	$739,259	$319,360
50	$1,735,276	$765,133	$330,538
51	$1,427,824	$791,913	$342,106
52	$1,084,189	$819,630	$354,080
53	$701,451	$848,317	$366,473
54	$276,481	$878,008	$379,300
55	−$194,072	$908,738	$392,575

The reasons that this 55 percent adjustment is less than the 92 percent additional savings in the retire-at-age-70 tables, are that the calculations to retire at age 65 already have adjustments in the savings for living five years longer, Social Security not kicking in for five years, and a smaller pension. So the 55 percent adjustment is being added onto a far larger savings base.

Testing the Retirement Tables with Inflated Funds

In this section we walk through each year of savings before retirement, noting the actual inflated savings each year. The desired income and Social Security are also indexed for these years, but their inflated values are calculated only for the purpose of later use in the second table, where we track what happens to the savings during each year of retirement.

Testing Example 1 from Chapter 14 with Inflated Dollars

A couple is 40-years-old and plan to retire at age 70. So they have 30 additional years to work. Their current combined income is $75,000 after taxes. Using 80 percent as the factor to determine their retirement income needs, their required retirement income will be $0.8 \times \$75,000 = \$60,000$ in current dollars.

The combined nominal company pensions that their companies have projected the couple would receive at age 65 is $40,000 per year (after taxes and in future dollars). The pension is assumed to be an additional 10 percent due to delayed retirement for five years. They currently have no savings specifically for the purpose of retirement.

In Table B.5, we will walk through each year of savings before retirement, noting the actual inflated savings each year. The Desired Income and Social Security are also indexed for these 30 years, but they are included here only for the purpose of monitoring their inflating values for later use in our next table.

So, at the time of retirement, the couple will have saved $1,036,802 in inflated funds. This sounds like an outrageous amount of money, but it is actually equivalent to $369,390 in current dollars. The diminished value of fixed funds, even at an assumed 3.5 percent annual inflation, can cause people to be radically underfunded at the time of their retirement, if the probable diminished future value of their savings isn't taken into account.

Since we saved funds in a Roth IRA, there will be no tax concerns on these savings. Since our initial savings amount was within the Roth limits, and this limit was adjusted up with inflation, all of the savings and related gains are tax free. Social Security benefits *are* subject to taxation, so the actual benefit amount shown in Table B.5 is reduced somewhat. The pension is also taxed, but we have already specified that the pension amount assumed should be after estimated taxes.

We will now want to track what happens to our savings during each year of retirement. In Table B.6, we start out with the $1,036,802 we just calculated. This is shown as the top value in the second column of the table. Each year we will include the inflation-adjusted Social Security and the $44,000 fixed pension amount, which includes the assumed additional 10 percent for delaying retirement, and stays constant throughout. The savings are reduced every year by the outgoing funds,

Table B.5   Savings Detail, 30 Years to Work, Initial Savings of $8,169, 3 Percent Interest, 3.5 Percent Inflation

Savings Year	Inflated Annual Actual Savings	Accumulated Savings Including Interest and Inflation	Desired Income Including Inflation	Social Security Including Inflation
1	$8,169	$8,169	$60,000	$25,920
2	$8,455	$17,155	$62,100	$26,827
3	$8,751	$27,021	$64,274	$27,766
4	$9,057	$37,834	$66,523	$28,738
5	$9,374	$49,668	$68,851	$29,744
6	$9,702	$62,598	$71,261	$30,785
7	$10,042	$76,709	$73,755	$31,862
8	$10,393	$92,088	$76,337	$32,977
9	$10,757	$108,831	$79,009	$34,132
10	$11,134	$127,038	$81,774	$35,326
11	$11,523	$146,819	$84,636	$36,563
12	$11,926	$168,289	$87,598	$37,842
13	$12,344	$191,572	$90,664	$39,167
14	$12,776	$216,800	$93,837	$40,538
15	$13,223	$244,115	$97,122	$41,957
16	$13,686	$273,668	$100,521	$43,425
17	$14,165	$305,622	$104,039	$44,945
18	$14,661	$340,148	$107,681	$46,518
19	$15,174	$377,431	$111,449	$48,146
20	$15,705	$417,669	$115,350	$49,831
21	$16,255	$461,072	$119,387	$51,575
22	$16,823	$507,865	$123,566	$53,380
23	$17,412	$558,289	$127,891	$55,249
24	$18,022	$612,599	$132,367	$57,182
25	$18,653	$671,071	$137,000	$59,184
26	$19,305	$733,996	$141,795	$61,255
27	$19,981	$801,687	$146,758	$63,399
28	$20,680	$874,477	$151,894	$65,618
29	$21,404	$952,722	$157,210	$67,915
30	$22,153	$1,036,802	$162,713	$70,292

which represent the inflation-adjusted desired retirement income being drawn out.

You can see how, for the first five years, the accumulated savings actually increase somewhat, and then they begin to go down. This is

Table B.6   Retirement Detail, Retire at Age 70, 3 Percent Interest, 3.5 Percent Inflation

Retire Year	Accumulated Savings Plus Inflation and Interest	Inflated Outgoing Funds (Desired Income)	Inflated Social Security	Pension
1	$1,036,802	$168,408	$72,752	$44,000
2	$1,049,181	$174,302	$75,298	$44,000
3	$1,058,799	$180,402	$77,934	$44,000
4	$1,065,352	$186,717	$80,662	$44,000
5	$1,068,511	$193,252	$83,485	$44,000
6	$1,067,923	$200,015	$86,407	$44,000
7	$1,063,204	$207,016	$89,431	$44,000
8	$1,053,945	$214,262	$92,561	$44,000
9	$1,039,700	$221,761	$95,801	$44,000
10	$1,019,993	$229,522	$99,154	$44,000
11	$994,310	$237,556	$102,624	$44,000
12	$962,098	$245,870	$106,216	$44,000
13	$922,762	$254,475	$109,933	$44,000
14	$875,665	$263,382	$113,781	$44,000
15	$820,118	$272,600	$117,763	$44,000
16	$755,384	$282,142	$121,885	$44,000
17	$680,671	$292,016	$126,151	$44,000
18	$595,128	$302,237	$130,566	$44,000
19	$497,842	$312,815	$135,136	$44,000
20	$387,833	$323,764	$139,866	$44,000
21	$264,051	$335,096	$144,761	$44,000
22	$125,369	$346,824	$149,828	$44,000
23	−$29,423	$358,963	$155,072	$44,000
24	−$201,619	$371,526	$160,499	$44,000

because the pension is fixed and becomes a smaller percentage of the total income with continuing years of inflation. You can see from Table B.6 that the inflated income needs actually double over the 23 years shown, while the pension contribution remains fixed.

You can see from Table B.6, by noting when the second column becomes negative, that we run out of savings after 23 years, which takes someone to age 93 if they retire at age 70. So the retiree's income at that point in time would only be the $155,072 Social Security plus the $44,000 pension, which is a total of $199,072. This is a shortfall of $159,891 versus their $358,963 inflated income needs. However, as we discussed earlier, the couple could then start draining values from other assets like their home, which presumably also doubled in value during the 23 years of retirement, just as their income needs doubled with inflation. This use of other assets would presumably allow them to continue in their current retirement lifestyle until they were 100 years of age or so.

For most people, it would not be worth the financial burden to try to save for living longer than this. This is especially true given that even saving the amounts shown in the previous tables will prove to be difficult for many people. However, savings anywhere close to what the tables specify will prevent you from being in the predicament in which many seniors now find themselves: getting ready to retire with only $50,000 or so in savings!

Testing Chapter 14 Example 3 with Inflated Dollars

A 40-year-old couple plan to retire at age 65. So they have 25 additional years to work. Their current combined income is $75,000 after taxes. Using 80 percent as the factor to determine their retirement income needs, their required retirement income will be 0.8 × $75,000 = $60,000 in current dollars.

The combined nominal company pension that their companies have projected the couple will receive at age 65 is $40,000 per year after taxes (in future dollars). They currently have no savings for the purpose of retirement.

Table B.7 is a test on the above example. Earlier, we had determined that we would have to start out saving $16,293 annually, then index the savings up every year with inflation, until retirement at age 65, which is 25 years of savings. The second column in the table below shows what the actual savings will be for each year, assuming inflation of 3.5 percent per year. You can see from the table that, by the time of retirement, the yearly savings will be an actual $37,202.

The third column, which is Accumulated Savings, includes each year's savings plus prior savings, including interest and inflation, which would be applied automatically when funds are saved in TIPS.

The fourth and fifth columns in Table B.7, which are Desired Income and Social Security, are only shown for future reference, because at the time of retirement we will then use the inflated values for each.

Table B.7 Savings Detail, 25 Years to Work, Initial Savings of $16,293, 3 Percent Interest, 3.5 Percent Inflation

Savings Year	Inflated Annual Actual Savings	Accumulated Savings Including Interest and Inflation	Desired Income Including Inflation	Social Security Including Inflation
1	$16,293	$17,352	$60,000	$25,920
2	$16,863	$35,343	$62,100	$26,827
3	$17,453	$55,094	$64,274	$27,766
4	$18,064	$76,739	$66,523	$28,738
5	$18,697	$100,424	$68,851	$29,744
6	$19,351	$126,303	$71,261	$30,785
7	$20,028	$154,541	$73,755	$31,862
8	$20,729	$185,315	$76,337	$32,977
9	$21,455	$218,815	$79,009	$34,132
10	$22,206	$255,244	$81,774	$35,326
11	$22,983	$294,818	$84,636	$36,563
12	$23,787	$337,768	$87,598	$37,842
13	$24,620	$384,343	$90,664	$39,167
14	$25,482	$434,807	$93,837	$40,538
15	$26,373	$489,442	$97,122	$41,957
16	$27,296	$548,553	$100,521	$43,425
17	$28,252	$612,460	$104,039	$44,945
18	$29,241	$681,511	$107,681	$46,518
19	$30,264	$756,073	$111,449	$48,146
20	$31,323	$836,541	$115,350	$49,831
21	$32,420	$923,336	$119,387	$51,575
22	$33,554	$1,016,907	$123,566	$53,380
23	$34,729	$1,117,735	$127,891	$55,249
24	$35,944	$1,226,332	$132,367	$57,182
25	$37,202	$1,343,246	$137,000	$59,184

This shows that the accumulated savings is $1,343,246. However, when we were setting up the savings plan shown in the table, additional funds were withheld because the initial savings exceeded the Roth IRA limits, so some of the earnings from the savings will be used for taxes upon retirement. We assume that only 85 percent of the proportion of the funds susceptible to tax can be used for retirement. This gives us a tax-adjusted savings of $1,265,424. These are the after-tax savings we must now use for testing whether funds are sufficient to last until age 93, which will be 28 years into retirement.

In Table B.8, Column 2 shows the current accumulated savings for each year of retirement. This accumulated savings is the starting savings, plus pension, minus the outgoing funds, which is the inflation–adjusted desired income. Although the Social Security benefits are shown in the table for the whole 28 years for purposes of monitoring their inflated values, they are not included in the first five years of accumulated savings

Table B.8   Retirement Details, Retire at Age 65, 3 Percent Interest, 3.5 Percent Inflation

Retire Year	Accumulated Savings Plus Inflation and Interest	Inflated Outgoing Funds (Desired Income)	Inflated Social Security	Pension
1	$1,265,424	$141,795	$61,255	$40,000
2	$1,239,265	$146,758	$63,399	$40,000
3	$1,206,120	$151,894	$65,618	$40,000
4	$1,165,351	$157,210	$67,915	$40,000
5	$1,116,270	$162,713	$70,292	$40,000
6	$1,058,138	$168,408	$72,752	$40,000
7	$1,067,644	$174,302	$75,298	$40,000
8	$1,074,202	$180,402	$77,934	$40,000
9	$1,077,496	$186,717	$80,662	$40,000
10	$1,077,185	$193,252	$83,485	$40,000
11	$1,072,900	$200,015	$86,407	$40,000
12	$1,064,245	$207,016	$89,431	$40,000
13	$1,050,793	$214,262	$92,561	$40,000
14	$1,032,084	$221,761	$95,801	$40,000
15	$1,007,622	$229,522	$99,154	$40,000
16	$976,875	$237,556	$102,624	$40,000
17	$939,269	$245,870	$106,216	$40,000
18	$894,190	$254,475	$109,933	$40,000
19	$840,975	$263,382	$113,781	$40,000
20	$778,913	$272,600	$117,763	$40,000
21	$707,241	$282,142	$121,885	$40,000
22	$625,139	$292,016	$126,151	$40,000
23	$531,726	$302,237	$130,566	$40,000
24	$426,059	$312,815	$135,136	$40,000
25	$307,125	$323,764	$139,866	$40,000
26	$173,837	$335,096	$144,761	$40,000
27	$25,030	$346,824	$149,828	$40,000
28	−$140,544	$358,963	$155,072	$40,000

calculations. This is because we are assuming that Social Security benefits will not start until age 70. We could have shown a much reduced benefit starting at age 65, but over the course of the 28 years shown this would have resulted in reduced overall savings. After five years, the Social Security benefits are included in the annual income. The accumulated savings also includes interest and inflation on any unused savings, which is consistent with TIPS savings. Note that the pension stays at a constant $40,000 per year throughout.

As you can see by looking at Table B.8, the accumulative savings column goes negative in 28 years, which means that savings are drained at age 93, which was the goal. At that point, only Social Security and the $40,000 pension will be available. As previously mentioned, draining other assets, like the value in a home, will probably allow a continued lifestyle until age 100.

So our tests of looking at actual inflated savings show that the retirement savings tables, although stated in current dollars, work to give desired retirement incomes when the savings amounts are indexed up annually with inflation.

Derivation of the Divisors and Multipliers in the Retirement Formulas of Chapter 15

In Chapter 15, we presented formulas for determining the retirement income. In this section we see how the above formula values were developed

In the formulas we used RI to represent "retirement income," SS for the "Social Security benefit," TS for the required "TIPS savings," and PN for the "pension benefit."

Here is one of the formulas from Chapter 15.

Retire at Age 65, Live to Age 93, Determine Retirement Income

$$RI = TS/19 + SS + 0.68 \times PN$$

Let's see how the above formula values were developed. First, notice that we divided the TIPS savings (TS) by 19. The reason this was done is that we wanted the savings to be reduced slowly every year and to run out in 28 years, which would get us to age 93, if we retire at age 65. We assume that the savings are getting 3 percent interest, and that inflation is 3.5 percent, so any remaining savings are indexed up 6.5 percent every year. Here is the spread sheet where we show that if we start out using $\frac{1}{19}$ of the savings for retirement income, then index that value up every year by 3.5 percent to account for inflation (we want to keep the purchasing

Table B.9   Table Showing Derivation of TS/19

Year	Accumulated Savings	Inflated Retirement Income
1	$50,000	$2,632
2	$50,447	$2,724
3	$50,826	$2,819
4	$51,127	$2,918
5	$51,343	$3,020
6	$51,464	$3,125
7	$51,481	$3,235
8	$51,382	$3,348
9	$51,156	$3,465
10	$50,791	$3,587
11	$50,272	$3,712
12	$49,587	$3,842
13	$48,718	$3,976
14	$47,650	$4,116
15	$46,364	$4,260
16	$44,841	$4,409
17	$43,060	$4,563
18	$40,999	$4,723
19	$38,634	$4,888
20	$35,940	$5,059
21	$32,888	$5,236
22	$29,449	$5,420
23	$25,591	$5,609
24	$21,281	$5,806
25	$16,481	$6,009
26	$11,153	$6,219
27	$5,255	$6,437
28	−$1,259	$6,662
29	−$8,436	$6,895

power of the retirement income constant), we run out of savings after 28 years (the savings go negative during the 28th year). See Table B.9. In this example, we used \$50,000 as the starting savings, but any starting number would show the same effect. The first number in the Income column below, \$2,632, is $\frac{1}{19}$ of \$50,000.

Similarly, in the previous formula we multiplied the pension (PN) by 0.68. This was done because, since the pension is fixed, its purchasing

Table B.10   Table Showing Derivation of $0.68 \times$ PN

Year	Accumulated Savings	Inflated Retirement Income
1	\$100.00	\$68.00
2	\$135.96	\$70.38
3	\$170.55	\$72.84
4	\$203.64	\$75.39
5	\$235.09	\$78.03
6	\$264.77	\$80.76
7	\$292.53	\$83.59
8	\$318.21	\$86.51
9	\$341.64	\$89.54
10	\$362.66	\$92.68
11	\$381.08	\$95.92
12	\$396.72	\$99.28
13	\$409.36	\$102.75
14	\$418.81	\$106.35
15	\$424.83	\$110.07
16	\$427.21	\$113.92
17	\$425.68	\$117.91
18	\$420.00	\$122.04
19	\$409.90	\$126.31
20	\$395.10	\$130.73
21	\$375.30	\$135.31
22	\$350.20	\$140.04
23	\$319.46	\$144.94
24	\$282.75	\$150.02
25	\$239.72	\$155.27
26	\$189.99	\$160.70
27	\$133.17	\$166.33
28	\$68.85	\$172.15
29	−\$3.40	\$178.17

power would go down if we used its initial full value every year. To keep a constant pension value, we assume that we only use 0.68 of the initial pension, indexing up that value every year with an assumed 3.5 percent inflation. Excess pension money is invested in a TIPS savings fund, getting 3 percent interest and 3.5 percent inflation.

Our goal is to have the pension "savings" go negative after 28 years. See Table B.10. We assumed a starting pension of $100, using 0.68 of that amount, or $68. Again, any starting pension amount would have shown the same effect.

You can see in Table B.10 that the savings column did not go negative until after 28 years, which was our goal.

You may have also noticed that the Social Security benefit had no corrective value. This is because it inflates automatically with inflation, so we don't have to worry about it running out or losing its purchasing power.

Understanding Logarithmic Charts

I n several places in this book, data are displayed on a logarithmic chart. This is because uniformly increasing (or decreasing) data displayed in this manner will show as a sloped straight line.

For example, suppose we had something that was increasing 20 percent every year, and the initial value was 1. Here is what that data would look like for 10 years.

Year	Value
0	1
1	1.2
2	1.44
3	1.728
4	2.0736
5	2.48832
6	2.985984
7	3.583181
8	4.299817
9	5.15978
10	6.191736

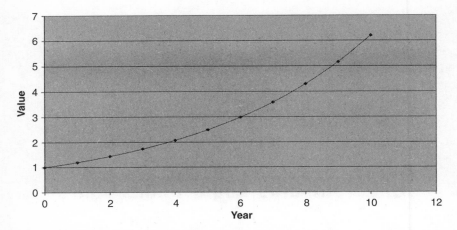

Figure C.1 Regular Chart, Data Growing 20 Percent Per Year

Let's plot these data on a regular and a logarithmic graph, Figure's C.1 and C.2.

Note that in Figure C.2 it is obvious that the value is increasing at a uniform rate. The reason this works is the log is the power to which base "10" must be raised to reach a given number. For example, in the following data, you plotted the "numbers" from the above, giving a curve with a dramatic upswing. However, if you plot the "power,"

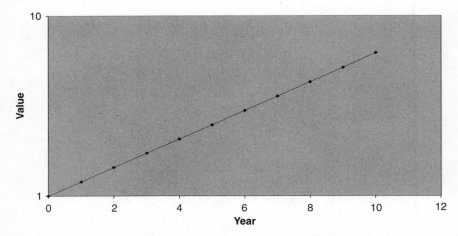

Figure C.2 Logarithmic Chart, Data Growing 20 Percent Per Year

the graph will be a sloped straight line. On a logarithmic chart (actually semi-log), rather than actually plotting the "power," the vertical axis is spaced equivalent to the power of the number. That is why you see the unusually spaced left-hand axis numbers on the log charts.

Base	Power	Number
10	0	1
10	1	10
10	2	100
10	3	1000
10	4	10000
10	5	100000
10	6	1000000

10 to the zero power is 1
10 to the 1st power is 10
10 to the 2nd power is 100
10 to the 3rd power is 1000

A logarithmic chart is useful for data that you suspect are increasing at a steady rate, like dividends increasing at a uniform rate for a number of years. The straight line on the plot tells you that this is happening.

APPENDIX D

Key Numbers Used in Stock Market Calculations

T here are many sources for the key numbers listed in Table D.1, and many of these sources may have slightly different values. This discrepancy is partially caused by the time of year when the numbers are assumed to be taken. Some data are from end-of-the-year, other data may compare averages of one year to the next or even use midyear values. These data are midyear. However, the differences between the different data sources average out and are not critical to the analysis done in this book.

Also, since the S&P 500 was not computed before 1926, all numbers related to the S&P 500 or its dividends before that time are based on estimates done in retrospect. The real (inflation adjusted) S&P 500 numbers are shown in 2007 dollars.

Table D.1 Key Numbers

Year	Real S&P 500 Value (Not Including Dividends)	S&P % Dividend	% Inflation
1900	168.4	4.35	8.00
1901	216.8	3.65	−2.47
1902	215.9	3.86	8.86
1903	180.0	4.74	0.00
1904	182.6	5.07	−1.16
1905	229.4	3.72	2.35
1906	234.9	3.92	3.45
1907	177.1	5.36	7.78
1908	191.1	5.50	−6.19
1909	216.8	4.29	8.79
1910	201.5	5.00	5.05
1911	216.0	4.86	−11.54
1912	208.3	4.96	9.78
1913	179.4	5.91	1.98
1914	165.5	5.54	1.02
1915	175.7	5.29	2.02
1916	181.8	5.29	6.93
1917	135.1	6.91	20.37
1918	105.0	8.46	13.08
1919	106.4	5.97	14.97
1920	82.4	6.57	23.67
1921	82.0	7.40	−15.79
1922	107.5	5.74	−5.11
1923	105.6	6.24	1.80
1924	113.0	6.26	0.00
1925	135.4	5.32	2.94
1926	150.8	5.33	1.14
1927	190.5	4.90	−0.56
1928	252.6	4.26	−2.84
1929	316.0	3.48	0.00
1930	260.0	4.53	−1.75
1931	180.9	6.49	−10.12
1932	106.4	13.84	−9.93
1933	149.9	4.52	−6.62
1934	152.9	4.48	5.51
1935	168.2	4.35	2.24
1936	239.2	3.74	0.73
1937	218.0	5.37	4.35
1938	173.4	7.25	−2.08

Table D.1   *(Continued)*

Year	Real S&P 500 Value (Not Including Dividends)	S&P % Dividend	% Inflation
1939	182.4	4.64	−2.13
1940	163.3	6.72	2.17
1941	137.6	7.07	4.26
1942	112.3	7.92	10.88
1943	141.4	4.88	7.36
1944	150.6	4.97	0.57
1945	181.4	4.31	2.84
1946	181.0	3.66	3.31
1947	141.7	5.12	17.65
1948	136.3	5.05	9.55
1949	136.1	7.30	−0.83
1950	163.0	6.40	−0.42
1951	182.5	7.24	8.82
1952	195.6	5.95	2.32
1953	194.0	5.93	1.13
1954	239.7	5.01	0.37
1955	323.9	3.95	−0.74
1956	361.2	3.89	1.87
1957	329.1	3.64	3.31
1958	345.8	3.87	2.85
1959	415.6	3.12	0.69
1960	398.1	3.41	1.72
1961	472.1	2.96	0.68
1962	431.6	3.70	1.34
1963	486.2	3.14	1.32
1964	557.4	2.97	1.31
1965	592.4	3.07	1.94
1966	547.1	3.29	2.53
1967	584.1	3.17	2.78
1968	598.7	2.98	4.20
1969	553.8	3.16	5.48
1970	450.9	4.21	6.01
1971	514.1	3.11	4.64
1972	554.6	2.84	2.71
1973	497.9	3.07	6.00
1974	342.8	3.90	10.86
1975	343.1	4.02	9.39
1976	378.1	3.69	5.97

(Continued)

Table D.1   *(Continued)*

Year	Real S&P 500 Value (Not Including Dividends)	S&P % Dividend	% Inflation
1977	335.7	4.39	6.87
1978	310.2	5.68	7.41
1979	298.5	5.25	10.89
1980	305.0	5.18	14.38
1981	292.0	4.83	9.55
1982	265.2	6.21	7.06
1983	341.8	4.17	2.58
1984	325.2	4.77	4.22
1985	370.5	4.10	3.76
1986	462.5	3.30	1.77
1987	528.0	2.83	3.65
1988	476.6	3.41	3.96
1989	553.5	3.18	5.17
1990	535.3	3.24	4.67
1991	592.0	3.21	4.70
1992	624.7	3.02	3.09
1993	661.2	2.79	3.00
1994	651.6	2.82	2.49
1995	763.7	2.48	3.04
1996	915.1	2.13	2.75
1997	1164.7	1.73	2.30
1998	1429.5	1.44	1.68
1999	1691.1	1.23	1.96
2000	1731.1	1.14	3.73
2001	1397.3	1.27	3.25
2002	1140.1	1.58	1.07
2003	1123.8	1.64	2.11
2004	1262.0	1.64	3.27
2005	1306.2	1.74	2.53
2006	1379.6	1.87	4.32
2007	1491.2	1.73	2.69

SOURCE: Stock Data, www.econ.yale.edu/~shiller/data/ie_data.htm.

Glossary

actively managed mutual funds These investments combine money from many investors into a fund that actively analyzes and buys stocks, bonds, or other assets.

Adjustable Rate Mortgages (ARMs) Mortgages that have periodic resets on their interest rate. About half of ARMs are tied to the 1-year Constant Maturity Treasury (CMT) index. ARMs have a set amount of interest in addition to the CMT rate.

bubble An economic bubble occurs when investors become so excited about a stock or some other financial instrument, that the price of the asset (or the size of a debt) rises so high that it is no longer rational.

buy-and-hold Buying and holding stocks for a long period of time with no regard to purchase price or other timing considerations when purchasing or selling stocks.

depression A severe or long recession is referred to as an economic depression.

dollar averaging Accumulating stocks by buying a fixed-dollar-amount of stocks on a regular basis. This is a type of market timing, in that you are buying more shares of a stock when the price is low and fewer shares when the price is high. The net effect is that, over a period of time, you will have bought stock at less than the mathematical average price of that stock over that same period of time.

efficient market theory   This assumes that all stocks are perfectly priced at all times, based on all information available, and that all information is instantly known by all.

Exchange-Traded Funds (ETFs)   Funds that track an index but can be traded like a stock.

fat tail   Where a normally balanced distribution of data now has a lot of data far out to one end of the distribution tail.

Fed (Federal Reserve System)   Established by Congress in 1913 as a means to foster a sound money and financial system. It basically is the central bank of the United States. The Fed has 12 regional Reserve Banks and a Board of Governors appointed by the president. They have a Federal Open Market Committee, with 12 members that set the overnight Fed funds rate. They also influence how much money is in the market, and therefore the interest rates, by buying and selling government bonds.

financial obligation ratio   The ratio of total debt obligation versus after-tax income. This debt obligation includes credit card debt, auto payments, and rent or house payments.

foreclosure   When a financial institution reclaims a home because of nonpayment of a mortgage.

GDP (Gross Domestic Product)   The GDP is the total market value of all final goods and services produced in the United States in a given year, equal to total consumer, investment, and government spending, plus the value of exports, minus the value of imports.

Hedonistic Adjustment of Price Data   This adjustment assumes that the cost of any improvement in a product should be discounted when comparing to an earlier price.

home equity   The value of a home minus the amount owed on the home.

index funds   An index fund enables investors to buy stocks in the same balance as in a particular index. An index fund makes no attempt to evaluate the individual merits of each investment within the index.

inflation   An increase in the costs of goods. Some people maintain that "real" inflation can only come from an increasing supply of money in excess of the growth of the gross domestic product.

interest-only mortgages   Where borrowers have some introductory time period where they need to pay only the interest on the mortgage with no payback of the mortgage principal.

IRA regular   When funds are saved in a regular IRA (Individual Retirement Account), the money is saved pre-tax, and you pay all taxes at a later date when the funds are withdrawn, generally after age 59½. Taxes are then paid not only on the initial deposited funds, but also on any gains those funds generated.

IRA Roth   In a Roth IRA, the funds are saved *after taxes*, so taxes are paid up front on the funds as they are being saved. There are no additional taxes on those funds, *nor on any of the related gains*, when the funds are withdrawn, again generally after age 59½.

Irving Fisher formula   A numerical way to determine a fair-market value of a stock or the stock market in general.

liar or no-doc loans   A loan requiring no documentation regarding income. Since surveys have found that many people lie related to the income they claimed on these mortgages, they have become know as liar loans.

liquidity   Refers to how quickly and cheaply an asset, like a security, can be converted to cash. Money, in the form of cash, is the most liquid asset.

logarithmic charting   On a logarithmic chart (actually semi-log), the vertical axis is spaced equivalent to the power of the plotted number.

market value   The calculated "fair" price of a stock or stocks. This number provides a reasonable baseline against which to evaluate a stock's actual price.

mortgage walkers   People who choose to walk away from their home rather than fighting to make payments that they have difficulty affording. In many cases, these people owe more than their homes are worth.

mutual funds   These funds combine money from many investors into a fund that actively analyzes and buys stocks, bonds, or other investments.

option mortgages   A loan where the buyer can make payments at several different levels, including the lowest payment that is less than the interest owed. These are also called negative amortization mortgages.

pension   A sum of money regularly paid as a retirement benefit.

price/dividend ratio   The stock price divided by the annual dividend paid on that share of stock.

price/earnings ratio   The stock price divided by its annual, after-tax, per-share earnings.

random walk   This theory was made famous by Burton Malkiel's *A Random Walk Down Wall Street*, which was published over 30 years ago; it basically means that a stock's price movement is truly random, and that any prior change in a stock's price has no influence on whether its future price will be higher, lower, or the same.

"real" price   Price adjusted to remove the effect of inflation.

recession   A recession is a significant decline in economic activity spread across the economy, lasting more than a few months, normally visible in real GDP, real income, employment, industrial production, and wholesale-retail sales.

regression to the mean   The tendency of a stock's price to revert to its historical average if there is no identified reason why the price should be higher or lower than the historical mean.

Social Security   A U.S. federal benefits program that includes retirement benefits.

Stock Index   A measure of the performance of a select group of companies.

stock index fund   Enables investors to buy stocks in the same proportion as the stocks in a particular index. For example, if someone buys shares in an index fund based on the Dow Jones, they are buying shares in all the companies in the Dow Jones index and in the same proportion.

subprime mortgages   These were given to people who did not have good credit ratings. These mortgages often had low initial teaser interest rates and usually had their interest rates adjusted after one year.

teaser rates   Low initial interest rates that encouraged borrowers to get mortgages larger than perhaps they normally would have.

TIPS   (Treasury Inflation Protected Securities) These securities have a periodically adjusted interest. Part of the interest is base interest that is assigned at time of purchase. The other adjustment is based on the government's reported inflation numbers.

upside-down mortgage   Where a borrower owes more on his house than the house is worth.

References

Baer, Gregory, and Gary Gensler. *The Great Mutual Fund Trap*. New York: Broadway Books, 2002.

Bernstein, William. *The Four Pillars of Investing*. New York: McGraw-Hill, 2000.

Bonner, William, with Addison Wiggin. *Empire of Debt*. Hoboken, N.J.: John Wiley & Sons, 2006.

Bonner, William, with Addison Wiggin. *Financial Reckoning Day*. Hoboken, N.J.: John Wiley & Sons, 2003.

Brussee, Warren T. *Statistics for Six Sigma Made Easy*. New York: McGraw-Hill, 2004.

Brussee, Warren T. *The Second Great Depression*. Booklocker.com.

Carlson, Charles B. *Winning with the Dow's Losers*. New York: HarperCollins, 2004.

Ellis, Charles D. *Winning the Loser's Game*. New York: McGraw-Hill, 2002.

Ellis, Joseph H. *Ahead of the Curve*. Boston: Harvard Business School Press, 2005.

Harding, Sy. *Beat the Market the Easy Way*. Wheatmark, 2007.

Kiplinger. *Retire Worry-Free*. Chicago: Kiplinger's Washington Editors, Inc., 2003.

Malkiel, Burton G. *A Random Walk Down Wall Street*. New York: W. W. Norton & Company, 1999.

Malkiel, Burton G. *The Random Walk Guide to Investing*. New York: W. W. Norton & Company, 2003.

Morris, Charles R. *The Trillion Dollar Meltdown*. New York: PublicAffairs, 2008.

Netti, Frank L. *Retire Sooner, Retire Richer*. New York: McGraw-Hill, 2003.

Ottenbourg, Robert K. *Retire & Thrive*. Chicago: Kiplinger's WashingtonEditors, Inc., 2003.

Prechter, Robert R. *Conquer the Crash*. Hoboken, N.J.: John Wiley & Sons, 2003.

Paulos, John P. *A Mathematician Plays the Stock Market*. Cambridge, Mass.: Basic Books, 2003.

Shiller, Robert J. *Irrational Exuberance*. Princeton, N.J.: Princeton University Press, 2005.

Smithers, Andrew, and Stephen Wright. *Valuing Wall Street*. New York: McGraw-Hill, 2000.

Stein, Ben, and Phil DeMuth. *Yes, You Can Time the Market*. Hoboken, N.J.: John Wiley & Sons, Inc., 2003.

Turk, James, and John Rubino. *The Collapse of the Dollar*. New York: Doubleday, 2004.

Woodward, Bob. *Maestro: Greenspan's Fed and the American Boom*. New York: Simon & Schuster, 2000.

Web Sites

401Kafé. "Planning to Retire at 65? You May Need to Think Again..." 2000. www.infoplease.com/finance/commentary/feature/feature_plan.html.

Baker, Dean. "Nine Misconceptions About Social Security." *Atlantic Monthly*, July 1998. www.theatlantic.com/issues/98jul/socsec.htm.

Bernstein, Jared, and Lawrence Mishel. "Weak Recovery Claims New Victim: Workers' Wages." Economic Policy Institute. www.epinet.org/content.cfm/issuebriefs_ib196.

"The Biggest Market Crashes in History." *Investopedia*, 2008. www.investopedia.com/features/crashes/crashes1.asp.

CNN Money Planner, *CNN Money*, 2008. http://cgi.money.cnn.com/tools/retirementplanner/retirementplanner.jsp.

"The Consumer, First Source of Dynamism, Piles on Debt to Sustain World

Growth," by E. Leser. *Global Policy Forum*, October 20, 2003. www.global policy.org/socecon/crisis/2003/1020consumerdebt.htm.

Damodaran, A. "S&P Earnings: 1960-Current" *Bloomberg and S&P.* January 5, 2008. http://pages.stern.nyu.edu/~adamodar/New_Home_Page/datafile/spearn.htm.

Dinnen, S. "Readers seek tips on Treasury Inflation Protected Securities." *Christian Science Monitor*, March 1, 2004. http//www.csmonitor.com/2004/0301/p16s02-wmgn.htm.

Dodd, R. "DSC: Greenspan's Fed and the American Boom." *Derivatives Study Center*, June 2001. www.financialpolicy.org/dscchallenge.htm.

"The Federal Reserve." BondKnowledge, 2002. www.bondknowledge.com/fed.html.

Federal Reserve Board. "FRB: Monetary Policy, Open Market Operations." April 30, 2008. www.federalreserve.gov/fomc/fundsrate.htm.

Federal Reserve Board. "Mortgage (ARM) Indexes: Constant Maturity Treasury Index (CMT)," 2008. mortgage-x.com/general/indexes/cmt.asp.

Greaney, J. "Using Treasury Inflation Protected Securities (TIPS) to increase your safe withdrawal rate." *Retire Early*, August 1, 2000. www.retireearlyhomepage.com/safetips.html.

Heylighten, F. "Occam's Razor." *Principia Cybernetica Web*, July 7, 1997. http://pespmc1.vub.ac.be/OCCAMRAZ.html.

"Historical data on S&P 500, interest rates, and inflation," Moody's Economy, 2008 www.economy.com.

Hodges, M. "Grandfather Family Income Report." *Grandfather Economic Reports*, June 2008. http://mwhodges.home.att.net/family_a.htm.

Lahart, J. "Spending Our Way to Disaster" *CNN Money*, Oct 3, 2003. http://money.cnn.com/2003/10/02/markets/consumerbubble/.

"London Fix Historical Gold-result." *Kitco Bullion Dealers*, 2008. www.kitco.com/scripts/hist_charts/yearly_graphs.cgi.

Savings Calculator used to calculate annual savings required, MSN Money, 2008, http://beginnersinvest.about.com/gi/dynamic/offsite.htm?site=http%3A%2F%2Fmoneycentral.msn.com%2Finvestor%2Fcalcs%2Fn_savapp%2Fmain.asp.

"The State of the Nation's Housing 2003." Joint Center for Housing Studies at Harvard University, 2003. www.jchs.harvard.edu/publications/markets/son2003.pdf.

"Treasury Inflation Protected Securities (TIPS)," 2008. www.savingsbonds.gov/.

U.S. Census Bureau. "Population Projections". January 13, 2000. www.census.gov/population/projections/nation/summary/np-t3-a.txt.

U.S. Census Bureau. "Projections of the Total Resident Population by 5-Year Age Groups . . . " January 13, 2000. www.census.gov/population/projections/nation/summary/np-t3-f.txt.

"United States – U.S. Statistics – Household and Family Statistics." Infoplease.com, 2006. www.infoplease.com/ipa/A0005055.html.

Weston, L. "The truth about credit card debt." *MSN Money*, 2008. http://moneycentral.msn.com/content/Banking/creditcardsmarts/P74808.asp.

About the Author

Warren Brussee spent 33 years at GE as an engineer, plant manager, and engineering manager. His responsibilities included manufacturing plants in the United States, Hungary, and China. He has multiple patents related to both products and processes.

Warren Brussee earned his engineering degree at Cleveland State University and attended Kent State toward his EMBA.

The author's earlier books, *Statistics for SIX SIGMA Made Easy* and *All About Six Sigma,* were written to make Six Sigma user-friendly, so that a more diverse group of people could use this powerful data-based methodology. *Getting Started in Investment Analysis* applies the same sort of philosophy to evaluating stocks and other investments. And his most recent book, *The Great Depression of Debt*, is geared for intelligent people who also want to use data, but in this case to help them navigate their own financial future through an economic depression.

Index